## Other Books by G. Michael Dobbs

**Escape.** *How Animation Broke into the Mainstream in the 1990's.*

**15 Minutes With...** *Forty Years of Interviews*

**Springfield.** *Postcard History of Springfield, Massachusetts*

**Tales from the Runway.** *Written as Bill Brazil with Danielle Holmes*

**Made of Pen & Ink:** *Fleischer Studios, The New York years*

# MADE OF PEN & INK:

## FLEISCHER
### *Studios*

## THE
# FLORIDA
## YEARS

## BY
# G. MICHAEL DOBBS

inkwell
productions ™

**inkwell productions** ™

Published by
Inkwell Productions
Office of Publication:
17 Spruce Street
Springfield, MA 01105  USA

In association with
Not Dog Books

First Edition: March 2024
ISBN 978-1-7330144-6-5

# Dedication

*Three people have played a huge role in this project and I would like to thank them by dedicating this book to them:*

**JJ Sedelmaier** is not only an award-winning producer of animation, he is also a historian and a tireless booster of the art. His support of this project has been phenomenal and deeply appreciated.

**Mark Masztal** is not just the designer of this book but has been a loyal friend and supporter.

**Mary Cassidy** is my wife and she has had to listen about the Fleischer Studio since we started dating in 1977. Thank you for your great patience.

# Table of Contents

# Introduction

Are you old enough to remember a time when someone could actually repair a television and these technicians actually came to your house to do so? Believe it or not in the 1950s and '60s that actually happened.

Our TV repairman went by the nickname of "Smiley" and he came to our house in Springfield, MA, often enough to notice something: I liked Popeye cartoons a lot. So much in fact he dubbed me "Popeye."

With this second volume of "Made of Pen and Ink: The Fleischer Studios," my intent is complete the story started in the first book and attempt to show the immense legacy of the cartoons made at the studio.

The simple truth is the cartoons made by the Fleischer Studios have had an immense and increasing influence on animation for the past 35 or more years. It took a while for this to happen, though.

When television firmly established itself as a commercial media in 1949, there was a huge demand for programming. Local stations had many hours to fill on their own with the networks only supplying shows at certain times. Movies started being offered to stations as well as cartoons.

The theatrical cartoons of the 1930s and 1940s proved to be a valuable commodity on television from the 1950s through the 1970s. Almost every local station bought packages of cartoons to run on their shows aimed at children.

The release of the Popeye cartoons in the mid-1950s proved to be so popular that King Features made their own series of Popeye cartoons for television in the early 1960s in order to financially benefit from the character's popularity.

The widespread broadcast of older cartoons created a generation of people who loved the Warner Bros. and Fleischer Studio cartoons, which were the main fodder for many of these shows. While the weekly long-running network Wonderful World of Disney TV show did present animation, it was primarily live-action programming. Disney made the decision not to release that library of its shorts to TV.

Although Max and Dave did live long enough to get any benefit out of this new awareness from a younger generation of fans, Max's family certainly have benefitted from it, with its recreation of the Fleischer Studios as a corporate entity and its licensing of Betty Boop.

I believe this exposure to the classic theatrical cartoons laid the bedrock for animation fandom that slowly but surely started in the 1970s. By the 1970s, the children who had loved Popeye and Bugs Bunny, among others, were now adults.

The popularity and financial success of the older cartoons on TV clearly started an interesting trend in the 1960s. There was now an effort to create animation for prime-time television, meaning it would have appeal for both adults and children. Examples of this would be "Rocky and Bullwinkle" as well as a string of Hanna-Barbara shows such as "The Flintstones," "Top Cat" and "The Jetsons." The Warner Bros. cartoons were packaged with new wraparounds for a weekly series.

The creation of "Jonny Quest" was an indication of the experimentation with the audience by producing a show that was animated but not humorous.

The idea of animated series that would appeal to whole families – just as the theatrical cartoons of previous years had done – was relatively short-lived, though. Not until the success of "The Simpsons," which made its debut in 1989, did broadcast decision-makers start to view animation differently.

One should note "The Simpsons" was seen as a radical departure for animation on TV at that time. The underground comics vibe to the show and its deconstruction of the TV sitcom family actually concerned some people. Initially scheduled against "The Cosby Show," with Bill Cosby heading up what was seen as television's ideal family, some people hoped "The Simpsons," with its outrageous humor, would not damage the other show's ratings.

During much of the 1960s through the 1970s, too much of the animation people saw was cheaply made, limited animated for kids on Saturday morning that might have been high on concept but low on quality. So much of what was presented created a true wasteland for the medium.

I should add the work of Ralph Bakshi in redefining animation in the 1970s and '80s should be acknowledged. Schooled at Terrytoons, perhaps the least respected animation studio of the golden era, Bakshi produced feature films that should have changed the course of commercial animation and, for a while, did have an impact.

His movies "Fritz the Cat," "Heavy Traffic" and "Coonskin" were personal, confrontational and adult. The first two films found an audience, but "Coonskin'" – also known as "Streetfight" was highly controversial and ended the initial personal part of his career.

Bakshi told me, "Hollywood forced me to change and said if you want to continue to do animation you have to clean up your act. [Go from R-rated material to PG] and make sure there are no ideas in the PG. I was very political."

Ultimately, the marketplace for animation wasn't seen as one that could support those kinds of films.

Bakshi added, "I love 'Wizards,' but I don't love 'Lord of the Rings.' I appreciate 'American Pop,' but I don't love it. And I appreciate 'Fire and Ice,' but I don't love it."

The rise of the VCR and the eventual affordability of VHS tapes meant that both protected and public domain animation was now available to see. One cannot underestimate the impact of the VCR technology in allowing people to collect films. It democratized what had been a very small hobby.

The growth of cable television in the 1980s and '90s brought about two services; both owned by Viacom, which also owned Paramount – Nickelodeon and MTV. When MTV started running "Ren and Stimpy," originally just intended for broadcast on Nickelodeon and aimed at kids, people understood the multiple generational popularity of "The Simpsons" had not been a fluke.

There was an understanding that a show such as "Ren and Stimpy" could appeal to a much broader audience and there was a golden era in creator-driven animated cartoon series aimed, not just at kids, but for everyone.

Linda Simensky, who in the 1990s was the director of Development at Nickelodeon, told me what she was looking for in a series at that time. "It has to be beyond being 'rad surfer dude.' It has to be smart. It has to be really funny. And fun – the super intangible. Does it feel like a fun prop if I wear a tee shirt with that character embroidered on the pocket? Would I buy one for my younger cousin or would I cringe when I saw it?" she explained.

The Nickelodeon shows were largely reflective of the "creator-driven" concept unlike the dreck of the 1970s and '80s television animation. Fans realized the shows were the work of actual artists who guided their ideas to realization.

I will contend that with this huge shift on TV coupled with the growth of VHS and the release of many animated properties on that medium, animation started to be considered something much more than just throwaway pop culture for kids. I detailed this shift in my book, "Escape! How Animation Broke into the Mainstream in the 1990s."

The explosion of the sale of animation art in the mid-90s, the attention paid to veteran animators from the past and the existence of magazines such as Animato!, which I co-owned and edited, ushered in a very important period when animation was being seen in a very new light.

Combining the power of fan-owed physical media with a new adult interest in animation created an environment for a rediscovery of the work of the Fleischer Studios and subsequently an increase in licensing of Betty Boop. Part of this was nostalgia from adults who remembered the Betty Boop and Popeye cartoons on TV from their youth and shared them with their children, while part of the interest came from people discovering the cartoons for the first time.

While some Fleischer vets were alive to benefit from this renewed interest, many of the key people were not. If the new interest had come earlier, performers such as Jack Mercer and Mae Questel would have been pop culture convention favorites, for instance.

Artists Myron Waldman and Shamus Culhane both benefitted from participating in the limited edition cel market that arose in the 1990s. That market included many other artists as well and eventually crashed through way too much product as well as the veteran artists who provided the art passing away.

All of these factors brought renewed and well-deserved attention to the work of the Fleischer Studio. Today, thanks to the efforts of historians such as Tommy Jose Stathes and his Cartoons on Film company and Steve Stanchfield and his Thunderbean Studios, more and more classic animation is being made available, including Fleischer cartoons.

*G. Michael Dobbs*
2024

# A Word About These Cartoons:

This book is about an animation studio active from just after World War I through the spring of 1942. This was a time in American popular culture when ethnic humor and stereotypes were every day elements of vaudeville, movies, radio shows, comic strip and novels.

This was an era in which one of the most popular radio shows in the nation starred two white men portraying stereotypical and racist depictions of African-Americans. It was a time the sound movie that was credited with ending the silent period had sequences of its star in black face. It was also a time one of the most highly visible and highly paid African-American actors in film portrayed a character that was slow, lazy and dim-witted. The most popular Asian-American character in movies was played by succession of white actors and Native American characters in film and radio were almost always played by white actors, as well.

Although the Fleischer Studios did not have on-going characters that were negative stereotypes – unlike other studios – there are moments of ethnic humor that are not positive, especially when viewed today. There are Asian and Black stereotypes in some of these cartoons and especially through the early 1930s, there are gags revolving around Jewish elements, often a reflection of the ethnic backgrounds of some of the Fleischer staff members.

I don't agree with the use of ethnic stereotypes in pop culture, but I have to acknowledge their existence and the pain they can cause today.

When examining any element of popular culture, context is essential and discussion is important. The Fleischer Studio made many wonderful and groundbreaking cartoons that are still influencing animation today. It should be celebrated for that accomplishment without ignoring moments that are no longer justifiable.

## *Architectural Record January 1939*

Max's new studio in Miami was going to be quite different than the studio's former home in New York City. In New York, the studio occupied several floors at 1600 Broadway. That building was well known as being a center for offices related to the film and entertainment industry.

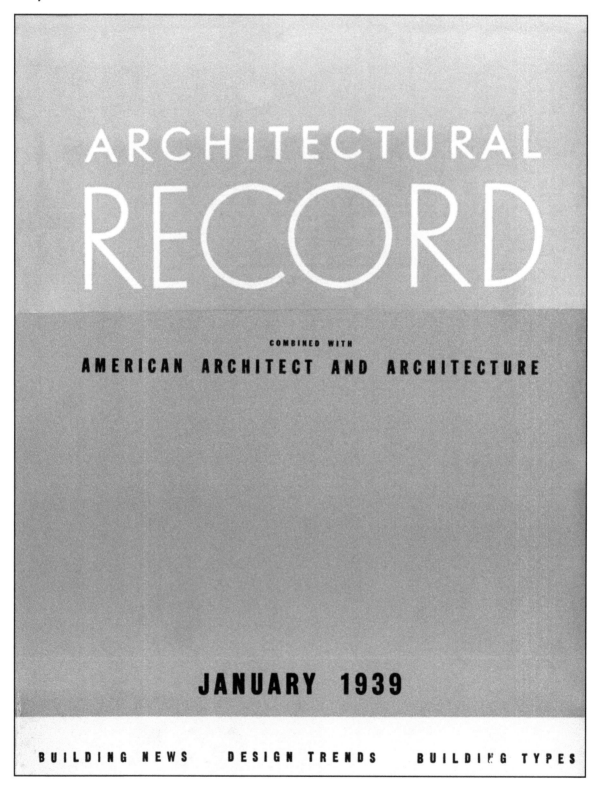

The new studio, all on one level, had air conditioning necessary for the Florida climate, as well as an open patio area in the center of the plant.

## LIGHT, SOUND, AND ATMOSPHERE CONTROLLED IN STUDIO DESIGN

C. SHELDON TUCKER, Architect

JOHN M. LYELL, Associate

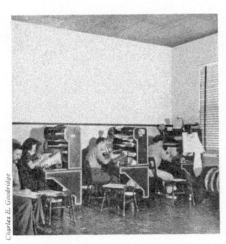

Charles E. Goodridge

Typical animators' room

THE NEW Fleischer Studios are located in a part of Miami that had been neglected in the hasty, boom development of the city. The area is now being re-subdivided, and many streets are being closed or re-located. In the area southwest of the building, a rental housing project of 41 houses, similar in construction to the Studios, are being built.

The plant has been designed for the production of "animated cartoons." A "cartoon" consists of a series of photographed drawings, each slightly different from the one preceding it; so that when they are projected rapidly on a screen, an illusion of action is produced. A cartoon that runs for 7 minutes may include 11,000 to 14,000 separate drawings. Production of such a film involves the preparation of stories; of key drawings—usually every fourth "frame"; "inbetween" drawings; inking; coloring; photography; and sound synchronization.

The cost of the plant was approximately $300,000.

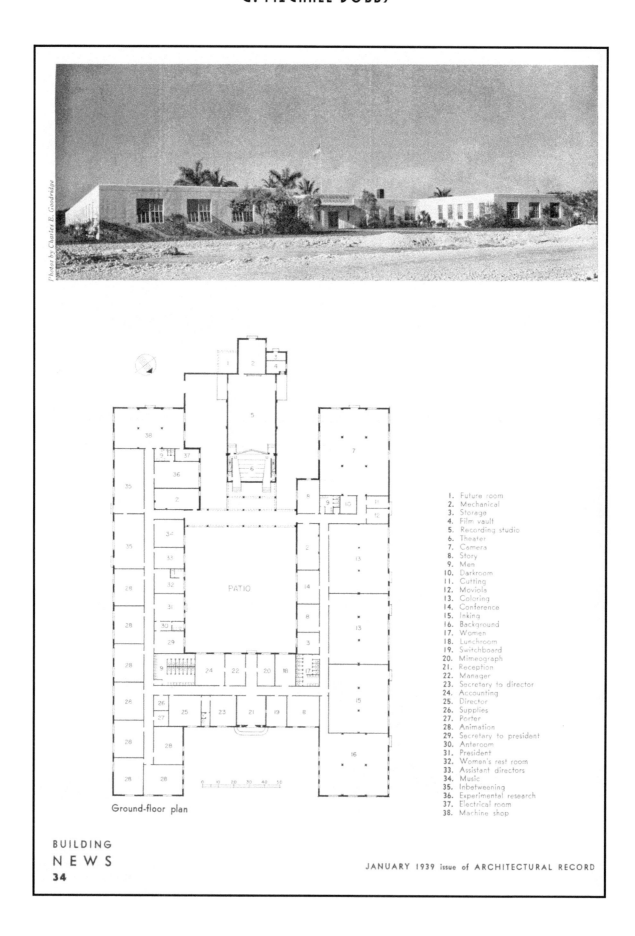

Photos by Charles E. Goodridge

PATIO

Ground-floor plan

1. Future room
2. Mechanical
3. Storage
4. Film vault
5. Recording studio
6. Theater
7. Camera
8. Story
9. Men
10. Darkroom
11. Cutting
12. Moviola
13. Coloring
14. Conference
15. Inking
16. Background
17. Women
18. Lunchroom
19. Switchboard
20. Mimeograph
21. Reception
22. Manager
23. Secretary to director
24. Accounting
25. Director
26. Supplies
27. Porter
28. Animation
29. Secretary to president
30. Anteroom
31. President
32. Women's rest room
33. Assistant directors
34. Music
35. Inbetweening
36. Experimental research
37. Electrical room
38. Machine shop

## FLEISCHER STUDIOS

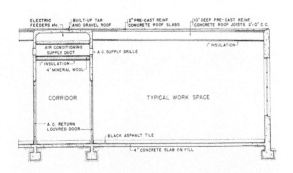

THE STRUCTURE of the Fleischer plant is poured reinforced concrete, except for the roof, which is built of precast concrete slabs over precast joists; the roof slabs over the corridor, however, were poured to obtain greater rigidity as well as to facilitate construction. Prefabricated metal forms, arranged in module units, were used with door jambs and steel windows, which were locked into the formwork before pouring began.

The plant is completely air-conditioned: constant temperature and humidity are essential; for the gelatine coating on motion-picture film is not only temperature-sensitive but also hygroscopic (moisture-absorbing).

There are three central plants delivering conditioned air to work spaces; air is sent through the adjustable grilles of supply ducts located between roof and corridor ceiling. The air is returned to the conditioning plants through louvered doors on the corridors; corridors are used as plenum chambers. The recirculated air is combined with fresh outside air, passed through filters, then over refrigerating coils or electrical unit heaters, and through blowers into the supply ducts. The duct work is fabricated of composition hardboard.

Air from public toilets is returned through ventilating exhaust fans in the ceilings; this to avoid circulating obnoxious odors in the corridors; a direct exhaust was further needed against the possibility of plant shutoff. (Toilets have no outside fenestration.)

To avoid glare, the Venetian blinds are kept down during working hours. There is local lighting at the drawing desks, which are equipped with circular, rotating glass surfaces, "lighted" either from above or from below. Only under such lighting can a drawing be made to resemble a projected screen image. To avoid glare from corridor lighting, 25-watt deflecting lights are used the length of the corridors, illuminating only the floor edges. General lighting has been provided, however, for the use of porters in cleaning up after working hours.

The corridor is a plenum chamber for the air-conditioning system.

combined with AMERICAN ARCHITECT and ARCHITECTURE

## SOUND-RECORDING BUILDING, FLEISCHER STUDIOS

*Photos by Charles E. Goodridge*

THE SOUND-RECORDING building has been isolated structurally to check vibrations originating in other parts of the building; it is connected to the rest of the plant by an open cloister, with expansion joints for isolation. Monolithic poured-concrete construction has been used largely to satisfy acoustical requirements.

The walls of the sound stage are insulated in "soft" and "hard" areas. The soft areas are insulated mostly with mineral-wool batts, covered with galvanized wire mesh, and the hard areas either with flat surfaces of composition hardboard or with hard plaster baffles. The baffles serve to reflect sound waves to other locations to produce a balanced sound composition at the recording microphone. Walls are insulated above a line three feet from the floor; below this line insulation has little effect on acoustical results.

For sound insulation, all glazed openings to the sound stage are made double, with glass set in sponge rubber. Openings larger than motion-picture projection and observation ports have one thickness of ¼-in. plate glass and one thickness of ⅛-in. plate glass; the two panes are set not parallel, but at a slight angle to each other—about three inches apart at one jamb and six inches apart at the other; this, and the difference in glass thicknesses, breaks up the sound-transmission harmonic and prevents accidental noises from reaching the recording microphone. A system of piping to all glazed observation openings and machine ports was necessary for dehumidification, as well as for equalization of air pressure inside the double-glazing. To facilitate cleaning, panes were made easily removable. (A type of glass like Pittsburgh Crystal-X is needed to minimize the cloudy effect produced by chemical changes at the glass surface.)

The Monitor room (for the sound-recording engineer) is the "brain center" of the recording operation: it must command a clear view of the screen and of the stage floor; it must be close to the projection room and to the sound-recording machinery room. In the Monitor room are located the sound-control equipment and the control of communications from outside the building (telephone and fire-alarm systems, etc.).

There is a separate air-conditioning plant in the recording building with separate supply ducts over the roof to the sound stage and to the control section of the building. Circular air deflectors deliver air horizontally at the sound-stage ceiling, reducing objectionable air currents. Air velocity in the supply ducts has been decreased by enlarging the ducts.

Control of the air-conditioning supply is located at the Monitor's desk. Because of duct or machine vibration and the effect of air currents, the conditioning system is shut down during recordings. These periods are short: a completed film runs only seven to nine minutes, and the recording is done step by step to synchronize the sound track with the animation; hence the heat build-up during recording periods is relatively small. Moreover, the only persons on the sound stage in these intervals are a recordist, voice characters, and musicians; this is a very different situation from that on a sound stage making "live" movies, in which hundreds of persons may be on the stage at once, and in which the lighting and the heat which it generates are usually much more intense.

JANUARY 1939 issue of ARCHITECTURAL RECORD

Historian Jerry Beck noted the building at 1701 NW 30th Avenue was the home of the Miami-Dade County Child Development Center for decades but became the Miami Police Grapeland Height Substation in 2007.

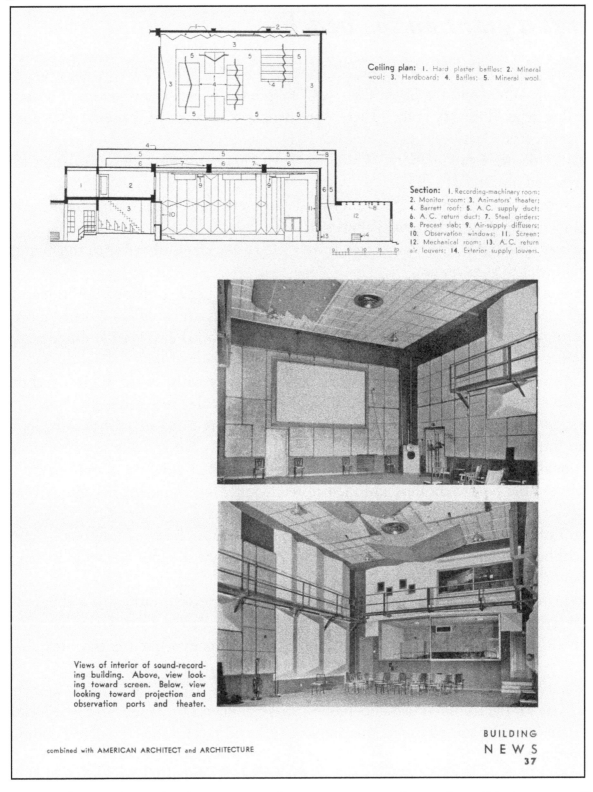

Ceiling plan: 1. Hard plaster baffles; 2. Mineral wool; 3. Hardboard; 4. Baffles; 5. Mineral wool.

Section: 1. Recording-machinery room; 2. Monitor room; 3. Animators' theater; 4. Barrett roof; 5. A.C. supply duct; 6. A.C. return duct; 7. Steel girders; 8. Precast slab; 9. Air-supply diffusers; 10. Observation windows; 11. Screen; 12. Mechanical room; 13. A.C. return air louvers; 14. Exterior supply louvers.

Views of interior of sound-recording building. Above, view looking toward screen. Below, view looking toward projection and observation ports and theater.

combined with AMERICAN ARCHITECT and ARCHITECTURE

BUILDING
NEWS
37

A check of the website for the Miami Police Department shows that of 2023, it is still being used as a substation.

# Chapter One

## *There's a giant on the beach!*

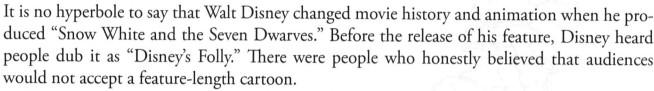

It is no hyperbole to say that Walt Disney changed movie history and animation when he produced "Snow White and the Seven Dwarves." Before the release of his feature, Disney heard people dub it as "Disney's Folly." There were people who honestly believed that audiences would not accept a feature-length cartoon.

Those critics were wrong. "Snow White" was both a huge critical and box office success when it was released on Dec. 31, 1937.

The success of the film and the money made on merchandising certainly impressed many people, including the executives at Paramount.

The first Fleischer feature, "Gulliver's Travels" (GT) has long suffered with the myth that it was a failure at the box office.

The truth is that GT was widely hailed by critics in 1939, provided additional money through licensing of merchandise and was a box office success. It could have earned more if the European market had been open. The first year of World War II eliminated a huge market for Paramount and the Fleischer Studios.

So much of the issue with GT has been its comparison with "Snow White" and the fact that, for the last 30-plus years, the film has not been seen with a restored print.
The best way – the only way – to see the film today is the restored Blu-ray released by Thunderbean (https://thunderbeanshop.com).

National Telefilm Associates (NTA) bought the rights to GT from Paramount in the 1950s. It re-released the film to theaters and then to television. Unfortunately, the film fell into the public domain.

That status ensured with the home video revolution that GT was ubiquitous – there were dozens of bargain tapes featuring the film – but it also meant the film was seldom seen as the Fleischer Studio had intended.

Too many people have seen dupey, splicy versions with washed-out color and have judged the film accordingly.

While GT does have problems in storytelling, there are many sequences that are quite wonderful.

It is not an excuse, but a reality, that the Christmas 1939 release date came at an incredibly chaotic time for the studio. It had undergone a strike, followed by a move to a new location in a new state. The film started production in New York and was finished in Miami under a very tight deadline.

The studio, of course, had to maintain its promised schedule of shorts during this time as well.

Longer formats were nothing new to the studio has it had produced three Popeye two-reel specials to great acclaim. A feature-length cartoon, though, was seen by many in the industry has something audiences might not accept.

It should be noted that Disney and his staff started working on the Snow White feature in 1934. That long gestation period helped make sure the final film met with Disney's high expectations.

Max Fleischer did not have that kind of time. He had about a year.

And he had a studio to build and a union still to be convinced.

This photo shows the front exterior of the new studio. In the foreground one can see the street still needs to be paved. (Photo courtesy of JJ Sedelmaier)

The Motion Picture Herald reported on Feb. 12, 1938: "Max and Dave Fleischer returned to New York this week from Miami with their plans set for the building of a studio in Miami at the approximate cost of $300,000. The studio is expected to be ready for occupancy on Oct. 1.

"Concessions were made by the city of Miami, Dade County and the Delaware housing Company of Miami, the principal factor being that the studio ground and building will be tax-free for 15 years. Also, a substantial part of the cost of the studio and ground will be absorbed locally, it was intimated. The city of Miami has pledged itself to build a road to cost $100,000 which will run in front of the building an connect with the Hialeah road leading to the race-track.

"The studio force of 200 in New York has been asked whether or not they want to make the move and 70 percent have already signed up, according to the studio. Last summer the studio was confronted with labor troubles when the commercial artist and designers walked out on strike, followed by the musicians' union, the projectionists' union and the cameramen's union. It is said that labor troubles have no bearing in the situation.

"The building will be one-story of poured concrete and steel and will have air conditioning throughout. It will have 30,000 square-feet of space, an increase of 25 percent over the present premises at 1600 Broadway. With the additional plot for recreation and parking and a patio in the center of the development, it will cover a total of two square blocks, Mr. Fleischer said.

"The Delaware Housing Company is planning to build low-cost homes for the employees to be financed in part by federal housing loans, which will be rented or sold. The dwellings will be offered to employees for about $4,500 it was said.

"All functions now performed in new York will be handled in the Miami studio. Paramount will continue to handle the printing in New York. As in the past, color developing and printing will continue to be done by Technicolor on the coast.

"The Commercial Artist and designers Union, a Committee for Industrial Organization affiliate, said Monday that the move 'will be of no ultimate benefit to the employees.'

"The studio termed the statement 'a surprise, in view of the cordial relations existing with our employees.' Of the 200 Fleischer employees, 64 are members of the union, the studio said. At a conference in the offices of Phillips and Nizer, Fleischer attorneys, the studio agreed to accept without reservation the demands made by the union.

"Demands were that wages be not reduced in Florida; guarantee of one full year's employment and maintenance of hours, vacation, sick leaves and other benefits. Mr. Fleischer volunteered to pay the employees' traveling expenses, their hotel accommodations there for a month and traveling expenses to any employees who decided to return to New York within a year."

A story in 'Box Office' on March 11, 1938, had a different figure for staff, putting it at 387 people with a weekly payroll of $18,000 or $385,322 in 2023 dollars. The story also noted there would be an air-conditioned cafeteria with the cost of $20,000 in 1938 dollars.

The story ends with a quote from Max, "Many persons, high in production circles in Hollywood, are watching with definite interest the success with which the Fleischer Studios are operating in an area which it has refused to believe would be suitable as a studio locale."

Max didn't figure in one major issue with a Miami Studio. With the exception of motion picture production, New York was the center the American entertainment industry. With radio production, the recording industry and Broadway, New York had a huge talent pool. It also had the motion picture infrastructure consisting of labs and stores that carried cameras and other equipment.

Moving from New York to New Jersey or Connecticut, for example, could have lowered Max's costs in some ways and still would allowed him to tap into what New York had for producers.

Granted, Miami was offering tax breaks and saw the studio as the start once again to establish an east coast Hollywood, but Max was definitely rolling the dice.

This photo was taken in November 1938 showing artists at work at their desks. (Photo courtesy of JJ Sedelmaier)

In its Feb. 23, 1938, edition, 'Variety' reported the possibility of a feature from several studios. "On top of this, Paramount has decided to go into the field at once with Max Fleischer producing a feature for that organization."

Just a few weeks later, March 3, 1938, 'Variety' reported "Under the deal with Fleischer, who makes Betty Boop and Popeye cartoons for Paramount, both will jointly be interested in the project. Paramount has already made the first advance to cover partial costs of production. The budget is not known, probably being dependent on the story to be chosen. Paramount has two stories in mind but is keeping the identity a secret for reasons."

The 'Variety' article did rule out both "Alice in Wonderland" and "The Blue Bird" as potential subjects. Paramount had produced a live action version of "Alice" in 1933, a production that featured Paramount contract stars (Gary Cooper, Cary Grant, W.C. Fields, etc.) under heavy make-up that attempted to reproduce the drawings from the original book. Bordering on the surreal, it must be seen to be believed.

"The Blue Bird" was a 1908 play for which Paramount had made a silent version in 1918. 20th Century Fox would make a live action version in 1940 as that studio's attempt to produce its own "The Wizard of Oz" with Shirley Temple in the lead.

'Variety' continued, "Fleischer will start the feature cartoon in New York and finish it in Miami, which will be ready for operation about Aug. 15. Consequent upon decision to go for full length cartoons, Fleischer is altering the original plans for the Miami plant, increasing the space on which he will build, to nearly 32,000 square feet to about four city blocks. It will be located towards Coral Gable, a Miami suburb and will employ 300 to 400 people. Construction begins this week."

The enormity of the task at hand cannot be under-estimated. Max was responsible for getting a new studio built, producing his roster of shorts and making a feature-length film. To make it more challenging, he had to increase the staffing of the studio enlisting experienced artists from other studios.

GT was made in the background of these events.

On June 22, 1938, 'Variety' reported that Max had signed a contract with Paramount to create a musical adaptation of Jonathan Swift's "Gulliver's Travels."

The next story about the studio in 'Variety' noted the on-going fallout of the strike. On Aug. 3, 1938, it reported, "Negotiations have been opened for a renewal of the contract with Max Fleischer cartoon producer covering the artist and animators who are members of the Local

United American Artist of the United Office and Professional Workers of America, a CIO affiliate, whose present agreement runs out in three months.

"The new contract is being sought in advance of plans to move production to the new studio he is building in Miami, FL.

"In additional to a guarantee of one year's employment, the union seeks the payment of transportation costs and all extra expenses for the first moment in Florida for shifting.

"Fleischer consented to negotiate after six weeks of deliberations. Louis Nizer, attorney for the cartoon producers, finally indicated his client was willing to discuss a renewal of the present signed last October, after many months of intensive picketing."

In its Oct. 13, 1938, edition, 'Film Daily' reported Fleischer Studios in New York was closing over weekend "with all effects and employees of the organization either in Florida or en route to the new studio in Miami by that time."

It was the end of an era and the start of the eventual demise of the studio.

\*\*\*

While Walt Disney used a well-known fairy tale, the decision was to use a story that had name recognition but certainly not a fairy tale: Jonathan Swift's "Gulliver's Travels."

Looking at the decision now, it strikes me as remarkable that this was the story the Fleischers and Paramount chose.

Swift was a satirist with a very sharp world view. An Irish patriot living under British rule, Swift became known for his brutal "Modest Proposal," in which he suggested that the English eat the bodies of impoverished Irish children as they had already consumed their souls.

While not as brutal as that essay, "Gulliver's Travels" certainly was a satire. Swift once said, he wrote the book "to vex the world rather than divert it."

This was not a children's book by any means and the Fleischers used only the part of the journey as the basis for their film. In that section of the book, Gulliver arrives in his ship to Lilliput where he finds he is a giant. The residents tolerate him and he helps them fight a war with neighboring Blefuscu.

Gulliver will only go so far in helping them and he is branded a traitor and sentenced to be blinded. He escapes, however, to Blefuscu, and eventually returns home.

Since its publication in 1726, the fantasies the book presents had been seen as something that kids as well as adults might appreciate. Certainly, the book was still well-known and had a fantastic theme, both of which were valuable to an animated feature.

Essentially, the studio elected to turn the film into a musical love story involving the princess of Lilliput and the prince of Blefuscu. The conflict came between their fathers, the kings, concerning which national song should be played at the wedding. The disagreement leads to a war and Gulliver not only ends it by hauling the fleet of Blefuscu up onto the beach of Lilliput but also by suggesting both songs should be combined and sung together.

The center figure of the film is the Lillputian town crier Gabby. Gabby discovers the unconscious Gulliver on the beach, alerts the king and apparently organizes the townspeople to secure Gulliver and to take him to the king.

The comedy built around the character is that Gabby is a blowhard. He is quick to brag and quick to be frightened. The character comes from a tradition of making characters who stretch the truth as the stars of animated productions. Producer J.R. Bray's silent star Col. Hezza Lair and Ub Iwerks' Willie Whopper both did that.

This photo shows members of the story department with storyboards for "Gulliver's Travels" on the walls. (Photo courtesy of JJ Sedelmaier)

The result is far from what Swift had intended. In the book, Gulliver is the star of his own adventures. In the film, the emphasis is placed on the Lilliputians and Gulliver is in some ways a secondary character.

An article in the January 1940 edition of 'Good Housekeeping' magazine has a remarkable feature story about the creation of the film. It's fascinating as it purports to report the evolution of the script and quotes a variety of studio staffers, from Max to writer Bill Turner to Seymour Kneitel and Edith Vernick. Jack Mercer is mentioned as the voice of King Little and other characters, as well as well Pinto Colvig as the voice of Gabby. The writer does not note that Mercer was Popeye and that Colvig was known for his work at Disney as Goofy.

The story also mentions background artists Robert Little, Louis Jambor and Shane Miller, and Esther Dayton, is identified as the head of the in-between department.

The story read in part, "When Max Fleischer decided to make an animated cartoon of the famous voyage, he reread Gulliver. 'Humph,' he said to himself, the fellow's self-centered to say the least. I wonder how the poor Lilliputian's felt when Gulliver picked them up by the scruff of the neck and dangled them on his thumb?' Right then and there Max Fleischer decided the movie would present the Lilliputians' version of Gulliver's saga."

"'Gulliver's had his say. It's time for the little man to speak up,' said Mr. Fleischer. 'I'll take a five-inch citizen of Lilliput view of the adventure.'"

The article credits Turner as the one who had a town crier discovering Gulliver.

The article does not mention Dave Fleischer at all and puts forth a version of the background story in which Max is sitting in story sessions and character development. It would be tempting to see this omission as another skirmish in the increasing war between Max and Dave, but that is just a theory.

Undoubtedly a first for an animated feature, there was a guide for teachers about the film, prepared by William Lewin, the chair of the English Department of Wequatic High School in Newark, NJ, in January 1940. The guide offers a detailed synopsis of the film, but also a look at the making of the film, based on interview with Max. It was published in Photoplay Studies.

The story reported that Popeye was considered to be "cast" as Gulliver, but that was ultimately rejected.

An excerpt from the publication noted, "Max Fleischer wanted a truly sociological picture retaining the full weight of Swift's satirical theme, with modern implications. David Fleischer, held out for a light Gilbert-and-Sullivan treatment. A compromise was finally reached. The film as produced retains the essential satire of Swift but is also abounds in humor, color and spectacle. It moves with a charming musical flow. Music is indeed an essential part of cartoon technique. Every bit of action must follow the tempo of the musical score."

The challenge for the studio was not only in making the film, but making it for a Christmas 1939 release date. The studio needed help well beyond the capacity of the New York crew that had come down to Miami.

Fleischer Head Animator Myron Waldman explained to me that there were many people hired in a rush but not all of them were qualified.

"Many of the people who came from the [west] coast thought they were better than us," he said. The new influx of people didn't help the mood of the studio still hurting from the strike, he added.

Waldman also attributed the uneven quality of the animation to the skill level of the new enlarged staff.

Waldman was kept on the shorts while GT was in production, but he was called into duty on the scene in which Gulliver is dragging the Blefuscu ships towards the beach.

\*\*\*

There were two key people who returned to the studio from their time working on "Snow White" at Disney: Grim Natwick, and James "Shamus" Culhane.

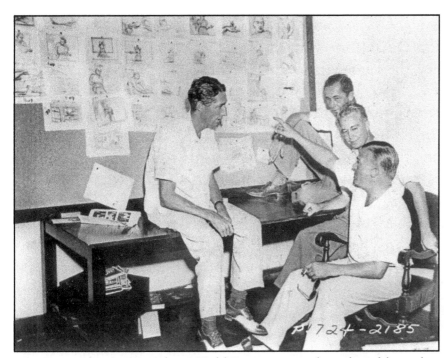

More story men are seen here. Tedd Pierce is seated on the table to the left. Jack Ward and Cal Howard are on the right with Edmond Seward is pointing to the 'Gulliver's Travels' storyboards.
(Photo courtesy of JJ Sedelmaier)

Culhane was not happy with his initial assignment: crowd scenes with the Lilliputians.

"Mob shots. I came right in at the end of the picture and they had a whole mess of them waiting for this very end of the job. I got things like the whole crowd is waving at Gulliver as he leaves. Jesus Christ! After being a specialist on 'Snow White' I got this junk to do. But because of my background at that time, I could do it very well but it was a pain in the ass. I hadn't done that kind of thing since I started at Walt," Culhane told me.

There were plenty of scenes in the film involving many characters and apparently, they were not popular to animate. Animator John Walworth, who had come from a stint at Screen Gems, recalled with a laugh to me, "Joe [Oriolo] sub-contracted some of these scenes to me to do under the table. So, I did them along with my other work."

Natwick was given scenes with Princess Glory as he was viewed as an expert in animating female characters. He reportedly was given Dave Fleischer's office in which to work and was assigned 1,000 feet of film to direct.

Natwick told me, "Even though Max made 'Gulliver's Travels,' on which I worked on a couple of years [sic], something like that, the characters are still clowns. Disney characters have a certain amount of refinement about them; there's much more difficult drawing about them. They're harder to do and call for greater skill…That doesn't mean he [Disney] always succeeded in getting a better piece of entertainment. We kicked this thing about yesterday [referring to a discussion he had] in their own way 'Gulliver' and 'Mr. Bug' are highly rated pictures. Nobody in the world had quite gone past them. But Disney has done things that have artistic excellence."

Al Eugster also came back to Fleischer. He told me after having worked at Disney where animators had their own rooms "when I came down to Miami there were so many people there for the feature. The animators were placed in large rooms, it was noisy. When they went to 'Mr. Bug Goes to Town,' they had learned from experience and had a very good system. The working conditions were much better and there wasn't all that noise."

He called GT "an interesting experience."

Eugster added, "I felt more of a camaraderie with the Fleischer organization. I guess the organizational know-how at Disney, the regimentation, was to the point we couldn't create. I might say it was a little too orderly."

Making a comparison between his Disney and Fleisher experiences, he said that comparing the output of the two studios was comparing "a potato and a peach, pardon my analogy. A potato is more durable. … At times, the Disney animation was overly refined."

Like Waldman, he knew there were "artists hired who had lied about their abilities and experience."

Eugster received $135 a week at the Miami studio, a $35 a week raise from Disney. He said that after GT he was cut back to $115. When he joined Famous, he got a boost to $125. To put that into perspective, $100 in 1939 had the buying powers of about $2,195 today.

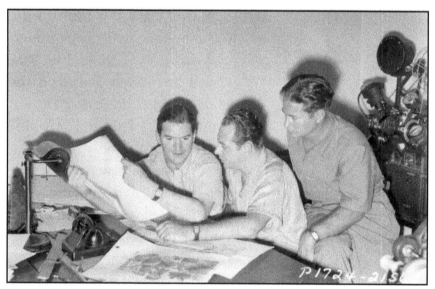

Willard Bowsky, Seymour Kneitel and Myron Waldman are conferring over drawings for "Gulliver's Travels." (Photo courtesy of JJ Sedelmaier)

New to the studio was another person who had worked at Disney, Pinto Colvig. Colvig was an animation veteran having worked as an artist with J. R. Bray. He had also tried to set up a studio with Walter Lantz. He had worked with Walt Disney from 1930 until 1937 where, among his other accomplishments, he provided the voice for Goofy. He was also a writer.

For GT he provided the voice, sped up slightly for Gabby, the star character of the film.

Jack Mercer played King Little of Lilliput and writer Tedd Pierce provided the voice for King Bombo.

GT has a unique distinction in that it was the first animated feature film that credited vocal performances from well-known performers. In this case, Lanny Ross and Jessica Dragonette, both recording and radio stars, were hired to perform the singing voices of the prince and princess.

Ross had been educated at Yale and earned his law degree at Columbia. He abandoned law when he learned he could earn more as a singer. He had appeared in several musicals prior to was a substantial star into the 1940s. He stayed active into the 1980s and passed in 1988.

Ross was one of the first interviews I did for this project back in the late 1970s. We met at his club in New York City, one of those exclusive clubs with quiet rooms filled with leather upholstered chairs. Ross was quite friendly but could offer only a few memories of his involvement in GT.

He had known Max, as they lived in the same building, and accepted the job like any other offer. "I was told the prince was very small, and I thought I should do something that made my voice sound small. So, I stood on my knees on the recording studio," he said.

Ross noted he didn't receive any direction on how to perform, so he sang the two songs for the film in his usual style. The prince character has one moment of dialogue but Ross did not perform it.

Dragonette was also a very popular singer on radio and had provided a voice for Disney's Silly Symphony short "The Goddess of Spring."

Having these two accomplished popular radio stars contribute to the production was a solid publicity angle for GT and the Fleischer studio. It was also a natural progression as the studio had repeatedly used radio, recording and Broadway performers in its Screen Song series.

Both Dragonette and Ross were guests at the Miami premiere of the feature.

For the role of Gulliver, Sam Parker, a Miami radio announcer was hired for the job. The pleasant baritone had a bit of Southern accent and also served as one of the live-action models for Gulliver. According to a column about studio employees that appeared in the Flipper, a studio newsletter, "Did you know that the various models for different portions of Gulliver's anatomy included Dave Fleischer, Seymour Kneitel, Willard Bowsky, Doc Crandall, Jack Ward, Frank Paiker and Thomas Moore. Nelson Demorest did all of the modeling for the full figure from the beginning of the feature to the scene where Gulliver was drawn into the courtyard by his captors. It was at this point that Sam Parker stepped into the picture, or should we say arose to the occasion."

'Variety' reported on March 15, 1939, Max "will begin shooting his full-length cartoon Gulliver's Travels the end of April or early May. He has imported 75 animators from Hollywood and estimates that shooting will be completed in October so the picture can be scheduled for a Christmas release."

The story continued, "Fleischer is turning the picture out at his new Miami studio, one of the most modern in existence, including features for sound control as well as mechanical inventions of Fleischer's. The cartoon producer is going to be able to furnish stills immediately through a new printing process for the purpose with the result that Paramount will have these available on the cartoon as regular features, prior to the completion of the finished picture."

In the same edition, the licensing of GT was discussed, "A new department is being organized by Paramount under Lou Diamond, who heads shorts and music, for the commercial licensing of products based on cartoons, characters developed by Max Fleischer, producer of Betty Boop, Popeye and Color Classics shorts. Fleischer is now making his feature length cartoon in color."

"The department will be headed for Diamond by Harry L. Royster, along with a Paramount theater department executive, who returned last week from Miami conferring with Fleischer on plans for the new division of activity. Formally a district manager for Paramount during the last two years, Royster has been in charge of commercial film in the company's theaters."

A story in 'Variety' on April 12, 1939, detailed that Royster would be responsible for making the deals for tie-in merchandise such as toys, children's costumes, books, cartoon books and candy.

Although there had been a number of products with Betty Boop's image, some illegal and some legal, Max had not been focused on that kind of revenue. He did not benefit from any funds from Popeye merchandising as he only owned the rights to make the animated cartoons. GT provided the opportunity for Max and Paramount to increase profits through another revenue stream.

There were many GT products including coloring books, adaptations of the story, a Big Little book, dolls, postcards and many more items. A story in October in 'Variety' noted there were at least 65 merchandising tie-ins set up. Stores reported using Gulliver material as window displays and "a giant figure" of Gulliver was in the Macy's Thanksgiving Day parade. The final count of licenses for merchandise was above 100.

Paramount started running trade ads for GT in June 1939. The ads proclaimed "the biggest news of the year! A full-length feature cartoon completely filmed in color."

'Variety' reported in August 1939, that the cost of GT had risen above the $900,000 mark and was expected to go to $1.5 million. "This is a higher budget than originally figured," the story noted.

Several editions later, Paramount ran an ad in 'Variety' that the radio and television rights for GT were for sale.

The movie was heavily merchandised.
(Photos of mugs courtesy of JJ Sedelmaier)

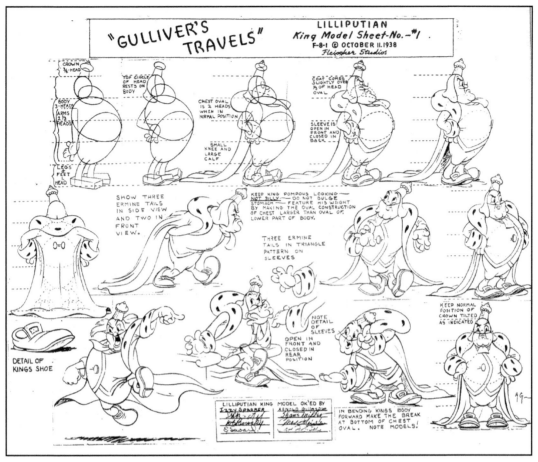

These two model sheets show earlier versions of Gabby and King Little. Despite the various approvals, changes were made.

Memos from Paramount execs suggested there was a time in which actor Gary Cooper was considered for the role of Gulliver. It was theorized that Cooper, under contract at that time to producer Samuel Goldwyn, would be too expensive to engage for the film.

The memos suggest a real disconnect between what Paramount officials envisioned the film to be and what the Fleischer staff was developing.

***

Max was running a race to release GT when Paramount wanted it, but he faced another race. On Feb. 1, 1939, 'Variety' noted that was "a race threatened between Max Fleischer and Walt Disney in getting to the market with their respective cartoon features 'Gulliver's Travels,' and 'Pinocchio.' Present indications are that neither picture will be ready for release until November or December."

GT was released in December of 1939 and "Pinocchio" was released widely on Feb. 23, 1940. With a release schedule that took longer to complete, this meant that, to a certain extent, GT's release and "Pinocchio" overlapped.

'Photoplay,' in its January 1940 issue, ran a photo spread from both animated features and wrote, "At opposite ends of the United States, two brilliant rivals – Walt Disney in Hollywood and Max Fleischer in Miami (he was the father of the first life-like animated drawings on the screen) – coaxed their artist-assistants to finish film version of two beloved classics for your winter's entertainment."

Here are more variations in developing the design of King Little. (Photo courtesy of JJ Sedelmaier)

'Variety' noted on Nov. 22, 1939, that Paramount had put nine special sales reps on the road to do advance work for GT.

Paramount treated this as a major Christmas release, as reported in the Motion Picture Herald. In the Motion Picture Herald in December 1939, the sales aspect of GT was detailed. The film would have "no minimum, no maximum rental stipulation – prices depending on the best bargainer."

The story reported how GT would open Christmas week in 41 key theaters and in about 40 more for New Year's week. The World premiere Dec. 18 at the Sheridan Theater in Miami Beach with a program on 52 CBS stations originating from WMAM Miami at 11 a.m. and 1:45 p.m. for rebroadcast to the West Coat. Jessica Dragonette and Lanny Ross were on the program. A later story noted that Paramount had increased the number of prints to 45 with the number jumping to 60 after New Year's Day.

On Dec. 6, 1939, 'Variety' announced that a Spanish language version of the film was being prepared. Along with a Spanish version prepared, The Motion Picture Herald reported on June 3, 1939, that a Russian version was ready with about five minutes of footage cut that was considered "propaganda." A live action prologue was added showing a boy reading "Gulliver's Travels."

'The Motion Picture Daily' reported in its Dec. 5, 1939, edition, "Max Fleischer is conferring in Hollywood with Cal Howard and Eddie Seward of his scenario 'gag' staff on the next feature-length cartoon to be produced for Paramount release. While 'Gulliver's Travels' is being scored and prepared from Christmas week, in eight reels, Fleischer is preparing a new fantasy subject which has not yet been decided. Luigi Luraschi, Paramount censorship editor, is supervisor on the Spanish version of the cartoon feature."

Seward is an interesting character in the story about the production of GT. He is credited as being an important writer in the development of the adaptation. Animation historian Devon Baxter shared research he has done about Seward, who was born in 1908 and was a journalist and a commercial artist before entering motion picture work. Baxter noted Seward "migrated to California in 1931, where he joined Walt Disney's studio for a brief period ['Mirror News,' Feb. 16, 1954]; hired at Warner Bros. (with Warren Keefe) to develop original story ideas by August 1932 ['The Hollywood Reporter,' Aug. 23, 1932]; collaborated with Warren Duff in writing the screen version of 'The Way of All Women' for KBS-World Wide by January 1933 ['The Hollywood Reporter,' Jan. 11, 1933]; co-wrote the screenplay for 'Walls of Gold' for Fox Film Corporation and 'Wild Innocence' for Cinesound Productions Limited, an Australian film studio, both released in 1933."

Baxter's research continues: Seward "co-wrote the screenplay for 'The Duke Comes Back' Bryant, over to Broadway producer Sam Harris by March 1937 ['The Hollywood Reporter,' Mar. 12, 1937]; worked at MGM in their animation department by February 1938 ['MGM Studio Club News,' Feb. 8, 1938]; became head of the story department on 'Gulliver's Travels' (1939) at Max Fleischer's studio in Miami; worked on a second feature based on Pandora's Box, officially announced in March 1940 ['The Hollywood Reporter,' Mar. 29, 1940]."

The new production based on the Greek myth did not happen and Baxter noted Seward continued his career in animation. "[He was] hired at Screen Gems under the supervision of Dave Fleischer by June 1942 [The Hollywood Reporter, June 30, 1942]; he is credited as a story man on five theatricals released from 1944-45; became a story man at George Pal's studio (joined by Webb Smith) by October 1944, according to 'The Animator;' wrote 'Jasper and the Beanstalk' (1945), 'My Man Jasper' (1945), and 'Together in the Weather' (1946) with Webb Smith ['The Hollywood Reporter,' Oct. 1, 1945; 'The Hollywood Reporter,' Oct. 9, 1945]; continued to write for Pal as late as February 1946 [The Los Angeles Times, Feb. 10, 1946]; co-wrote screenplays for several entries in the Bowery Boys films for Monogram in the late 1940s, and is credited for additional dialogue in 'Bela Lugosi Meets a Brooklyn Gorilla' (1952); died from a cerebral hemorrhage on Feb. 12, 1954."

'The Film Daily's' columnist Phil M. Daly wrote the following for the Dec. 11, 1939, edition: "Whatever you can say about it, dear old 1939 A.D. has been the most animated in pix history and if there is any doubt on your mind, we refer you to Messrs. Disney, Fleischer, Schlesinger, et al.

"There's been more drawing in the above gent's studios during the past 12 months than you're likely to find in all the realm of contemporary poker. For example, in the case of Max Fleischer 'tis authoritatively said that 700 artists were on the boards to turn out some 500,000 celluloids and backgrounds which go to make up 115,200 composite scenes for 'Gulliver's Travels' and that approximately 16 tons of drawing paper were used plus 12 tons of paint, which sounds like enough."

"Not only on the statistical side but from that of entertainment, 'Gulliver' is a big pro-

These two photos show two different production elements at work. At top, in-betweeners work in their new area of the studio. At bottom, cel painters are replenishing their stock. (Photo courtesy of JJ Sedelmaier)

Artists Roberta Bottcher and Aaron Krawetz work on a drawing from "Gulliver's Travels." (Photo courtesy of JJ Sedelmaier)

duction and is certain to make a gargantuan pile of dough for the producers, distribs, and exhibs. It cost a pile, too, a mere million or more. Isn't the pix biz wonderful?"

There must have been a huge sigh of relief at the studio when GT was finished. Seymour Reit, a writer at the studio who would later create Casper the Friendly Ghost, wrote in the studio's newsletter 'The Flipper,' the following poem:

### A Song of Impatience

The feature's finished,
The feature's done,
Work is over and worry's begun
Come bite your nails,
Come tear your hair
Come harry the gods in
Hysterical prayer.

We mumble morosely,
All joy we despise
As we watch the growth of rungs 'neath our eyes
And we wait for the day that
the critic unravels
The wondrous merits of "Gulliver's Travels."

Hark Winchell and Fidler and Nugent
and Nugent and all!
When Gulliver opens
Heed promptly the call.
We know it's a wow
And we're sure it will click, but hurry, we beg you,
And tell us that quick.

Gullivers travels trade ads. Paramount clearly wanted a winner and presented evidence that "Gulliver's Travels" was going to make money for everyone.

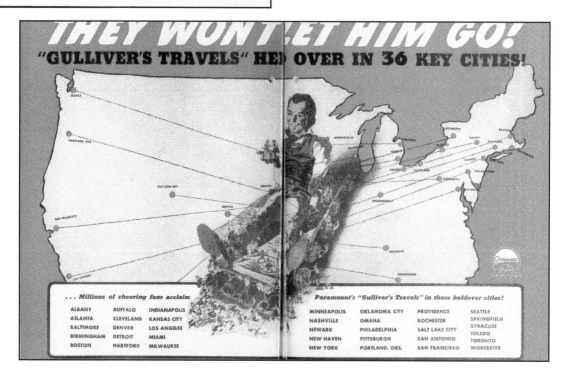

The same issue of 'The Flipper,' issued in time for a December dinner dance for Fleischer employees, is filled with references in cartoons about the challenges GT brought to the studio. It's also evident from the booklet's lengthy description of the various sports teams and other activities in which employees could participate, there was a big difference in the lifestyle as opposed to New York City. (See following pages for pages from the booklet).

The contents reflected both a hope the film would succeed as well as plenty of references to the difficulty of the task.

The Miami premiere was Dec. 18, 1939, in two theaters: The Sheridan and The Colony. Paramount brass, entertainment figures and local officials joined audiences for the event. Overhead floated a balloon with the theaters' names and "Gulliver's Travels, World Premiere." 'The Miami Herald' gushed over the assembled dignitaries and made special note of how the popular CBS radio announcer Ted Husing tried sneaking through the crowd disguised by a pair of amber glasses.

Gulliver himself was represented – not by Sam Parker, but a very tall man in a Gulliver costume.

# G. MICHAEL DOBBS

## UNIVERSAL EXECUTIVES MEET; GULLIVER IN MIAMI; OTHER ITEMS OF NOTE

FROM ALTEC TO CONRAC. A. A. Ward, formerly in charge of the Altec Service Corporation's special development work, is named chief engineer for Conrac, Inc., ticket register manufacturers.

"MEET DR. CHRISTIAN." That is just what vice-president Ned E. Depinet (left) did when Jean Hersholt, star of the RKO-Radio picture, visited the home office.

"GULLIVER" IN MIAMI. At the Miami premiere of "Gulliver's Travels" is seen (upper left) Max Fleischer, whose first feature-length, Technicolor cartoon is this Paramount release. Upper right shows director Dave Fleischer with the rubber models of Gulliver and Popeye. Bottom shows Dave Ballard, Paramount's eight-foot "Gulliver", and Leslie Harris at the picture's recent opening at the Sheridan, Miami.

UNIVERSAL EXECUTIVES MEET. Leading a product discussion last week of home-office and field executives, President Nate J. Blumberg and general sales manager William A. Scully (right photograph) faced (left picture, left to right in front) Chicago's E. T. Gomersall, West Coast's Al O'Keefe, New York's A. J. Her- man, Pittsburgh's Dave Miller, Kansas City's Pete Dana, New York's Dave Levy, (back row) Atlanta's Harry Graham, eastern sales manager Frank J. A. McCarthy, home-office's James Jordan, Andrew Sharick, Morris Alin, eastern sales manager William J. Heineman and told them about future product.

*December 27, 1939*

The Exhibitor rans this coverage of the Miami premiere. That is not the voice of Gulliver, Sam Parker, in the Gulliver costume.

Looking at 'The Miami Herald' coverage, it's clear the success of the Fleischer Studio had economic implications for the Miami area and for the state of Florida.

According to the story that appeared on the front page of the Dec. 19, 1939, edition, "Mayor E.G. Sewell and President John C. Hall of the Miami Chamber of Commerce, declaring Miami definitely was 'in the market' for more locally made movies, proffered their official assistance at a gathering of 200 civic and business investors in the Columbus Hotel."

The story noted, "Some 17 pictures had been made in that initial attempt."

Florida had a history of filmmaking starts and stops. In the early days of silent cinema, according to an essay by Bill DeYoung, the state's filmmaking activities centered around Jacksonville. The pioneering Norman Film Manufacturing Co. made movies featuring all black casts. Kalem Studios, of New York City, also opened a facility in Florida to take advantage of mild winter weather for production.

The producers shifted their operations from New York City to southern California to escape the agents who enforced the Edison Trust – which held patents for the production of movies and made sure producers paid for the rights to use the technology – and the film industry in Florida suffered. With the growth of Hollywood as a production center the idea of establishing a second center was made difficult.

There were attempts in the 1920s and '30s to establish independent production in Florida but without great success. One notable one involved a producer who lured Buster Keaton after he left MGM in the early 1930s with a plan to build a huge soundstage and to make features there. In James Curtis' biography of Keaton, he notes the funding for the soundstage and the features fell apart.

It is little wonder then, when the new Fleischer Studio opened in Miami in October 1938, it was celebrated. There were congratulatory ads in 'The Miami Herald,' including one from theaters owned by Paramount telling movie-goers to watch for the first Fleischer cartoon made in Miami.

In a front-page story in the Motion Picture Daily (Dec. 5, 1939) the effort in Florida to bring motion picture production was emphasized. The successful production of GT made John Hall, the president of the Miami Chamber of Commerce say, "Florida has plenty of offer film producers and we will match anything that Mayor La Guardia offers, plus a little more."

Apparently, the mayor of New York City didn't like to see the Fleischer Studio relocate from the city.

Jack Mercer and his first wife, singer and voice actress Margie Hines are seen in this publicity shot in the *Motion Picture Herald*, (April 15, 1939).

Hall continued, "We offer tax exemption for 15 years and a year-round climate that makes even Californians want to change the subject when you speak of the weather."

The studio made news in Miami. The marriage of Jack Mercer and Margie Hines – the singer who was one of the early voices of Betty Boop and now provided the voice of Olive Oyl – made front page news at 'The Miami Herald' on March 10, 1939.

The pair either lied about their ages for the story or reporter Vernon Van Ness had his facts wrong. Hines was 21, according to the story, but was actually 30 and Mercer was listed as 24 but was actually 29. They were married March 3 in Fort Lauderdale.


At the event on Dec. 19, Max, Ross and Dragonette and Paramount officials met at special luncheon. It was a self-congratulatory event but Max added a little reality to the situation. He was quoted by 'The Miami Herald' about how difficult this assignment had been.

"Eighteen months ago, when the decision was made to produce Gulliver's Travels as a feature, we faced some very real problems. For example, more than two years is required to produce an animated cartoon feature in color and sound, provided one has a large enough staff sufficiently experienced and coordinated to do the work.

"When we started this picture, we lacked space, manpower and the machinery for feature work. We only had one and half years instead of two years in which to build, move, organize, equip and complete the picture for distribution by Christmas, 1939."

Generally, the reviews were positive. Walter Winchell, whose highly popular radio show was part gossip, part news and part opinion, raved about the film.

*Harrison's Reports* in its December 1939 edition noted, "Delightful entertainment. The material lends itself perfectly to cartoon work, for it is mostly comic. It is grand entertainment for children, since there is nothing in it to frighten them and adults too, should enjoy it for the action is fast, the ideas ingenious and the material comical and there is plenty of music that gave the film its "Blue Ribbon Award" for December, only the second Paramount film of that year to earn the distinction."

*The New York Times* said the film "was a fairy tale for children," while "Snow White" had been a "fairy tale for adults." It deemed the movie entertaining, though.

*Variety* described the movie as "an excellent job of animation, audience interest and all-around entertainment." Newsweek called it "diverting."

*The Boston Transcript* wrote in its review, "The younger patrons ought to be properly grateful for it. For if the Fleischer Brothers had not turned out a picture in the inspired or Disney sense, they have least contrived an hour and a half of bright colors, broad humor and tuneful music … the irony of Swift's tale, it seems scarcely necessary to note, is missing."

*The Film Daily* carried a front-page review of the film presented as a letter to the editor on its Dec. 19, 1939, edition. The interesting thing is how it approaches the issue of comparisons to "Snow White" head-on.

It read, "I am happy to report that 'Gulliver's Travels' is a great and glorious picture. I report this on the highest authority and with complete awareness of the importance of the occasion.

My authority for this assertion is the young lady, then 11, now 13, who accompanied me to the world premiere of 'Snow White and the Seven Dwarfs' on Dec. 22, 1937, and authorized me to announce in your paper the next day that the first feature length cartoon film would 'captivate the population as no other motion picture ever has.' This young lady authorizes me to repeat the same eminently substantiated statement here.

"You will remember, I'm sure, this young lady's opinion about 'Snow White' was, at the time of utterance, distinctly a minority vote. The adult experts were full quibblings and questions about such things as the expertness of animation, the possibilities of making audiences sit still and stay interested for 82 minutes. The experts found out about those matters the hard way. The eyes of youth saw only what the eyes of paying audiences saw, about seven million dollars' worth.

"The experts were quibbling and questioning about the same sort of things last night at the Village Theater in Westwood, but your informant and his informant knew before the film was five minutes old on the screen that here was another box-office natural set for terrific grosses and as sure to thrill the world of entertainment seekers as anything a camera can produce.

"We talked about it in detail afterward and my companion became very explicit. Although they are beside the point and completely irrelevant so far as the audience value of the picture is concerned, these are her observations:

"'Gulliver is a much more amusing picture that 'Snow White,' much stronger in comedy values. 'Snow White' is a tenderer, sweeter picture, stronger in sentimental appeal. The musical numbers run neck and neck. The pictures are as different as any other two pictures and the fact that there are now two of them proves that other extremely important, and until now unestablished fact, that there can be many more of as there can be pictures in any medium.'

"I am able to report on my own, that Messrs. Max and Dave Fleischer have supplied the art industry with a tremendous asset a magnificent picture which is as bright and entertaining as any adult or child ought to be in the market for a picture full of entertainment, an amusing picture, rich in invention and powerful in its ability to hold eye and ear, an altogether delectable screen experience."

"Color, now practically in full command in the cartoon field, here tightens its hold. Ralph Rainger and Leo Robin, long headliners in the field of popular composition, add to their stature by their musical contributions to 'Gulliver.' So do Sammy Timburg, Al Neiburg and Winston Sharples. And it is more likely that the voices of the unseen Jessica Dragonette and Lanny Ross, singing the love songs of the cartoon prince and princess, will gain fame and popularity as the films makes its way around the world. Victor Young's scoring of the picture is a triumph of brilliant consistency.

"The running time is 77 minutes and the picture is appropriate – indeed mandatory, if I say so – for the exhibition everywhere to any and all kinds of audiences. Yours very truly, William R. Weaver."

Looking at reviews of how the film played in local theaters, (*Motion Picture Herald,* April 13, 1940) the opinions were not always positive. "A much finer cartoon in every respect that grossed about one-third as much as 'Snow White.' The artwork, characterizations, and music

Copyright 1939, Paramount Pictures Inc. "GULLIVER'S TRAVELS" in TECHNICOLOR Produced by Max Fleischer Based on
Permission granted for Newspaper and Jonathan Swift's Immortal Tale. A Paramount Picture.
Magazine reproduction. Made in U.S.A.
"Imprime Aux Etats Unis D'Amerique."

were excellent, but the adult draw was very poor. Only criticism: it was too short," wrote the manager of the Ritz Theater in North Vernon, IN.

"You won't get rich on this one. Not enough adult business," wrote A.J. Turcotte of the Star Theatre in Newmarket, NH.

Other theater managers complained about the rental rates being too high.

GT was still in circulation several years later. There was a favorable review from a theater manager in Wyoming in the *Motion Picture Herald's* July 15, 1944, edition.

GT proved to a profitable film for Paramount. The box office gross for GT has been reported at $3.27 million, which would be about $65,105,700 today. *The Motion Picture Herald* in its March 2, 1940, edition noted the "January Champions at the Box Office." Six directors were noted for their recent releases: George Marshall for "Destry Rides Again," William Keighley for "The Fighting 69th," Victor Fleming for "Gone with the Wind," Sidney Lanfield for "Swanee River," William Dieterle for "The Hunchback of Notre Dame," and Dave Fleischer for GT.

Paramount ran a trade ad in the *Motion Picture Herald* touting the box-office results for the film. There are some people who purport that GT was a financial failure. It clearly was not according to the box-office figures and the fact that Paramount wanted a second feature from the studio.

GT opened Jan. 1, 1940, at the Carlton Theater in London (Film Daily Dec. 12, 1939) where a "huge success" was predicted.

Looking at GT today, there are scenes that work very well and those that are very curious choices.

The first stylistic decision one notices was to animate the Lilliputians as standard cartoon characters and to have a far more realistic approach to Gulliver by filming live action sequences and then rotoscoping them.

This creates an interesting visual statement by having more life-like animation for Gulliver as a way to underscore he is a stranger in a strange land. I don't believe that rotoscoping Gulliver was a means to speed up production or to give less experienced artists assistance with the character.

The plot has Gulliver wind up unconscious on the beaches of Lilliput after his ship is lost in a storm at sea. Gabby, the town crier doing his nightly rounds, discovers Gulliver, who is a giant to the Lilliputians. Gabby is unaware that King Little of Lilliput and King Bombo of Blefuscu had come to an agreement concerning the marriage of their daughter and son, respectively, and then broke the agreement because it was traditional for each country to play its own love song at state marriages and they would not compromise.

The discovery of the giant is a distraction for the king who is worried about his daughter since her marriage is now off.

Gabby organizes an effort to capture and bring the giant to the king. Naturally, everyone is afraid of the giant, but the Lilliputians soon learn he does not intend to harm anyone.

Bombo, however, is preparing for war, having left three spies in Lilliput. The spies understand that Gulliver must be neutralized and decide to steal Gulliver's pistol knowing that could kill him.

When Blefuscu attacks through the use of its fleet, Gulliver gathers up the fleet dragging them to shore. He stops the war and provides a solution to the marriage stalemate by showing how the two songs "Faithful" and "Forever" can be sung together.

To express their gratitude the Lilliputians build a ship large enough for Gulliver to sail home.

The film certainly has a different look than "Snow White" as it has a color design that strongly suggests the muted tones used by Arthur Rackham. It may not have taken full advantage of Technicolor, but it is striking and seems appropriate for a fairy tale style story.

The star of the film without a doubt is Gabby, who as I mentioned earlier, is a liar and blowhard. He is also a bit of a coward. I understand that in the American comic tradition such a character has been used many times, but in this film, one would think that Gulliver and his reactions to the Lilliputians would come to the forefront of the story.

The beach sequence opening the film with the Lilliputians figuring out how to secure and transport the giant is pure Fleischer studio convention. It's handled very well in both the animation and invention of the sequence.

Another scene that is quite effective has Gulliver and the Lilliputians celebrating with Gulliver sitting at an oversized table. It's a night scene and the use of light and shadow is impressive. There's a charming bit with King Little dancing with one of Gulliver's hands.

These positive aspects of the films are damaged, though, by the prince and princess being non-entities. There is only line of dialogue for the prince and none for the princess. It's impossible to care about them as characters.

Gulliver is also a bit of an enigma. There's little effort to develop him as a character.

The sequence in which Gabby is walking with Gulliver and spinning a tall tale through rhyme does not to advance either plot or characterization. Gulliver's rejoinder of saying "My, my" sounds odd.

The vacuum caused by the lack of characterization means more eyes are on Gabby. Perhaps that was the intent but as the following series of Gabby cartoons showed, the character is more acceptable in small doses.

One aspect of the film that is successful is the musical score by Victory Young and the six pop songs in the soundtrack. "All's Well," "Faithful Forever," "Bluebirds in the Moonlight," and "We're All Together Now," were written by the prominent team Leo Robin and Ralph Rainger. The team earned an Academy Award nomination for best original song for "Faithful Forever," but lost to "Over the Rainbow."

Several of the songs were recorded by some prominent artists, such as Glenn Miller and Judy Garland. According to *Variety*, Robin and Rainger spent a month in New York City in the summer of 1938 writing their songs. *Film Daily* noted in its Nov. 8, 1939, edition the songs yielded 60 separate recordings.

Sammy Timburg, Al Neiburg and Winston Sharples wrote "It's a Hap-Hap-Happy Day," which became very well used in subsequent Fleischer and Famous productions.

# JANUARY CHAMPIONS AT THE BOX OFFICE

*Victor Fleming, director*

*George Marshall, director*

*William Keighley, director*

**DESTRY RIDES AGAIN:** Produced and distributed by Universal. Producer, Joe Pasternak. Director, George Marshall. Screen play, Felix Jackson, Henry Myers, Gertrude Purcell. Cast: Marlene Dietrich, James Stewart, Charles Winninger, Mischa Auer. Release date, December 29, 1939.

**THE FIGHTING 69TH:** Produced and distributed by Warner Bros. Executive producer, Hal B. Wallis. Director, William Keighley. Cast: James Cagney, Pat O'Brien, George Brent, Jeffrey Lynn, Alan Hale, Frank McHugh, Dennis Morgan. Release date, January 27, 1940.

**GONE WITH THE WIND:** Presented by Selznick International in association with M-G-M. From the novel by Margaret Mitchell. Produced by David O. Selznick. Director, Victor Fleming. Screen play, Sidney Howard. Released by Loew's, Inc. Technicolor associates, Ray Rennahan, Wilfred M. Cline. Technicolor supervision, Natalie Kalmus. Cast: Vivien Leigh, Clark Gable, Leslie Howard, Olivia de Haviland, George Reeves, Fred Crane, Thomas Mitchell, Barbara O'Neill, Victor Jory. Release date: not determined. Special engagements began December 15, 1939.

*Dave Fleischer, director*

*William Dieterle, director*

*Sidney Lanfield, director*

**GULLIVER'S TRAVELS:** Produced and distributed by Paramount Pictures. Producer, Max Fleischer. Director, Dave Fleischer. Screen play, Dan Gordon, Cal Howard, Ted Pierce, I. Sparber and Edmund Seward. Music and lyrics, Ralph Rainger and Leo Robin. Singing voices of Princess Glory and Prince David, Jessica Dragonette and Lanny Ross. Technicolor adviser, Johnny Burks. Release date, December 22, 1939.

**THE HUNCHBACK OF NOTRE DAME:** Produced and distributed by RKO-Radio. Producer, Pandro S. Berman. Director, William Dieterle. Screen play, Sonya Lavien. Adaptation, Bruno Frank. Cameraman, Joseph H. August. Film editors, Robert Wise and William Hamilton. Cast: Charles Laughton, Sir Cedric Harkwicke, Thomas Mitchell, Maureen O'Hara, Edmond O'Brien, Alan Marshal, Walter Hampden. Release date, December 28, '39.

**SWANEE RIVER:** Produced and distributed by Twentieth Century-Fox. Producer, Darryl F. Zanuck. Director, Sidney Lanfield. Associate producer, Kenneth Macgowan. Technicolor director, Natalie Kalmus. Cast: Don Ameche, Andrea Leeds, Al Jolson, Felix Bressart, Chick Chandler, Russell Hicks, George Reed, Hall Johnson Choir, Richard Clarke, Diane Fisher, Charles Halton, George Breakstone, Al Herman. Release date, January 5, 1940.

Dave Fleischer was celebrated by *The Motion Picture Herald* on March 2, 1940, as being a "box office champion" for January 1940. He was honored alongside of directors Victor Fleming, William Dieterle, George Marshall, William Keighley and Sidney Lanfield.

Reportedly, Dave had given composer Victor Young some suggestions about his score. That apparently made Dave very happy.

*Motion Picture Herald* on Jan. 6, 1940, reported that GT cels and art were being sold to collectors by F.A.R Galleries in New York City. Another gallery was selling Disney cels.

*The Mami Herald* noted Paramount's approval of GT in its Dec. 13, 1939, story when it quoted Paramount President Barney Balaban saying, "So far, as we can see there is no limit to what this picture may gross. Evidence of our satisfaction with and confidence in this production is afforded by the fact at our meeting in Hollywood, we have given Fleischer a definite assignment to make another full-length Technicolor cartoon."

Culhane had plenty to say about GT in our interview. "But after it was over, a funny thing happened. Everyone was convinced this was a smash, that this was going to be as good as Walt's any day ... the valor of ignorance, because it wasn't. It was an improvement as far as Max's place was concerned, a big jump ahead, but it really wasn't their bag. They stayed with what I called a 'peasant approach.' Both Max and Walt in the beginning had farmer type jokes, barnyard jokes, a very low sense of humor. I say 'low;' not in the derogatory sense, maybe I should say broad. Kinda of pie in your face approach, and not much else. And Max stayed with except for these rare excursions into other type of jokes.

"They thought it was going to be a big hit. I knew it wasn't going to be. I didn't want to say anything. It turned out not to be the greatest thing. They thought it was going to make millions and it didn't."

When reminded it did make money, he replied, "It did well enough, but it was no 'Snow White.' That was a disappointment."

He continued, "Max had this approach ... let me give you the other side. At Walt's no one cared how much work you did in a day. I mean you could work all day and at the end of the day, look at your work and throw it in the wastepaper basket. The whole Goddamn thing and do it over again. And over again. But when you put it in front of Walt to look at it, it better be damn good. If it wasn't, if you made a mistake of putting in something inferior, you were in trouble. I mean serious trouble, If you did it often enough, you got thrown out without any recourse.

"At Max's things were different. My education at Max's was in fact wrong for working at Walt's because we just worked according to the mood on a picture we cooked up or started from someone else's idea. In my own case, I was very much an in-and-outer. One day, I felt like doing very good animation and I did. The next day, it wasn't good at all and it was used. Everything was used. Nothing was thrown out.

"So, when I went to Walt's every animator had their own Moviola to study your work – nitpick this and change that. And you could do this as often as you want – send it back and re-shoot it until you think it's right.

"Max, when he was working on Gulliver had one Moviola. One. For all of the animators. And he said anybody who didn't know what he was going to do is no animator. That's a different approach all together.

"So, the result was some of it was good and some of it was bad. I remember one time, I tried

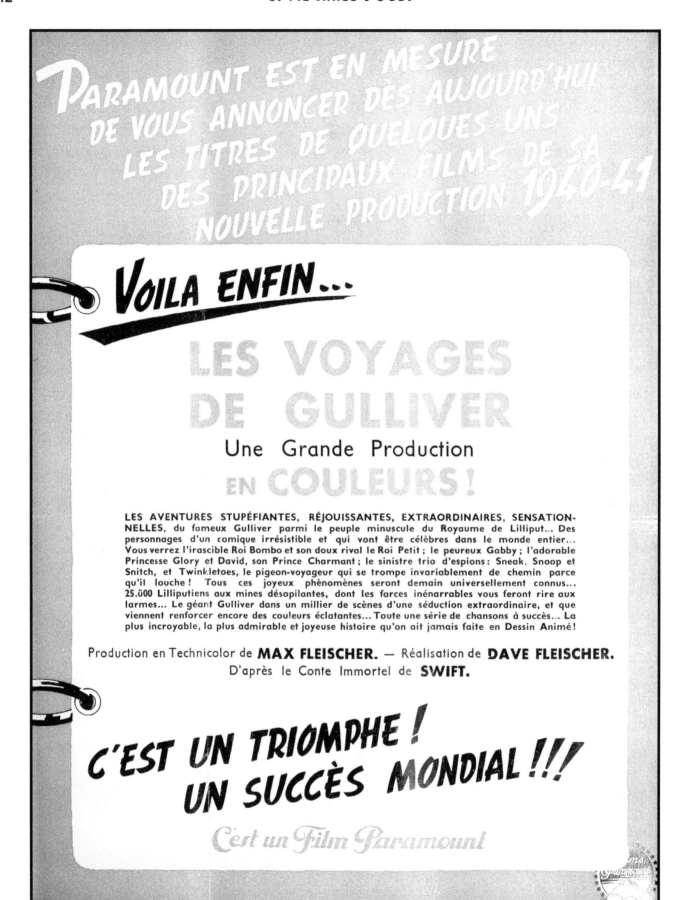

Paramount marketed the film to France in 1940.

### "Gulliver en el País de los Enanos" (Paramount) en Miniatura

En la isla de Liliput viven felices sus habitantes, pensando en las grandes fiestas que se preparan con motivo de la boda de la princesa Gloria, hija del Rey Little, con el príncipe David, hijo del Rey Bombo, cuando el sereno Gabby, en su recorrido por la ciudad, se encuentra un gigante dormido en la playa.

Gabby, aterrorizado, vuelve como una centella hacia la ciudad, despertando a todo el mundo con sus gritos de alarma. Todos le toman por loco y no pueden creer sus cuentos. Desesperado, decide llegar en busca de ayuda hasta el palacio del Rey Little, donde éste, con el Rey Bombo, discute los planes de la boda.

Inoportunamente, porque el Rey Little y el Rey Bombo acaban de pelearse por cual ha de ser el himno que se ha de cantar en la boda, habiendo salido del palacio el Rey Bombo en plan de guerra a muerte con el Rey Little, llega Gabby ante el trono. El Rey Little se espanta ante la noticia y ordena que Gabby convoque a todo su pueblo.

Al toque desesperado de la campana de la plaza, acude todo el mundo. Deciden ir todos en masa, con camiones y grúas, a prender al gigante. Y, aunque despavoridos por el miedo, los habitantes de Liliput ven en la llegada del gigante la salvación, tal vez, contra la guerra próxima que se ven obligados a librar con los ejércitos del Rey Bombo.

Aprovechando el sueño del gigante, con esfuerzos sobrehumanos logran encadenarle, moviendo sus piernas y brazos por medio de potentes grúas, hasta poderle subir a una plataforma, que, tirada por varios troncos de briosos caballos, le lleva hasta el centro del pueblo, deteniéndose ante el palacio del Rey Little.

Cuando Guliver despierta se encuentra encadenado por finísimos hilos de alambre, que rompe fácilmente, y se asombra de que los pequeños insectos que le cosquillean por todas partes sean hombres de carne y hueso, como él. Conminado por el Rey Little, pronto se pone al corriente de lo que ocurre y ofrece al rey su ayuda incondicional.

Al aparecer en alta mar los navíos enemigos del Rey Bombo, Gulliver los arrastra fácilmente hacia tierra, convenciendo a los dos reyes de que deben hacer la paz, uniendo los dos himnos nacionales en uno sólo y haciendo así felices a los jóvenes príncipes. A ello acceden los reyes complacidos, con gran contento de los novios y del populacho.

Y después de una serie de aventuras, a cual más curiosas y originales, en la isla de Liliput, Guliver abandona sus playas, a bordo del navío que le regalan los liliputienses, dejando un grato recuerdo entre los súbditos del Rey Little y del Rey Bombo, cuyos hijos, los príncipes David y Gloria, son felices por los siglos de los siglos. . . .

And the Spanish-speaking market was covered, as well.

some oddball approach on a piece of action and I sent it in to be shot and I was looking at it on the Moviola. Seymour Kneitel came over and said, 'What's that? That's wrong.' I said, 'Well that was just an experiment.' He said, "It's still wrong.' I said, "It was an experiment.' He said, 'It didn't come out.'"

Culhane asserted that Max would not "keep something in that was blatantly wrong, but he didn't believe in refining anything."

In a story about theaters in Paris after the Nazis fled the city, (*Film Daily,* Dec. 14, 1944) the Paramount exchange only had two films at its Paris office, GT and "Lives of the Bengal Lancers," both of which were reported enjoying "tremendous patronage." All other films had been either destroyed or removed by the Nazi forces.

It should be noted that GT still had a theatrical presence in Europe through the 1970s. There was a German print of the film with newly recorded dialogue and songs with the written introduction to the story also reshot in German. There have been reissues of the film in France, Great Britain and Poland.

Today, a film could have a second life or build an audience through home video and streaming. In the pre-home video era, a movie went from first run to second run theaters and, starting

This frame blow-up was part of a French revival of the film.

in the 1950s, then potentially to television. In 1940, when the first and second runs of GT ended, the film, like others, was simply stored away. It's conceivable a theater owner might want it for a Christmas vacation show, but the commercial value of a movie was bleak.

Then came television into the American pop culture life beginning in 1949. One thing local television stations needed was programming. There were shows offered by the three networks to them, but then local stations were expected to fill much of their schedule on their own. This is when the stations produced their own shows, as well as bought packages of old movies, as well as syndicated programs.

National Telefilm Associates (NTA) was a company that sold programming to stations. It was founded in 1954 and distributed cartoons, such as the Betty Boop series, which it controlled when the company bought U.M.&M, which had bought rights to the pre-October 1950 Fleischer and Famous shorts (excluding Popeye and Superman). NTA bought rights to features from Republic Pictures and 20th Century-Fox, among others.

It also wanted to build a network of local stations on which NTA's movie acquisitions could be seen. *Television Digest* wrote in its Oct. 13, 1956, edition that NTA bought Rainbow Productions from Paramount, which included the two Fleischer features, along with "Bells of St. Mary." The cost was $775,000.

*Motion Picture Daily* (Jan 22, 1957), noted that NTA had established a theatrical arm to distribute films, including GT. The plan was to offer GT and the renamed "Mr. Bug Goes to Town" to television stations one year after the theatrical arm.

In the July 21, 1958, *Film Bulletin*, in an article about whether or not blockbusters were the most reliable way to make money for theaters, various exhibitors offered their opinion. Robert Selig, president of Fox Inter-Mountain Amusement Corporation, mentioned how his organization was making double bills of family films to lure people away from television. One such double bill was GT with "Suzannah of the Mounties," a 1939 western starring Shirley Temple and Randolph Scott, that also had been acquired by NTA.

An ad in *Variety*, April 15, 1959, for ORB distributor in Great Britain noted the distributor was handling the re-release of GT in the United Kingdom for NTA.

NTA announced in a trade ad in *Broadcasting* on March 14, 1960, the availability for television for six "classics, timeless in appeal." These included "Tom Sawyer," Little

Reissue lobby card from NTA.

Women," "Bambutti" [a documentary set in Africa] and both "GT and "Hoppity Goes to Town." NTA certainly introduced the Fleischer brand to a whole new generation watching television.

Somewhere along the way, though, the copyright was not renewed, which created a real problem for the film's reputation when home video became popular in the 1980s.

# The Flippers Club

The vestiges of the strike were very real in Miami and the one-time family spirit that many people saw at the studio in New York clearly needed rebuilding. The following booklet was handed out at a celebration dinner at the end of 1939. One can see the jubilation that "Gulliver's Travels" was completed and notice many references to the hard work the feature represented.

DAVE TENDLAR
President

HAROLD WALKER
Vice-President

AARON KRAWETZ
Treasurer

FRANK KELLING
Secretary

CHARLIE SCHETTLER
Chairman, Board of
Directors

GRIM NATWICK
Vice-Chairman
Board of Directors

WILLARD BOWSKY
Director

SEYMOUR KNEITEL
Director

TOM MOORE
Director

"DOC" CRANDALL
Director

HAL WALKER
Director

BILL TURNER
Director

JOHN BURKS
Director

# GREETINGS

To:

THE FLIPPERS CLUB is now entering its second year of existence and its ambition to become better acquainted is certainly being realized.

The "Flippers," consisting of people actively engaged in the production of animated cartoons in Dade County, Florida, is a social and athletic club formed for the purpose of promoting good fellowship and mutual understanding among its members.

Tonight's dance and entertainment, which we hope everyone will enjoy, is an example of what the Flippers Club can and should do for its members and their friends. In the future we intend to plan outings, dances and parties which will develop social contacts and also promote healthful athletic activity.

No one can deny that the best way to become fully acquainted is to plan activities in which all can participate and find enjoyment. One very important point, however, for our members to bear in mind is this:

In order to have these gatherings, it is essential that each member feel an integral part of these activities, not merely a guest of the occasion.

There is no reason why the Flippers should not become one of the finest groups of its kind in the country. Of course this can only be accomplished by the fullest co-operation of all its members. If, in the planning of activities, each will contribute a little time and effort when called upon, then and only then can the final goal of the Flippers be realized.

We cannot form a club, then sit back and wait for things to happen, or hold dinners and parties without the co-operation of members, or have a Flippers Club at all if members won't all "pitch in."

I therefore urge each "Flipper" to make every effort to do his share and in doing so help to further the interests of all.

With sincere good wishes for a Merry Christmas and a Happy New Year.

Your President,
DAVE TENDLAR.

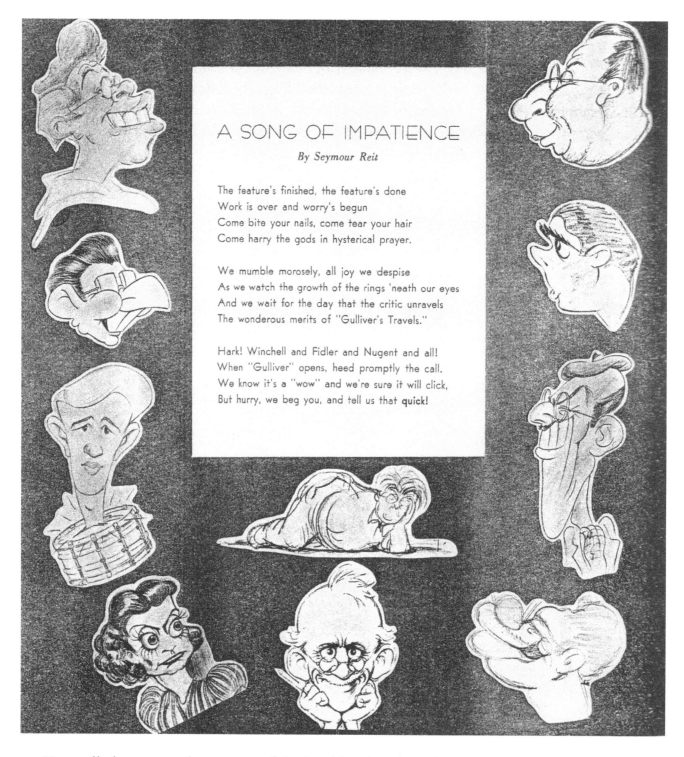

A SONG OF IMPATIENCE

By Seymour Reit

The feature's finished, the feature's done
Work is over and worry's begun
Come bite your nails, come tear your hair
Come harry the gods in hysterical prayer.

We mumble morosely, all joy we despise
As we watch the growth of the rings 'neath our eyes
And we wait for the day that the critic unravels
The wonderous merits of "Gulliver's Travels."

Hark! Winchell and Fidler and Nugent and all!
When "Gulliver" opens, heed promptly the call.
We know it's a "wow" and we're sure it will click,
But hurry, we beg you, and tell us that **quick**!

You will also notice the section of the booklet that described the many clubs and activities in which the studio employees were engaged.

They were in many ways strangers in a strange land. While plenty of people from the north were vacationing in Florida by this time, none-the-less Miami was certainly not New York City.

The Fleischer staff were trying to create their own community, their own home here. None of them knew just how short their time in Florida would really be.

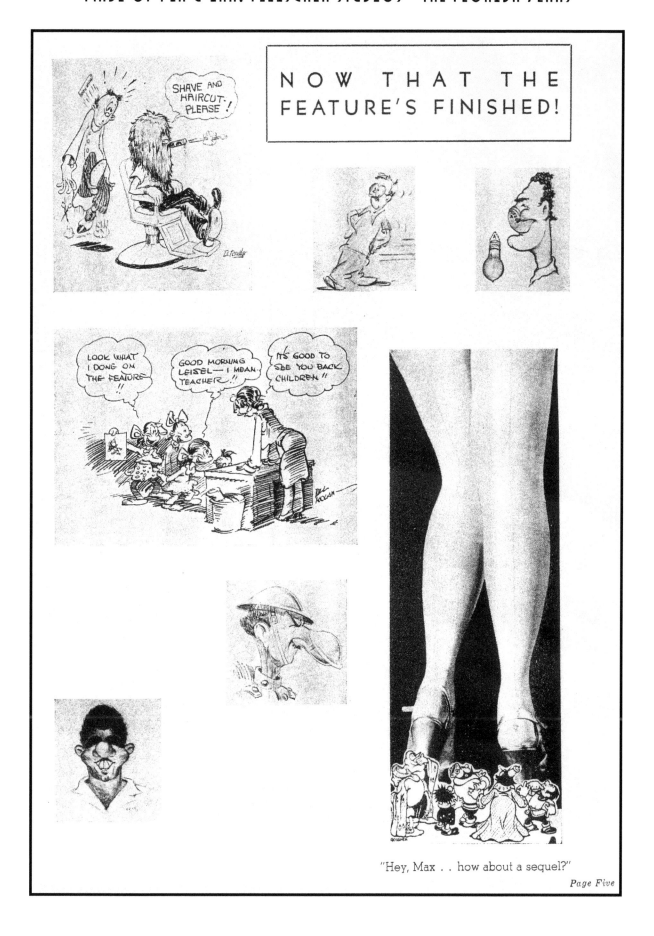

"Hey, Max . . how about a sequel?"

*Page Five*

## NOW THAT THE FEATURE'S FINISHED . . .

NOW THAT THE FEATURE'S FINISHED . . .

# OUT-WITTING DEMENTIA PRAECOX

| *Or* | *By* |
|---|---|

### *Why I Quit the Genius Racket!*

### "PINTO" COLVIG
(America's Problem-Child No. 1)

ACCORDING TO EINSTEIN, there are over 800 bald-headed bachelors in Greenland—all of which has nothing to do with what I am going to write about.

To begin with, I was born beneath a crazy-quilt and my first eight years were spent taking apart an old alarm clock and to this day the damn thing has never run and thank God for that!

One evening while sitting among my scattered clock springs, Father looked up from his newspaper and said to Mother: "That boy's a genius!"

"And, pray, what is a genius?" asked Mother.

"A genius," returned Father, "is a person possessing high mental powers or faculties, with a remarkable aptitude for some special pursuit."

"Such as tearing old alarm clocks apart?" retorts Mother.

"Hell no!" ejaculates Father. "That boy is a Genius-of-The-Arts. He shall delve into Poetry, Music ,Drama and Animated Cartooning!" (Animated cartoons were unknown in those days, but Father was 'way ahead of his time.)

Poetically, my first recognition came when as a valedictorian (Class of Ought-6) I composed and recited the following:

'Twas a dark and stormy, sunny night—

Th' moon came up like thunder!

Th' wind, it blew!

Th' snow, it **Snew**—

Or, **does** snow **snew?** . . . I (wonder!)

Then followed my Music, Drama and Art. For the nonce I tossed my Poetry aside, and into the remaining three arts I delved; until, one day I found myself playing E-flat clarinet with the Al G. Barnes' Big 3-Ring Wild Animal Circus Band.

Ere 'twasn't long, tho, when my artistic instincts overpowered my musical ambitions, so I traded my old clarinet for a little box of school crayons and set out to master Animated Cartooning—and, quicker than you can say Oblesquekomannahotuk, I was animating for one dollar per negative-foot by the old cut-out process for a San Francisco firm who owned an Ernamann camera.

Then came my Drama. Stellar roles—such as the voice of the canine in "The Hound of the Baskervilles"—and the screech of a sacred skunk on a Joe Penner program.

But, history repeats itself! My Art came back. The airplane was fast replacing the old ox-cart and Animated Cartooning zoomed into the field of Thespianic-expression. "Ah!" thinks I, "Animated-Cartooning—it embodies ALL of the Arts. Into it i

*Page Ten*

delved doggedly; (which accounts for my becoming known later as the pant, sniff and howl of Pluto, the Pup.)

Then came the screen version of GULLIVER'S TRAVELS!

Now, as I look back on it all, where has it got me? Recently, while reading "NORTHWEST PASSAGE,' by Kenneth Roberts, I read where his hero (Langdon Towne) wanted to paint Indians. He loved a preacher's daughter who didn't like artists; and her dad. too, (the Reverend Arthur Browne) tried hard to discourage the young suitor. I quote herewith, word-for-word, what the Reverend had to say. Page 36, Northwest Passage):

*"Now, my boy! You don't understand! Years ago, before I came to this country, I was secretary to Dean Swift in Dublin. It was while he was writing GULLIVER'S TRAVELS. As secretary to the Dean, I made the acquaintance of all sorts of folk: Actors—authors—artists. Almost the worst of the lot were the artists; a rude and clownish crew, unsavory and irreligious! Painters, actors, mountebanks! They were all in the same boat: a wicked and adulterous generation. They had no standing whatever! Even the family solicitor was preferable to an artist. I've seen artists left kicking their heels for hours in gentlemen's ante-chambers. They were poor men, too. All their lives they had lived miserably, in dire poverty. And for the most part they were drunkards!"*

So, THAT, My Dear EX-Associates, is Why I Quit the Racket!—and, in its stead, chose the godly occupation of Dahlia-bulb raising.

As I sit here now, basking my bunions beneath the old Banyan tree in the mostquito-infested Florida sunshine, my erstwhile poetic-sense surges to the fore . . . so, I shall compose an ode to something-or-other; and it might just as well be "To a Dahlia-bulb" as to anything else. Here goes!

*Oh, Dahlia-bulb—Sweet Dahlia-bulb,*

*So taut, so tense, so terse!*

*Four-score and twenty years ago—*

*(My God! What a lousy verse!)*

"I See that Guy from Fleischer's
Has Been Back Again Recently!"

"Okay! You Can Go in Free, But if You're Not
Jonathan Swift I'm Liable to Lose My Job!"

# On Renting An Apartment

### By Ted Pierce

"HULLO, BILL."

"Hi, Bob. Where ya been keeping yourself?"

"Aw, I been busy hunting an apartment."

"Yeah, you do look kinda like you'd been dragged through an inbetweening machine. How'dja make out?"

"Swell, Found a nice little place out at Northeast Southwest-by-South-Southwest 125th Terrace, and South Northwest Northwest by North-Northeast 125th Way. It's a garage apartment."

"Furnished or unfurnished?"

"Furnished; everything complete. The landlord supplies the walls, floors, hurricane shutters and bug spray—and pays for his own gas and lights; I only have to pay for his water and furnish my own roof and the plumbing fixtures. He'll connect them up."

"Say, not bad, Bob. We had to supply our own windows and door knobs at our place."

"Yeah, and I talked him into putting in a front door for us, too. These Miami landlords don't put anything over on me! I got it pretty reasonable, too—considering what they're asking for most places."

"I was going to ask you what they wanted for a place like that."

"Well, the guy wanted ten bucks a month in the summer and five hundred a month in the winter; fifty thousand for the season if ya paid it in one lump. But I got it for $250.00 a month by the year; ya see, the landlord's my wife's uncle, so I have kind of a drag. I only had to get three co-signers on the lease."

"I'll say you did all right! Gosh, I had to pay first and last eleven months rent in advance for our joint, and put up my ticket for the "Gulliver" premiere for security."

"Yeah, I know, ya gotta do that most places here; they're afraid you'll skip out on your lease after the season. But I got around that okay by agreeing to pay $1,000.00 a month for the first six months. Then a straight $100 a month for the next six months—and if there's an extra month this year we get it rent free. Of course we had to give him a second mortgage on our two kids and sign the car over in his name and agree to give him access to our ice box at all times and the right to entertain his friends in the living room on week-ends; he signed the lease without a whimper—after we waived extradition."

"Gee! That's swell, Bob. Ya got a good deal. I guess you're glad to be settled in a place."

"Yeah. I'd like to ask you over for dinner tonight, Bill, but we haven't got the lights and gas on yet; we're waiting for the oil well on Janet's property in California to come through so we can afford to put up a deposit."

"Well look, Bob. Why don't you come to our joint for dinner—you and your wife?"

"Well, gee,, thanks, Bill. *I'd* love to come. But I can't bring Janet; ya see I had to put *her* up for security on the lease and she can't leave the premises."

☆  ☆  ☆  ☆  ☆  ☆  ☆  ☆

## "Es Selemu Aleikum"

*from*

## Milton Stone

☆  ☆  ☆  ☆  ☆  ☆  ☆

### GREETINGS FROM

| | | |
|---|---|---|
| KEN BROWN | "POP" STONE | WILFRED SCHULER |
| ROBERT DAVEY | VINCENT NORDELL | THOMAS BITTNER |
| LORAN GIST | EDDIE POOLE | JOAN NORRIS |

### "OLD HICK" HIGGINBOTHAM

# CITY ICE & FUEL COMPANY

*Page Fifteen*

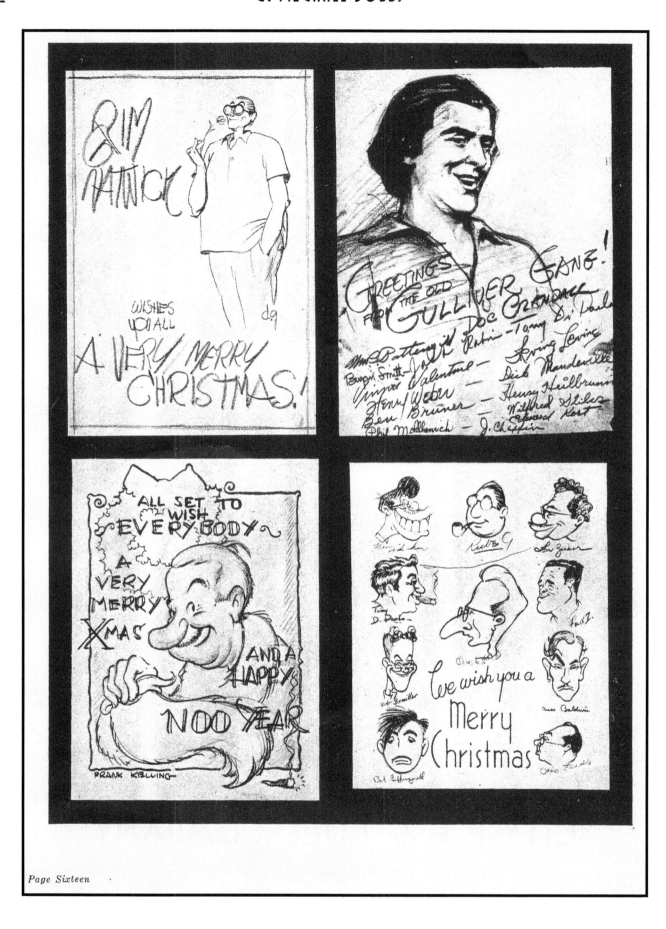

*Page Seventeen*

HOW THE REST OF THE STUDIO THINKS
THE STORY DEPARTMENT WORKS

(See Page 24)

HOW THE STORY DEPARTMENT
ACTUALLY WORKS...!

(See Page 18)

*"Say, Mary, do you remember in the second reel where Gulliver's eyelash quivered and the third wrinkle in his forehead moved? Well, I inbetweened that!"*

# SCOOPS & SNOOPS

*By Frank Paiker and Roberta Whitehead*

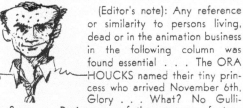

(Editor's note): Any reference or similarity to persons living, dead or in the animation business in the following column was found essential . . . The ORA HOUCKS named their tiny princess who arrived November 6th, Glory . . . What? No Gulliver? . . . During one of the numerous feature meetings on the sound stage the boys were in such rare form so far as wise-cracks go, that one was prompted to remark, ''Ah!—a meeting of the wits'' . . . In a moment came the obvious, ''How did YOU get in . . . on a half ticket?'' . . . And then the one about the new opaquer whose color scheme called for two brown . . . so he put on two coats of one brown. . . . . .

ROSALIND KNEITEL bids us adieu shortly after you read this . . . to return to the Big City . . . And speaking of the Big City, THOMAS MOORE was one of the first eleven hundred who passed the test to be one of ''New York's Finest.'' Thirty-three thousand took the test . . . Congratulations Officer Moore! ! ! ! ! . . . ARTHUR GREENBAUM spent an exciting two weeks recently in Gotham . . . running from one fire to another . . . Scallions to the Flipper members who did not attend the Xmas dance and sold their tickets for one dollar . . . Shame on you! . . . Wonder if Nick Gibson found out how the ''pan mover'' works? . . . George Lex will Wedding March it during the mistle-toe season.

Did you know that the various models for different portions of Gulliver's anatomy included: Dave Fleischer, Seymour Kneitel, Willard Bowsky, Doc Crandall, Jack Ward, Frank Paiker and Thomas Moore. Nelson Demorest did all the modeling for the full figure from the beginning of the feature to the scene where Gulliver was drawn into the court-yard by his captors. It was at this point that Sam Parker stepped into the picture . . . or should we say arose to the occasion. . . . Harold Straubing's gag collection is the result of many hours of clipping . . . so complete is his collection of giggle pictures that Harold was scheduled to appear on Radio's Hobby Lobby program . . . but Fate interfered and Harold's broadcasting is now confined to the Opaque Department P. A. . . . . . Mr. Roosevelt scored a big hit with Alice Morgan when he changed Turkey Day, making it possible for Alice's Ma to observe the twenty-third with her family up No'th and be with Alice for Florida's Day of Thanx a week later.

Debunking all rumors . . . Max's recent notice on the bulletin board . . . Hear Ye!! Hear Ye!! All ye Flippers and skippers, don't take a Cook's tour to the Keys. John will promise you ruby neck-laces and old Spanish coins . . . but you spend Sunday husking cocoanuts just for thé milk . . . . . Since Phil Mohullen knocked the mizzen-mast off his yawl he has taken to slooping. . . . Russ Baldwin has given it up entirely . . . claims he's not the fisherman type . . . Virginia (Sock 'em) Cagey hung a hay-maker on the proprietor of a local beanery . . . . An orchid to Verlin Blackwell whose painting won him a scholarship to the University of Pennsylvania . . . ''Alabam'' expects to journey to the City of Brotherly Love next summer . . . . . The Dave Tendlars are cradle shopping . . . so are the Rube Grossmans . . . so are the Nick Tafuris.

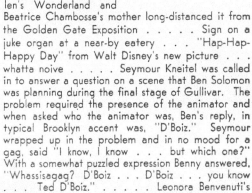

The Studio has been on the receiving end of 'phone calls from both of the recent Fairs . . . Larry Lippman's sister called him from Whalen's Wonderland and Beatrice Chambosse's mother long-distanced it from the Golden Gate Exposition . . . . . Sign on a juke organ at a near-by eatery . . . ''Hap-Hap-Happy Day'' from Walt Disney's new picture . . . whatta noive . . . . . Seymour Kneitel was called in to answer a question on a scene that Ben Solomon was planning during the final stage of Gullivar. The problem required the presence of the animator and when asked who the animator was, Ben's reply, in typical Brooklyn accent was, ''D'Boiz.'' Seymour wrapped up in the problem and in no mood for a gag, said ''I know, I know . . . but which one?'' With a somewhat puzzled expression Benny answered, ''Whassisagag? D'Boiz . . . D'Boiz . . . you know . . . Ted D'Boiz.'' . . . . . Leonora Benvenuti's California Romeo was here for a brief visit . . . returned to the land of Rose Bowl and in two weeks was back in Miami.

Faces About Town Again . . . Charlie Schettler, Maurice Manne and Lou Fleischer . . . Donna Clark will attend the opening of our epic at the Carthay Circle in Hollywood . . . ''Ten Boys and a Girl,'' the new picture to be projected into the in-betweening Department features; Richard Lang, Walter Kraemer, Jim Beatty, Stanley Faulkner, George Ottino, Clyde Wetherington, Eugene Mc-Gregor, Bernie Leiter, Harry Wichman, Frank Spangler AND Roberta Boettcher . . . Lotsa good luck for a swell performance . . . . . What bare-

CONTINUED FROM PAGE 25

footed animator gave Sam a run for auditor? . . . Ray Olsson, it seems, aspires to be another Benny Goodman. Ray swings a mean clarinet and has "sat in" with some of the jam sessions the University spreads on . . . . . Are any of you lassies interested in bowling? Kittie Pfister would like to know you.

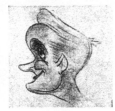

"Local Boy Makes Good" . . . Milford Davis holds the unique distinction of not being officially hired. Millie had a morning appointment to show samples of his work and upon arriving found the reception room crowded. Our young hero was soon to hear Ethel Munson's voice invite the room's occupants to "Come this way" and the group, including Millie, was ushered into the Opaque Dept. . . . Two days later Millie discovered all but himself had previously been hired. P. S. Millie's still here and is now one of Bill Turner's Lads . . . . . During the feature scoring Dave Fleischer wired to have Pinto Colvig record some Gabby cries. Through some misunderstanding almost every cry except that of fear was done and sent to Dave. Pinto, his eyes eager for a glimpse of California, thought it a good idea to put in a gag plea in hopes of acquiring said glimpse. Upon receipt of the sound track Dave and the rest of the gang sat down to select the 'take.' As the projection progressed the results were not what Dave wanted. Just about the time Dave had given up in utter despair Pinto's gag plea came along. This was it!! . . . Just what they wanted and what was originally intended as a gag turned

out to be the McCoy . . . . . Santa Claus steps out of his usual role this December 25th to put a wedding ring on Audrey Smith's finger . . . Audrey, as you no doubt remember, was recently chosen "Mayor" of Gullivar City . . . . . The lucky guy is D. C. Keisacker of midget auto racing fame.

Recollections of 15 years ago at the Bray Studios . . . Willard Bowsky coming to work in his Boy Scout uniform and getting an awful riding for same from Jimmie Culhane and Frank Paiker. Jeff Price trying to ink and at the same time duck a barrage of art-gums and film cans . . . . . The day Jeff forgot to duck and as a result getting so mad that he knocked the culprit through a glass partition. (Ed. Note—Man Bites Dog.) Frank Paiker is still picking splinters of glass out of his hide to this day.

FLASH!!!! . . . . Lorrin Gist cleans up!!! . . . He is exchanging his "coke" wagon for a laundry bus. Lorrin is opening a laundry in this vicinity and we hope his friends in the studio will continue to be his friends and let him do the dirty work. Remember Sam says to "Keep it clean" and Lorrin will be more than happy to serve . . . . . Here's wishing you the best of luck in your new venture . . . . . Many, many thanx to the lads who made it possible for this mag to be graced with photos of you and you and you . . . . . Bob Little's Frances is mending after parting with her appendix . . . . . The Merry Mac's arrangement of "Bluebirds In the Moonlight" heard on the Fred Allen show t'other night was swell.

## MERRY CHRISTMAS AND A HAPPY NEW YEAR

*In substantiation of Joe Stultz's claim that "They must put something in the water," we list the following marriages and births which have taken place since the Studio's removal to Florida:*

## INTRAMURAL

Sophie Delnick to Felix Zelenka.

Margie Hines to Jack Mercer.

Ruth Thompson to George Hill.

Zona Atherton to John Chaffin.

Rosemary Mullin to Dave Higgins.

Tillie Player to Larry Lippman.

Amita Calpini to John Cuddy.

Gene Sites to John Immerman.

Barbara Nicholas to Arman Williams.

Ann Alexander to Frank Endres.

Mildred Conroy to John Walworth.

Carol House to Tony Pabian.

Margaretha Felger to Ralph Wolfe.

Barbara Black to Ben Bruner.

## EXTRA CURRICULLAR

Tom A. Moore

Jim Lunnon

George Germanetti

Jim Culhane

Walter Cunningham

Tony DiPaola

Lloyd Von Hadin

Vincent Valentine

Bill Gerke

Bill Seeschaaf

Carl Arpe

Dick Mann

Jim Beatty

Bernice Orr, now Mrs. Frensdorf.

Rita Bryan, now Mrs. Myron Willison.

Frances Allison, now Mrs. Andrew Albertson.

Janice Doll, now Mrs. Thomas Rome.

Emily Jones, now Mrs. Wallace Dicks.

**HOMEWORK:** Barton Krawetz, Phoebe Ann Sturm, Steven Stone, Robert Morris Dressler, Joan Virginia Oriolo, Gary Gist, Glory Houck, Nancy Young, Marie Ehret, Judith Ann Willis.

**FLASH!** Johnnie Gibbs has married Tommy Parker's cousin, Helen Seidel.

## AFTER THE OVERTIME SESSION

EDITH VERNICK.

I came home late one nite at three,
Upon the staircase, I did see
A little man upon the stair,
It was the guy who wasn't there.

He didn't have a high silk hat,
A long white beard or things like that,
He wasn't even one inch tall,
From head to toes, he was so small.

I watched him standing on the stair,
The little man that wasn't there,
And, all around me, then, I saw
A hundred little men, or more.

When the keeper left, by gar,
The little men they weren't thar,
The last words that I heard em say,
Was, "goo-bye, it's a Hap-py day."

Our duty's done, so now we're thru,
"All's well" for us, but not for you,
It really is a bloomin shime,
Y'got like this from overtime!

## LAMENT

*By Seymour Reit*

Oh, I don't like the P. A. system,
I hate its clarion call,
Which summons others the whole day long,
But mentions me never at all.

Oh, it shouts for Willard and Myron,
For Liesel and Aaron and Bea,
But for all I care it can jump in the lake
'Cause it never shouts for me.

*Page Twenty-seven*

GREEN

## By Jack O'Sullivan

SINCE SPORTS ARE usually considered somewhat of an interloper about this time each year, we believe the Editor has been extremely farsighted in looking beyond his New Year's Day hang-over to permit us to publicize what sports hold for the Fleischer employees during the next semester.

With the overtime behind us we want all of you to feel free to acquaint yourselves with athletics, either as eager participants or diligent observers.

Well under way and spinning along in splendid fashion are our basketballers who are entered in the Y. M. C. A. Commercial League. The boys, led by Hal Robins and assisted by such Gulliver-like artists as Lars Bourne and Tom (Big) Moore, play every Monday evening starting at 7:30 o'clock at the Miami High school gym. So get out and give them the once over folks and you'll be itching to return.

Now that the cooler weather is upon us, all you tennis followers will be glad to know that a tournament has been arranged by Phil Di Paola of the In-betweening Department with play commencing about the first week of January. To avoid over-matching or under-matching, as the case may be, a preliminary tournament is now in progress and participants will be seeded (not seedy) for the matches to follow. This arrangement gives little opportunity for even our most modest netman to say he doesn't stand a chance. And while we are on tennis, Phil recommends Vic Gerstal, with premises opposite Sears-Roebuck on the Boulevard, for racquet repairs. Gerstal also accepts old racquets as part payment on the purchase of a new one.

Of course basket-ball and tennis are merely athletic infants with a bustling future ahead as compared to the two old 1939 stand-bys, bowling and softball.

One of our more sturdy band of athletes is the bowling team which has seen action for the greater part of the year and more particularly in the last

four months, at the Miami Recreation Center where the team has been representing the Studio in an eight team league. To date it has maintained the highest team average in the league but since the tournament is run on a handicap basis the club must pay for its expert marksmanship by conceding a set number of points to its competitor before the first ball is rolled. Matches are played every Thursday evening at 8:30 o'clock up to and including December 21st and Frank Paiker says you haven't seen all the comedies in town until you have taken in at least one of these. Following are the team members and their individual averages as this goes to press:

|  | Games | Average |
|---|---|---|
| Frank Paiker | 39 | 176 |
| Frank Scheidenberger | 45 | 172 |
| Capt. Max Jaeger (Mr. Kittie Pfister) | 44 | 172 |
| Hilmer Swens | 39 | 160 |
| Max Fleischer | 30 | 148 |

Holding the sportlight during the Summer months was the Studio softball team which went to battle twice a week at Riverside Park against the Y. M. C. A., the Chamber of Commerce, Circuit Court Clerks and its most deadly foe of all—old over-time. When the final tabulations were made the Fleischerites stood but a scant half game from first place, ceding that position to the "Y" who later went on to reach the semi-finals in the Golden Ball Tournament which embraced all the leading teams of Miami. Five of our batsmen hit over .300 percent while Ernie (Camera Room) Arcella finished with a neat .454 to top the league.

The squad thanks all those who regularly attended the games and hopes others who remained away toward the latter part of the season will return in 1940 to watch the play at a different park. Since the season doesn't start 'til early Summer, practice will not commence before the middle of February and new candidates will be welcomed. At this writing only one major change looms . . . the boys have agreed to furnish Doc Ellison with a "seeing eye" dog and a Western Union messenger to better patrol the dark expanse of center field and bring a certain timeliness to the progress of the game. We feel that Doc, being anything but a disinterested ball player, should be brought into closer contact with events at the plate.

Other activities which claim many devotees but as yet have not been organized are badminton, ping-pong, golf and handball.

A goodly number of employees would welcome the erection of one or more handball courts on the grounds north of the Studio because of the scarcity of courts in Miami.

A small group of badminton players saw a little activity during the Summer on the sound stage. As this is no longer available however they seek a good sized indoor court. Anyone knowing of such a location will find Hilmer Swens an eager listener. Swens is also interested in forming an inter-studio ping-pong competition.

Since golf seems to claim many followers the coming year might be made more interesting for them by the formation of different units to compete one against the other. Dave Higgins has been recommended to sound out the boys on this idea.

So much for 1939 and the early part of '40. More sports news will be forthcoming and we sincerely hope that each and everyone will support some sport by direct participation or as a spectator.

☆　　☆　　☆

*"Boy, He Sure Takes His Ten-Minute
Rest Period Seriously!"*

# Chalk Talks

## THE FIRST FEATURE CARTOON →

"THE ADVENTURES OF PRINCE ACHMET," A FEATURE ANIMATED CARTOON WAS PRODUCED IN GERMANY IN 1926 BY LOTTE REINIGER.... THE ENTIRE FILM WAS EXECUTED IN SILHOUETTE CUTOUTS.

## CARTOONS IN EGYPT

CARVINGS OF VARIOUS STAGES OF ACTION WERE PLACED ON SOME EGYPTIAN TEMPLES — POSSIBLY FOR THE ENTERTAINMENT OF PASSING CHARIOTS ....

5¢ A PEEK

## THE "PHENAKISTASCOPE"

THIS WAS THE EARLIEST DEVICE FOR VIEWING ANIMATED DRAWINGS ....

## EARLY CARTOON DRAWING

THIS IS THE FIRST DRAWING FROM THE FIRST FILM OF EMILE COHL, THE EARLY FRENCH PIONEER.. IT WAS MADE IN 1907...

Woody Gelman

# THE HISTORY OF ANIMATED CARTOONING

*By*

## MAURICE SUSSMAN

THE RUDIMENTARY developments of the animated cartoon industry antedated the development of the motion picture itself. As early as the year 1892, for example, cartoons were projected on a screen by a Frenchman named Emil Renaut—cartoons which depicted by means of "an endless band of graduated drawings" a rather long pantomimic story.

It was not until stop-motion photography was developed, however, that American pioneers in the cartooning field set to work in earnest. The first developments of this work included the attempts of J. Stuart Blackton and also those of Windsor McCay who, after much experimentation, achieved more than a small degree of success with the now historic "Gertie the Dinosaur."

Other artists, usually newspaper cartoonists, entered the field. Undoubtedly, these newspaper experiences exerted a strong influence on the animated cartoons then produced, for most of the characters employed in animation were either based directly on newspaper comic strips or were indirectly imitated. At this time "Mutt and Jeff" was a current favorite both on the screen and in the journals of the period.

At this point in the growth of the industry two very important developments were introduced by Max Fleischer and Amedee Van Buren. The former with the "Ko-Ko the Clown" series, the latter with "Aesop's Fables."

These two series, by virtue of their fresh viewpoint and originality, did much to open new avenues of endeavor in the field of animation. A departure from the usual formula, also was Pat Sullivan's "Felix the Cat" which shortly followed the series introduced by Fleischer and Van Buren.

As with the development in all new industries, constant experimentation was the keynote of animation. Thus in 1922, Fleischer followed his "Ko-Ko the Clown" series with the introduction of the "Out of the Inkwell" series, a new approach which utilized a photographic background upon which were superimposed cartoon characters. Undoubtedly it was this idea which suggested another to a newcomer in the field, Walt Disney, who, with his "Alice" series, reversed the procedure using a photographed character with a cartoon background.

From that time to this, endless experimentation has uncovered great possibilities which at this time are far from exhausted. The use of sound, of descriptive music and of technicolor are a few relatively recent contributions. Technical advances, though intricate, have also contributed vastly to present development of the industry. A development which finds its culmination in such feature length productions as "Snow White" and "Gulliver's Travels."

From this point onward, the future of the industry is a matter of speculation only so far as its possibilities are concerned. Undoubtedly animation has "arrived" as a top-notch form of theatrical entertainment.

"STAY THRU MAY"

MYRON WALDMAN

*Page Thirty-one*

WIN HOSKINS

## THEME SONGS

Eli Brucker—"Somebody Loves Me."

Fritz Kuhn—"Time On My Hands."

Bill Turner—"It's Funny to Everyone But Me!"

## THEME SONGS

Franklin D. Roosevelt—"Four or Five Times."

Eleanor Roosevelt—"It's a Hap-Hap-Happy My Day."

Walt Disney—"Who's Sorry Now."

Walter Bradfield—"Little White Lies."

WIN HOSKINS

*Page Thirty-three*

# Flipper Activites

### BASEBALL

The studio baseball unit had its inception at 1600 Broadway, New York, a year or so ago with only a handful of members. It started when a group of boys began donating a small sum weekly to go for equipment when we reached Miami.

The first real sign of activity at the studio was when a few of the boys decided to limber their joints by throwing the ball around during lunch hour. It wasn't long, though, before the bug started to bite many of the others.

Word was sent around that practice games would take place on Sunday mornings, and what with the studio officials graciously donating a splendid ball diamond for the purpose, the boys went to work in earnest. Each Sunday the response grew stronger until it became impossible for all who wanted a game to get it. So, after a few meetings and the appointment of officers, six teams from various departments throughout the studio were formed. A perfect schedule was arranged by Jay Morton and played thru. After the smoke had cleared it was discovered that the team known as the "Camera Dept." were champions and each of the players on this winning team was awarded a small silver soft ball.

This arrangement of games was ideal because it not only gave every one exercise and pleasure, but it also gave the baseball committee a wide range of players from which to select a number one team for entry into the Civic League. The committee did this and the team finished a half game behind first place.

### RACQUETEERS

Last Spring, a group of enthusiastic tennis players headed by Bob Schwartz, Phil Di Paola, Carl Wessler, Ham Butts, Chas. Schettler and Els Barthen got together and decided to form a club which would afford an opportunity for members to play against each other, hold matches and gain instruction. The club was not restricted to advanced players but membership was permitted anyone interested in playing the game. The club now numbers 22 members, ranking from novice to the more expert player. At present, these Racqueteers are holding a tournament for seeding.

In the future, the club will sponsor cup tournaments and will provide instruction for those desiring it. (A professional has volunteered his services as instructor to members). Records will be kept of progress and ratings of players and a contact service will be available to assure members a game at any time.

Any Flipper member interested in learning and playing tennis is invited to join the club. For further information see Phil Di Paola.

The club offers to assist in the formation of a similar organization for women players.

### DRAMATICS

It seems hardly less than inevitable that, given a group of artists of such wide and varied experience as the Flippers Club, a dramatic unit should be heard from.

Since all Flipper members and their respective tastes are treated impartially, this group from its inception has received its full share of attention. Several meetings were held during which ways and means of producing a play were discussed. It was finally agreed that old plays, rewritten in a humorous vein, would be the common vehicle of expression. At the last meeting the play "Rain" was decided upon as first for production. Very likely this much satirized work would have to be re-shaped to give it freshness, but that job would be left to the talents of several of our embryonic playwrights. How successfully it can be done is a matter of special interest to those involved.

However fantastic the idea of a dramatics unit in the Flippers Club may seem, actually it can be a most successful group if given the proper sort of interest and support. The interest and support should be forthcoming, since a successful dramatic unit can be very profitable to the "parent body," which is more than most of the units can claim.

CONTINUED ON PAGE 36

CONTINUED FROM PAGE 35

## GOLF

Wherever a gang of Americans can be found, a certain percent will be golf goofy. This is especially true of the Studio rabble. Quite a few have blown themselves to clubs and golf togs and taken to the bunkered pastures in pursuit of the little white ball.

The frenzy has risen to a pitch (and a putt) where it is almost out of hand. A tournament is now in progress, the winner to get a ticket to the Orange Bowl football game.

Among those who are marching through the traps, trees, canals, brambles and just plain dirt to the tune of profanity and groans, are the following:

Jack Willis, Win Sharples, Doc Ellison, Myron Waldman, Joe Miller, Sidney Pillet, Joe Oriolo, Frank Scheidenberger, Arnold Gillespie, George Waiss, Jim Davis, Lod Rossner, Tom Moore, Bill Morrison and Bill Nolan.

Among those resting on the sidelines through this tournament, but who will probably take part in our next, are Sam Buchwald, Dave Higgins and Phil Lepinsky. Phil was the winner of a tournament last Spring.

Golf being an incurable disease, it would be best to take all due precaution when associating with any of the Studio golfing bugs.

## BASKETBALL

The Fleischer Studio basketball team composed of the following players: George Ottino, Ernie Arcella, Herbert Frankel, Bill Gerke, Milt Fine, Tom Moore, Hy Neigher, Dave Higgins, Jerry Dvorak, John Clopton, Milt Wohl, Earl Klein, Walt Kraemer, Harold Robins and Irving Rabb have joined the Commercial League sponsored by the Y. M. C. A. All games are played at the Miami High School Gym, every Monday night. The schedule calls for 15 games with the following teams in a round robin tournament

Graham Dairies.

Pan-American Airways.

Miami Recreation Department.

Dade Teachers.

Naval Reserves.

Many of the players are former stars of High School and College teams. In the event any of you birds have nothing to do on Monday nights, drop around for a couple of laughs.

## PIGSKIN PATTER

To help digest lunch a bunch of us guys have been getting out on the baseball field and booting the oval about. Usually about four fellows start the play, then the guys on the side lines who have been watching and thinking what dopes we are to be playing in the heat of the day, can't resist the temptation and join in the game. We've had as many as twenty to thirty guys out there tossing or kicking. Everyone's welcome!

Our trick plays are wonderful . . . we think the Miami Hurricanes could learn something from us . . . and vice versa. We're so hepped up about our noon games that we've decided to organize a few touch-ball teams and play inter-studio touch-ball on the same basis as our softball games. There will be a notice in the very near future giving more details.

## BOWLING

New blood, in the form of ten new members, was injected into the Weekly Bowling Club which for nine years consisted of twelve men who called themselves bowlers.

After approximately six months of friendly throat-cutting, the "newies" had the last laugh on the "oldies" in that one of their members, Frank Scheidenberger, finished at the top of the list in the season's averages. However, the "oldies" did manage to save something out of the wreckage by sewing up the next three positions in the persons of Frank Paiker, Charlie Schettler and Willard Bowsky respectively.

Each group ran its own handicap tournament at the end of the regular bowling season and in each instance, competition was so keen that it took the final of the 24 game set to determine the winners who were Frank Scheidenberger, Hilmer Swens and Bob Little for the newcomers and Willard Bowsky,

CONTINUED ON PAGE 38

# FLIPPER MEETING

THE FIRST ANNUAL meeting for the election of officers to the Flipper Club was held at the Alcazar Hotel Roof Tuesday, November 21st.

Well, we can hardly say that the polls were overcrowded, but by the time the boys were pulled away from the bar on the mezzanine and a few night clubs had let out, we counted noses and finally found we had a quorum.

With a few more delays, such as Nick Tafuri appearing in a new kind of coat with no collar which he says helps him keep on his feet when the bouncer grabs the nape of his neck, and Grim coming in late as usual to find out he is really early, the meeting was finally called to order by the President, Dave Tendler, and we all got down to the serious business of electing new officers for the following year.

Roll call and the reading of the minutes of the last meeting by the secretary, Frank Kelling, was soon over. Aaron Krawetz next gave the Treasurer's report which we were all happy to find was well out of the red. A number of suggestions were made as to what to do with the surplus, such as: Pass out drinks all around, build a subway from here to New York, present Admiral Byrd with an animator's pencil, push Aaron out the window and run like hell, etc.

By this time, all the boys and girls were in the groove so two election inspectors were appointed, Tom Golden and Frank Paiker, to conduct the election.

Dave Tendlar was re-elected president, Aaron Krawetz re-elected treasurer, Frank Kelling re-elected secretary, and Harold Walker re-elected vice-president (it looks like the Tendlar machine was really oiled up).

Candidates for the auditing committee now weighed in, lined up for the gun and were off with a clean break. At the first quarter, Ann McLoughlin was on the inside, next came Elizabeth Touma, then Sam Buchwald, Doc Ellison, Lou Fleischer, Bob Little, Harold Robins, Carl Wessler and Mort Greenbaum bringing up the rear. Rounding the corner for the first half was Doc Ellison in the lead, Sam Buchwald two lengths behind and Ann McLoughlin dropping back in third place. At the three-quarter mark, Sam Buchwald still out in front, Doc—wait a minute! Look there towards the back, look at that horse go! It's a dark horse! He's coming to the front by leaps and bounds, he's nosed out McLoughlin, he's overtaking Ellison, he's about to pass him—it's Ozarkowitz! It's an upset!

But hold on, the two lead horses have him in a pocket, they won't let him pass—there they go across the finish line, Sam Buchwald first, Doc Ellison second, and you know who, taking third money. Whew! What a race, what excitement and what next.

Well, next we have results of the Nominating Committee election, they are: Tom Golden, Gordon Sheehan and Tom Moore.

The Board of Directors added three new members to their list, Tom Johnson, Frank Paiker and Izzie Sparber.

With good wishes all around for the newly elected officers, a few college yells with confetti and streamers, back slapping and shin kicking, everybody went to their respective homes or night clubs, as the case might be, thus finishing the first anniversary election of the Flippers Club.

Frank Kelling, Secretary.

CONTINUED FROM PAGE 36
Bill Turner and Charlie Schettler for the veterans.

Hostilities will be resumed at the first of the year and for the benefit of prospective new members, may we inform you now that it is the intention of the club to expand and that information on joining will be posted shortly on the Flipper bulletin board in the patio.

## WILDCATS

The girls bowling club of Wildcats was formed in 1937. At that time most of the ten members had never seen the inside of a bowling alley. Most of us had an idea that all that was necessary was to pick up a heavy ball and throw it in the general direction of the pins and to "watch 'em fall." (Ed. note: What makes ya think it's different now!!)

Some of the boys in the Men's Bowling Club joined in helping us and before long the Wildcats were able to equal and beat the scores of men bowlers. (Not to mention any names.)

The highest average reached by a Wildcat bowler when the club started was 97, made by Kittie Pfister.

Any Wildcat who would like to have her name engraved on the official cup need only roll better than an average of 170¼ for four official games in one evening. Our current membership numbers eleven: Edith Carey, Janet Fay, Hemia Calpini, Helen Sparber, Anne McLaughlin, Kittie Pfister, Marianna Butts, Liesel Howson, Kay Blitz, Helen Lane and Vera Coleman.

## BOATING & FISHING

The question arose as to the activities of the Fishing and Boating Committee but the answer to that is in Doc Crandall's hands—namely, "Gulliver." So instead, we will give you some data on the gentlemen in the picture who have all been too busy to "get out and get 'em."

Harold Walker, a fair sort of fisherman who would like to get them but can't seem to get to the right place at the right time. Result—not so much fish.

Johnny Burks, owner of the Bishkaboo, 26 Ft. Crosby Cat, Commander of the Miami division of the United States Power Squadron, too busy getting his boat and his classes in navigation in tip-top shape to do any fishing.

Bob Leffingwell, owner of an Atkins 28 foot Cutter, who has only done bottom fishing with fair results. Wait till the trolling bug bites him. Then it will be a different story.

Ralph Tiller, one boy who can brag and get away with it. Landing a 40-pound Blue fin tuna is a nice job for anyone.

Nelson Demorest, not so much on fish. He prefers to battle them in their own territory, resulting in getting his face and figure in the movies—as in the shipwreck scene in "Gulliver."

Thurston Harper—one of the better anglers who has tried everything in that line and landed a beauty —a sail weighing 55 pounds. Not bad at all—and can he tell fish stories!

Doc Crandall, owner of the Jeroda II, 39-foot Cabin Cruiser, his home and playground, who likes fishing but was too busy to go after the big ones. He will make up for that, though, now that he has more time.

Henry Rehe, a real (?) authority on fishing. He catches only the babies who don't know any better— as witness his baby barracuda. The sail fish in his hands belongs to his wife, who only catches the big ones.

## BADMINTON

To those spry and ambitious folk who aspire to strenuous sports, the game of badminton offers a definite challenge. Like basketball, handball or squash, it is not only a body conditioner but it also reqires excellent stamina to pass the "dub" class.

It seems this game requires more than a net, shuttlecocks and racquets . . . there is the very important matter of a court with a high ceiling, a court which is walled in on every side, because the slightest wind will throw the feathery "birds" off their course. Through the gracious good offices of the Studio management the sound stage was marked off into a court and the Studio went so far as to make curtains to protect the projector screen.

Now with the strenuous schedule of overtime over, the sky is fast clearing for all the different units. Whenever the sound stage isn't being used for mere business reasons it can and will be used for badminton and there is talk of sandwiching badminton before and after the basketball games (another Flipper unit) at the Y. M. C. A. All you who are interested in this hectic (but so far frustrated) sport are cordially invited to investigate.

# Chapter Two
## *Many misses and a hit*

Simply looking at the cartoons that came out of the Miami studio one can easily see the problems that came with the move to Miami and the demise of the Betty Boop and the Screen Songs series. The studio seemed to be floundering in the period following the successful release of "Gulliver's Travels."

Three series were released during 1940 and 1941, with all of them critical flops: "The Stone Age," "Gabby" and the "Animated Antics" cartoons.

*Box Office* had a lengthy story on May 25, 1940, detailing the entire list of up-coming productions to be released by Paramount. Included in it were 12 Popeye cartoons, eight Gabby shorts, and the Raggedy Ann two-reeler. A trade ad released Aug. 10, 1940, also noted 10 Animated Antics shorts on the schedule.

The Stone Age shorts were the first out to the theaters on Jan. 26, 1940, followed by Animated Antics, which started its series release on Sept. 20, 1940. The first Gabby cartoon release on Oct. 18, 1940.

It's clear looking at reviews from theater managers that in 1940, black and white cartoons were seen as inferior to color shorts and that theater audiences were reacting better to a cartoon in color. The two black-and-white series were not helped by it's lack of color.

## *The Stone Age cartoons*

Some people have commented "The Flintstones" built off the comedy established by "The Stone Age" series, but the kind of humor in the Stone Age cartoons was nothing new.

There is a long tradition in treating prehistoric man as a foil for jokes and the perhaps the best known of the earliest efforts came from British cartoonist Edward Tennyson Reed.

The book "The Lost Art of E.T. Reed: Prehistoric Peeps" details the cartoonist's work and collects many of his caveman cartoons, many of which appeared in the venerable English humor publication, *Punch*. Although he did other kinds of cartoons and illustrations, it was his cavemen pieces for which he is best remembered.

Reed essentially set the model with his first such cartoon in 1893. The book shows how this influenced other cartoonists at the time and that influence certainly paved the way for other caveman comedy.

As cartoonist and historian Stephen R. Bissette wrote in the book's introduction, "No doubt about it, Fred and Wilma, Barney and Betty owe their existence to E.T. Reed. In fact, every comic or cartoon mashup of the modern and prehistoric featuring English-speaking suburban cave-dwellers, saurian flivvers and the like originated with E.T. Reed."

The great stop motion animator Willis O'Brien, years before his work on "The Lost World" and "King Kong," had animated several shorts, including "R.F.D. 10,000 B.C." and "Prehistoric Poultry" in 1915. The surviving prints show the same kind of humor that was seen later in other animated comedies: caveman society as seen through a 20th century lens.

A trade ad for Bray Studios from 1915 lists a cartoonist named L.M. Glackens "formerly of 'Puck' drawing Stone Age Adventures."

Buster Keaton had a great caveman sequence in his 1922 feature "Three Ages," which even included a stop motion dinosaur.

V.T Hamlin's "Alley Oop" comic strip with its caveman hero launched Dec. 5, 1932, and is still running today.

So, there was little unique or different in what the Fleischer Studios planned in its "Stone Age" series of shorts in terms of humor. In 1940, the studio's newest series, "The Stone Age Cartoons," made its debut and the results were less than impressive. What was interesting is the film "One Million B.C." was also released in 1940 meaning there was suddenly quite a lot of "prehistoric" material in the popular culture.

A brief in the *Showman Trade Review,* (July 29, 1939) noted, "The Fleischer studios are working at top speed on the filming of short cartoon features including 12 Popeyes, six Color Classics and a new series of 12 Stone Age cartoons. The Stone Age features supplant the Betty Boop cartoons on the Paramount schedule."

The series had several problems. First, they were all produced in black and white when the industry was increasingly using color, something noted in many of the reviews sent to the trade papers by theater managers and owners.

The second is they were all conceived as one-shots. The studio did not develop a cast of recurring characters for the shorts loaded with gags and puns. Considering how important merchandising had been for GT, it is surprising the studio didn't want to establish a new group of characters from which it could benefit.

Promo ads from Paramount for the series had an image of a married cave couple with kids with the title "Introducing the 'Stonebroke' Family," suggesting a cast of recurring characters. Other promo ads continued with the theme of a family of sorts.

The other problem with these shorts is they seem to be a huge step-backwards in quality and imagination. Even though they were animated by some great talent, such as Roland "Doc" Crandall, Grim Natwick, James "Shamus" Culhane, Al Eugster and Myron Waldman, the concepts and the scripts were sub-par.

Waldman told animation historian Mark Langer, "With the caveman shorts, we knew right away that they were stinkers. I haven't the least idea where the idea came from, although I suspect it was Max Fleischer. The old humor magazine *Life* had a good illustrator called Lawson who drew monkey characters. Max was fascinated with them. When we were still in New York, Max asked me to draw some monkeys. I think that he kept working on this idea and it eventually turned into the caveman films.

"They were horrible. We wanted to discontinue them immediately, but Paramount wouldn't let us. They had sold an entire year of them to theaters and had to deliver, no matter how bad they made us look. And they looked bad."

Waldman told me that a pilot cartoon was usually done and if approved a series of 12 would be sold for that year. He said the Stone Age pilot was okay, but the "execution" of the following cartoons wasn't.

The Popeye cartoons had continued to develop in terms of animation, design and characterization and, in comparison, the Stone Age shorts were greatly lacking.

The series started with "Way Back When a Triangle Had its Points" released in January of 1940. In its review, *The Showman's Trade Review* ran in its Feb. 24, 1940, edition, "This is the first of Max Fleischer's new series of cartoons. It is not up to the standard set by Popeye or some others that have come from the Fleischer studios. The characterizations are not good and the movement is jerky. There are a few little laughs in it but they can barely be called chuckles. Dave Fleischer directed."

A theater manager in Penacock, NH, wrote to the *Motion Picture Herald*, (March 9, 1940) "Fair start on this new series. Part of it is funny and some of it dull. Hope it improves. It has possibilities."

The second short was "Way Back When a Nag was only a Horse," released in March 1940. "Way back in the Stone Age, 10,000 years ago the world wasn't so different," the narrator

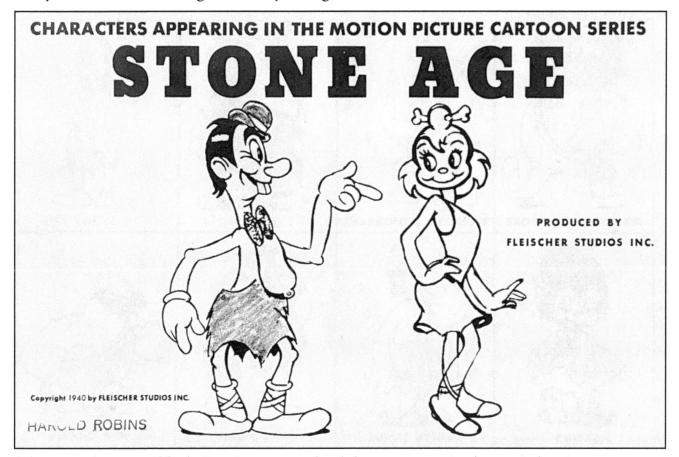

A character guide was printed for the Stone Age series even though there were no recurring characters in the series. (Photo courtesy of JJ Sedelmaier)

intoned, opening the short. We are then introduced to a cave couple. The wife wants to go to a big sale, but the husband doesn't. He hits his wife over the head with a club and then drags her by the hair to the store.

For fans of "The Flintstones," this short will seem very familiar. There is a vacuum cleaner that is actually a goose on a stick, an escalator that is the back of a dinosaur, a turtle as a waffle iron and a kangaroo as a cocktail shaker. At the conclusion of the short the wife discovers her husband dancing with a song promoter and the wife tells him to take her home. He hits her over the head again and drags her and her packages home. The narrator assures us that women loved such treatment.

Next was "Way Back When a Nightclub was a Stick." In this short, a dominated husband successfully sneaks out of the house and goes to a casino where his wife finds him and beats him just as he gets a jackpot on a slot machine after many attempts. In many ways, this was a 20th century story simply transposed to prehistory.

In "Granite Hotel," the third short, there was a framework of a telephone operator saying over and over "Nothing ever happens at the Granite Hotel." Unrelated gags and puns were the backbone of that short that proved her wrong.

"We've never enjoyed these cartoons and this was no better than the rest." John Grabenstein the manager of a theater in Eustis, NE, wrote for the *Motion Picture Herald* in Aug. 17, 1940.

"The Foul Ball Player" is simply a baseball short that could have been easily a Popeye cartoon. While set in the studio's version of prehistoric times, there is nothing particularly Stone Age about it. A team of short guys is playing a team of bigger men. The bigger guys dominated the game until it's discovered the pitcher is allergic to golden rod and the small guys, dubbed "the midgets," use this to achieve a victory.

"The Ugly Dino" is the well-known ugly duckling story only with newly hatched dino eggs instead of ducks. The ugly dino saves his siblings from being eaten. It does little

Model sheet for "The Ugly Dino."

to change what audiences would see as a story they had witnessed many times before.

The review in *Box Office,* (July 13, 1940) noted, "The ugly duckling cliché has been transferred to a prehistoric setting and a few variations from routine animation procedure have been injected in this item. Mama dinosaur hatches a brood of five. Four are grey, the fifth black. The usual happens but this time the black one saves the others from a saber tooth tiger. It is effective entertainment."

In "Wedding Belts," Stone Age lovers are getting married, which is an essentially armed conflict. Both of them go to trainers to prepare them for their evening's bout. For example, the young woman learns how to throw rolling pins while the groom learns to duck them. The female trainer advises the bride, "Enough of this love stuff, dearie. You're just getting married, that's all." The pair enter the ring at a coliseum and go after each other with clubs. The woman wins and is declared married.

"Wedding Belts" was deemed "very good for a laugh. A change from all other cartoons," by a theater manager from Missouri (*Motion Picture Herald,* Nov. 3, 1940).

"Way Back when a Razzberry was a Fruit" the cartoon newsreel again depicts the goings-on in the age of the prehistoric man and the dinosaur. This series of Stone Age cartoons can provide considerable humor and this issueis up to par," the reviewer wrote in *Motion Picture Daily* on Aug. 14, 1940.

This trade ad shows a group of theater owns praising Paramount shorts with one actually affirming the decision to make Gabby the star of his own series.

"Fulla Bluff Man," revolved around a door-to-door salesman making the rounds in "Rockville." The salesman eventually makes money by selling clubs to the cavemen who have an epic fight. The skills of Natwick and Crandall could not save this short.

Waldman once told me that he brought a script for a Stone Age short hanging off a long stick into Dave Fleischer's office. When asked by Dave why he was doing it, Waldman replied,

"It stinks!" In the short on which he was head animator/director, "Springtime in the Rockage," a farmer growing flowers is attacked by giant grasshoppers that eats the crop, moth eats fur coat, flies beat him and tie him up. It's not very good.

In "Pedological Institution (College to You)" a young guy finds out that he needs to be a college graduate and enrolls in a school. He is a dumb as a rock and his lack of intelligence is the basis for gags, many of which have nothing to do with cave dwellers. The professor is modeled a bit after Kay Kyser, a popular big band leader and light comedian. Again, there is nothing in this short that couldn't have been done in a cartoon set in contemporary times.

In the last cartoon in the series, "Way Back When Women had their Weigh," a young attractive diner owner opens the short with a song in which she expresses her preference for a slim man. An overweight man walking by is smitten but hears her song and heads over to a "reducing parlor." He is put through treatments, exercises, etc. Naturally, he reduces and naturally, he returns to the diner to find the young woman married to a man larger than he was.

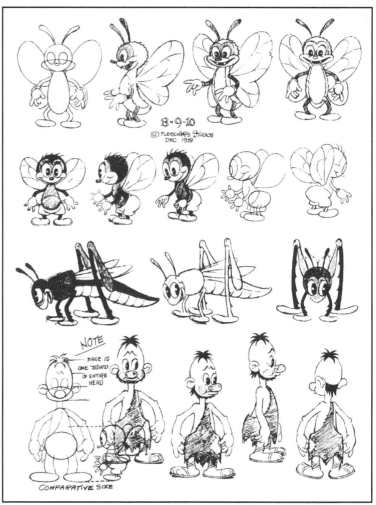

This model sheet is from "Springtime in the Rockage.
(from Michael Sporn website.)

This story could have been adapted to several other settings – there was nothing special about being in the "stone age." That is one of the problems of the shorts in general. The stories were not distinctive enough.

"Better than usual Stone Age cartoon" (*Motion Picture Herald* Nov. 3, 1940), wrote a theater manager from Oklahoma.

The 12 shorts were all released by Sept. 26, 1940. The reviews were very mixed. Some people did seem to like some of the entries, but for the most part, the series was not a favorite. Rather inexplicably, Joseph Priore writing a piece titled "The Most Popular Shorts of 1940" for *Box Office Barometer* (Feb. 22, 1941) included, "Paramount's new series of Stone Age cartoons were smartly humorous."

# *Animated Antics*

Next up came the "Animated Antics," a series of one-shots and the use of several supporting characters from GT.

Watching these shorts in order, one gets a sense of a certain kind of desperation. The series did attempt to build cartoons around several of the GT characters – the carrier pigeon Twinkletoes and the three spies – but the characters clearly did not catch on with audiences.

The Color Classics – with the exception of the Hunky and Spunky shorts – were also one-shots, but clearly, they were more of a prestige series with color and the 3-D effects. I think it was fair to say that more story care was given to that series.

"The Dandy Lion" has a terrible premise as mountain lion – is it a mountain lion who just looks like an African lion? – is adopted as pet by a young Native American child. The lion's mane is cut by the young boy to make it look more like a dog and when he manages to save a baby from death, he is accepted by the tribe.

In a review of "The Dandy Lion," "Just a cartoon," wrote Harry Shaw a theater manager in Missouri (*Motion Picture Herald*, Oct. 30, 1940). *Box Office,* reported, "It is average stuff. The comedy element will suit youngsters (Oct. 5, 1941)." The theater manager review in the *Motion Picture Herald,* (Nov. 23, 1940) was favorable: "Very good cartoon."

Model sheet for "The Dandy Lion" by artist Charlie Thoren.

In "Sneak, Snoop and Snitch," the cartoon opens with King Little of GT closing and locking a box while being observed by the three spies. It's decided the smallest spy, Snitch, will go down the chimney of the castle to steal the box while the king sleeps. He has to steal the key, as well. He manages to do it, but unknowingly drops it. The other two spies are angry and throw him against the lock box that pops open revealing what the king has been carefully guarding: his "Junior G-Man" badge.

This cartoon relies completely on whether or not the viewer has seen GT. There is no set-up to introduce any of the characters. Again, there is the use, as in the Gabby series, of a punchline that references a popular radio show, which makes little sense within the context of the time of the story.

A theater manager in Anamosa, IW wrote, "One of Paramount's very funniest Animated Antics. Will surely please all seeing it." On the other hand, a theater manager in Indiana wrote in the *Motion Picture Herald,* (Jan. 17, 1942), "As bad as any I've ever seen."

The cartoon was reissued in 1946 and the review by a theater manager in the *Motion Picture Herald* that year noted, "A reissue cartoon in black and white which looked its age."

"Mommy Loves Puppy" is set in the Arctic at a station where there are rescue dogs. A Saint Bernard sent her puppy back to the station as he is too small to carry the small barrel of brandy around his neck. He disobeys and comes across a snoring seal to which he gives some of the brandy. The seal enjoys the alcohol and fakes an injury to lure the puppy closer and drinks the entire barrel. The seal gives the pup a fish, which he doesn't like and then chases the pup. The pup is recused by his mom who gives him a dose of castor oil.

*The Showman's Trade Review,* (Nov. 23, 1940) advised, "Dave Fleischer directed this cartoon, which is average as far as this type of

Original concept art from "The Dandy Lion."

entertainment goes. Try to plant announcements of your showing in pet shop windows."

"Bring Himself Back Alive" is set in Africa, where we see the hut of "Hyde Skinner and all-around dirty guy." He sets a bear trap in his cabin, hits a parrot, test the traps with a touch of one of the bird's feathers. He has a turtle who he uses as transport. So, intent on trapping, he even places a tiny bear trap on an ant hill to capture ants. The action cuts to an egotistical lion who encounters other animals and scares them with his boasts about being the king of the jungle. "Why aren't you big and strong like me?!" he asks. The lion and the trapper meet and the lion escapes to a cave. The trapper has surrounded the entrance with traps and is ready to throw in a stick of TNT to drive the lion out. Instead, the trapper is caught in one of his own traps and the lion places the lit stick of TNT near the trapper, which explodes off-camera.

*The Showman's Trade Review,* (Dec. 21, 1940) said in its review, "The cartoon has some good gags and should please both adults and children."

"Twinkletoes Gets the Bird" shows the GT supporting character working at a delivery service and he is charged with delivering a box with a rare parrot inside to the zoo. Flying exhausts him and he crashes, with the parrot escaping from the box. He then tries to recover the bird, who refuses to cooperate. Threatened with a beating if he doesn't make the delivery Twinkletoes bursts into tears and makes the delivery or so he thinks. Just as Twinkletoes is about to get hit by his boss, he hits him.

In "Triple Trouble" (1941) the three GT spies are in jail and are trying to escape. While thinking about a plan, a pardon is slipped under the door and Snitch tries to tell the other two they can leave. Naturally, they hit him and tell him to be quiet. They draw out a map for an undercover tunnel on the back of the pardon and start digging. Their tunnel is eventually discovered and because they tried to escape the pardon was revoked.

There is a real Three Stooges vibe to the short in terms of slapstick and farce. The short is written that audiences wouldn't have to know the GT references. The three main characters could have been generic prisoners.

"Good enough black-and-white cartoon," wrote a theater manager from Oklahoma in the *Motion Picture Herald,* May 10, 1941.

In "Zero the Hound," a hunter and dog are trying to bag some ducks. The dog, named Zero, reluctantly follows a swimming duck in a pond. While Zero started enjoys the water and bathing himself, he quickly catches cold. The dog sneezes, throwing the duck in the air with a couple of fish. The hunter shoots the fish and proclaims, "Holy mackerel!" when he sees the bullet-ridden fish. Several sneezing gags later, the duck is uncovered. The hunter tries to club the duck but winds up hitting a bear, which chases him. The bear catches the dog's cold and the hunter and dog escape. The hunter then catches the cold, he sneezes and his rifle goes off into the air killing a huge number of ducks.

What I liked about this cartoon was its structure. The story builds to a climax and while it may not be the best cartoon the studio produced, it has some funny and unexpected moments. In a review from a theater manager in Oklahoma, "Zero the Hound" was described as an "average black-and-white cartoon." (June 7, 1941, *Motion Picture Herald*). In the Showman's Trade Review (May 31, 1941) the reviewer noted, "Much ado about nothing is this Max Fleischer cartoon. Zero and his master are not particularly captivating creatures and their antics while out hunting ducks do not provide the entertainment audiences expect from cartoon characters."

The review in *Showman's Trade Review,* (June 28, 1941) for "Twinkletoes: Where he Goes, No One Knows" noted, "Twinkletoes is in the mail-carrying business and receives a call to deliver a heavy package neatly wrapped by a horrific fiend to 'a friend.' The bundle contains a time bomb and the pigeon has a time flying the mail, returning it to the address he lost and arriving in time to have the bomb demolish the ghoul's hovel. It is a very routine cartoon comedy. There's a stock one-sheet for lobby display and if you have some carrier pigeon fanciers in your locality you might stage a race or exhibit one in the lobby."

"Copy Cat" features a young cat walking along a fence, following an adult cat who doesn't like it. The older cat challenges the younger cat to copy what he is doing. The adult cat sees a mouse and captures mouse, which the "copy cat" is supposed to accomplish as well but initially fails. He keeps failing which amuses the older cat. There's not much to this short.

A cartoon that is nothing but a stream of standalone gags and puns, "The Wizard of Ants" features a wacky sculptor who guides the audience through his studio gallery. The artist has a voice like Jerry Colonna, then a very popular comedian who worked with Bob Hope. Jack Mercer provides the vocal performance. It's not unlike the Tex Avery shorts at Warner Brothers that were also a parade of gags. While some of the jokes are clever, there is no story and the characterization relies on the impression.

There is always the sense that this format of cartoon is essentially lazy. It is just a format to place unrelated gags together.

In his final cartoon, "Twinkletoes in Hat Stuff," Twinkletoes answers the phone at the delivery service office and speaks to Mysto the Magician who wants to know what happened to his suitcase. If he gets the suitcase by 3 p.m. – about five minutes away – the bird is promised a big tip. What is preventing him from doing that is the fact he accidentally glues the telephone receiver to his ear. In his struggle, the suitcase breaks open spilling out the magician's props and tricks, most importantly his hat. After much effort he gets the hat and props to the theater and gets his big tip – an oversized nickel.

Paramount then added two more shorts to the slate of 13 from Max, the stop motion short "Pop and Mom in Wild Oysters" made by Charlie Bowers and "Speaking of Animals: Down on the Farm" by Jerry Fairbanks and animation great Tex Avery, which was nominated for an Academy Award.

# *Gabby*

On paper, the Gabby cartoons made a lot of sense. GT had been a hit and audiences seemed to like the little blowhard. It was logical to capitalize on the success of GT by having several of the characters star in their own shorts.

From a business point of view, extending the life of the characters could have resulted in more merchandise licensing. Max already had a staff who knew the characters. There wouldn't be any need to invent designs, etc., other than suitable stories. Much of the music was recycled from GT.

Of course, the assumption was enough people had seen GT to understand who these characters were and the universe in which they operated.

The problem is, while solid talent at the studio was used in these GT spin-off cartoons, the gamble did not pay off in the long run. There were eight Gabby cartoons produced in color in this series, while the other GT inspired shorts were black and white.

Looking at the Gabby shorts first, released in 1940 and 1941, one sees the studio was stuck with a character who was a vain incompetent. Simply put, Gabby wasn't very likable. The humor in the shorts revolved around Gabby screwing something up and then getting his comeuppance. For Gabby, there is no moment at which he understands his near psychopathic behavior has made him a pariah in Lilliput.

Pinto Colvig provides the voice of Gabby, while Jack Mercer does many of the other voices, including King Little.

The catch phrase, "All kinds of things and stuff like that there" that Gabby uses in GT is repeated several times in the series. Reportedly, it became a catch phrase used by some radio comics.

Starting with the first short, "King for a Day" (1940), Gabby delivers a letter to King Little in which the anonymous sender writes he is coming that day to shoot the king. King Little sees the opportunity to satisfy Gabby's fantasy of making him "king for a day," allowing the real king to hide and avoid death. Naturally, the payoff is there isn't an assassin coming, but a photographer.

That's the kind of story point that today would drive fans crazy on social media. Afterall, the Lilliput we know from GT exists in the late 1600s. There were no photographers then. *The Showman's Trade Review* published its review, "Featuring the little busybody of 'Gulliver's Travels,' this is the first of a series of Gabby cartoons. It is not, unfortunately, a very impressive beginning, but the kiddies won't complain. The story reveals what happens to Gabby who takes place of the real king, who has gladly given up his throne after receiving a note that someone is coming to shoot him. For the climax, the king is 'shot' all right, but by a camera fiend. To arouse interest in this Technicolor cartoon, which was produced by Max Fleischer, get the kiddies to form a Gabby Club. Use Gabby pins as giveaways."

Many theater owners used the popularity of the Popeye cartoons to form Popeye Clubs as successful marketing device. It's difficult to imagine how kids would be similarly impressed by Gabby.

A theater manager from Iowa wrote in the *Motion Picture Herald's*, Aug. 7, 1940, edition, "This is the first of this series we have played and it is certainly a weak sister. The Paramount Color Classics were excellent. Why this series? We certainly have to move them off of our good days."

In his second short, "The Constable," Gabby is a police officer of sorts and goes undercover as a pig – yes, that's right – to catch the persons who has been raiding the mayor's sty. Snitch, the small spy from GT, makes a guest appearance as the person being forced to steal the pigs.

Gabby creates a pig costume to catch the thieves red-handed. He is literally about to go into the oven when he makes his move against the pig-nappers.

"All's Well," opens with the song that introduced the Gabby character in GT. The cartoon starts with Gabby actually doing good deeds. He happens upon a crying baby whom he becomes determined to entertain and figures out he needs to change the kid's diaper.

This cartoon casts Gabby in his most favorable light, but the more he fails at the task the more determined he gets and the unpleasant Gabby returns.

"Two for the Zoo" is a bit of showcase for Colvig, who gets writing credit as well as performing Gabby's voice. Gabby usurps a deliveryman's job of bringing a new animal to the zoo. Gabby thinks he is escorting a small animal that looks like a kangaroo with a long snout, but in reality, he is bringing the small animal's mother, who towers over him, along as well.

Again, it is a short that emphasizes that Gabby is a constant braggart and liar.

"Swing Cleaning" has Gabby taking over the spring cleaning of King Little's castle. The king admonishes Gabby not to break anything, which sets up the rest of the action. Through his ignorance and incompetence, he breaks everything.

"Fire Cheese" sees Gabby taking over the Lilliput Fire Department, which is called to a house fire. The fire wins through his actions and somehow this is supposed to be funny.

In "Gabby Goes Fishing" Gabby encounters a little boy who is successfully fishing on a pier. Declaring the kid doesn't know what he is doing (despite a bucket full of caught fish) he takes over. He soon is outwitted by a large fish causing him to redouble his efforts.

"It's Hap-Hap-Hap Happy Day" was the final film in the series and reprises the opening of GT with Gabby as the night watchman. On his rounds in the morning extinguishing the gas lights, Gabby encounters the mayor, who is leaving for a solo camping trip. Naturally, Gabby invites himself along. Disaster follows Gabby's every move.

Although some theater managers thought some of the shorts were "good," generally the reviews from exhibitors were not positive. "Few laughs here and there," was an assessment for "Two for the Zoo." Another manager from Alabama advised, "Will do. Play it." (June 7, 1941) *Motion Picture Herald.*

A theater manager in Indiana wrote about "All's Well," "I am still waiting to see a good Gabby cartoon. They are far below Paramount's average." Another exhibitor wrote about the short, "Just another seven minutes running time used up."

A rare positive review came for "King for a Day," "Good color cartoon" wrote the manager of a theater in Dewey OK.

*The Showman's Trade Review* in its Aug. 23, 1941, edition published a review of "It's Hap-Hap-Hap Happy Day." It read, "Gabby insists on going on a camping trip with the mayor, although the mayor wants to be alone. Gabby succeeds in ruining everything beautifully. This is the last of the Gabby cartoons. Gabby hasn't been nearly as successful as it was thought he might be following 'Gulliver's Travels' and none of the cartoons has been particularly good. This swan song of the series measures up to the rest of them."

# *Finally, a hit*

Despite the extensive schedule of one-reelers, the studio also undertook the production of another special two-reeler, but this time, it did not feature Popeye.

Instead, the production was based on the very popular children's book character Raggedy Ann, created by artist and writer Johnny Gruelle.

Gruelle patented the Raggedy Ann design in 1915 and then created the first book in 1918. It was a success which led to a long series of books and the main character proved to be a merchandising staple. Kids wanted to read the stories and own the doll.

Interestingly enough, Gruelle created a cartoon series at the Bray Studios in 1917 called "The Quacky Doodles," a group of duck characters.

Raggedy Ann was still very popular in 1940 was the Fleischer production was first announced.

The cartoon is one of unabashed sentimentality, which harkens back to the some of the Color Classics. Myron Waldman and Joe Oriolo are credited as the head animators and it certainly matched Waldman's sensibilities. He did not enjoy, although he was capable of

Paramount suggests a booking of the new "Road to Zanzibar" with the Raggedy Ann two-reeler.

delivering, the violence of the Popeye cartoons and preferred what he called "oooh, aww" pictures.

The film opens with a young girl rushing to a toy story to buy the Raggedy Ann doll in the window. What she does not know is the doll has her hand sewn to the hand of a boy doll that looks like her and she does not have enough money to buy both.

The shopkeeper tells her the story of why the two dolls must always stay together. Set in Ragland, where most things are made of cloth, Raggedy Ann and Raggedy Andy are made at the doll factory where anthropomorphized spools of thread, scissors and tape measures bring the two dolls to completion.

To give them life, though, candy hearts are slid into their mouths. Neither has a name, though and they are advised to go to the castle before dark to get their names. If they don't get there by sunset, "you will be nothing but rags."

Another Gruelle character, the Camel with the Wrinkly Knees, then offers to take them to the castle. When the camel can't go any further, the dolls drag him to a filling station where he receives a fresh amount of sawdust in his hump.

While that is happening, a Spanish doll starts singing and Andy is seduced and abandons Raggedy Ann. Dejected, Ann heads to the castle on the camel. She worries about him not getting a name.

Arriving at the Castle of Names, she collapses and is in pain. The doll doctors discover her candy heart is broken. "There is nothing doctors can do about that," the doctors say together.

Andy, though, having realized his mistake, rushed to the castle, gets their names and Ann is revived.

They are subsequently married by the king, who sews their hands together. The shopkeeper gives the little girl the dolls.

The model sheets show an effort to keep the look authentic from the children's books. (Michael Sportn website)

The short harkens back to a style of storytelling seen in the early 1930s at Fleischers, as well as other studios, with ordinary objects coming to life. I liked how the animation conveyed the softness of the dolls. The Technicolor pastel color design works wonderfully with the subject material.

Sammy Timburg's score and songs are also sweet and sentimental.

Jack Mercer provides many supporting voices, while Pinto Colvig used his Goofy voice for the camel. Lou Fleischer's son Bernie plays Andy and Joy Terry is Ann.

The trade reviews were among the best the studio received in 1940. *Box Office,* (Dec. 21, 1940), noted, "A delightfully entertaining novelty reel which will find favor with the youngsters and even garner chuckles from adults. The color, music and animation are expertly handled. The material finds root in the Raggedy Ann books originated by the late Johnny Gruelle. It concerns the brief adventure of the little miss who most anxiously wants the Raggedy Ann doll she has seen in the window. But Raggedy Ann is attached to her boyfriend and they cannot be separated. The storekeeper then proceeds to tell his customer the story behind the attachment. Dave Fleischer directed, Sammy Timburg took charge of the musical arrangement and Myron Waldman, Joseph Oriolo, William Henning and Arnold Gillespie cooperated on the animation. It is being released for the Christmas holidays in key spots and will out generally next Easter."

"Raggedy Ann" was originally scheduled for Christmas release but was moved to Easter as not to compete with the release of the first Superman cartoon, Film Daily reported on Nov. 12, 1940.

*Motion Picture Herald,* (Dec. 28, 1940,) reported, "Mr. [Max] Fleischer and his staff have worked a colorful background into and throughout the subject with the various sewing implements giving a musical review while constructing the dolls."

*The Film Daily's* reviewer wrote, (Dec. 18, 1940) "As a Christmas release this cartoon number should appeal particularly to kids. It is sentimental and the story is nicely worked out. Max Fleischer produced, with the story adopted from the works written by Johnny Gruelle. A little girl goes to a toy store to buy the Raggedy Ann doll in the window, but she is told by the owner that she must also buy Raggedy Andy as they go together. She only has the price of one and he tells her the story of why the two dolls are joined together, finally giving her both of them as she dejectedly turns to leave the shop. Subject is in Technicolor."

"This two-reel Fleischer cartoon in color is exceptionally well done in all departments and should make a distinctive addition to holiday programs everywhere," declared the *Motion Picture Daily* on Dec. 20, 1940.

Theater owners seemed to have given it their approval. "Special – double length color cartoon that is very well done and although not very funny seemed to be enjoyed," one theater manager in New York wrote.

"Will pleases the kiddies. We made a mistake in playing it on Saturday date, although was very good," offered a theater manager in Alabama.

*Motion Picture Herald*, (Jan. 11, 1941) ran the results of its annual short subject poll. The leaders of the survey of exhibitors had the following top ten: Walt Disney Cartoons, March of Time, Crime Does not Pay, Pete Smith Specialties, Merrie Melodies, Three Stooges, Popeye the Sailor, Information Please, Our Gang and Passing Parade.

It's interesting to note that only three animated series were in that list: Merrie Melodies, Disney shorts and Popeye.

Later, after the demise of the Fleischer Studio, its successor, Famous Studio revisited the character twice in its Noveltoons

The Raggedy Ann two-reeler proved to be a hit.

series, "Suddenly It's Spring," (1944) and "The Enchanted Square" (1947). Both were very well-done tear-jerkers.

The Fleischer connection to the character re-surfaced many years later.

In 1977, a new feature length Raggedy Ann film was released with Richard Williams as its director. The film, according to Steve Stanchfield's great essay on Cartoon Research, had a complicated production history, but what he discovered was the involvement of several Fleischer alumni in the new production.

Stanchfield wrote, "When ITT [the company whose subsidiary Bobbs-Merrill owned the rights to the character] needed to find a studio to produce the Raggedy Ann and Andy feature, they did a search all over New York by tapping on lots of different studio doors. Several studios spent some time trying to budget the film for ITT, and several produced demo animation to try and convince the company to send the work entirely their way. Shamus Culhane was hired and paid to complete a production outline, including a budget, sometime in mid 1974, with a production solution that involved studios in New York, California and overseas to complete the film by March 1976, for release in the summer. Culhane had made many suggestions on sources to use that had various production capabilities – with many of those suggestions being awarded the final work.

As part of the studio selection process, Joe Oriolo produced a short pencil test as a demonstration reel for ITT. "This demo seems to fit into the timeline before [Abe] Levitow was hired [as the film's first director], as ITT was looking for possible studios. It's a pencil test of several scenarios from the film. My guess is that they were asked to visualize a few key moments from the script," wrote Stanchfield.

"It's a pretty short test, but interesting to see. It appears to have been animated by New York veterans Myron Waldman and Bill Sturm. I'm not sure who else worked on it, if anyone, but it was produced as a demo to show ITT," he concluded.

Williams told me in a letter that while he admired much of what Max had produced, he didn't think too much of the studio's rendition of Raggedy Ann. Interestingly enough, among the many animators Williams used in his film was another Fleischer vet, Grim Natwick.

## Toys Worth $200 Promoted by Stoltz in 'Raggedy Ann' Selling

It was only a letter. But directed to the right person—Johnny Gruelle, creator of the Raggedy Ann newspaper stories that have thrilled children for the past 30 years—it brought Gruelle to Utica, N. Y., where he arranged with Manager Arnold Stoltz of the Avon Theatre to have eleven firms furnish Stoltz with $200 worth of dolls, toys and books as giveaways in advance of the engagement of "Raggedy Ann."

The publishers of the Raggedy Ann color book also furnished tear-sheets which were distributed to 1,200 first and second-grade pupils in public schools for coloring purposes.

A week was set aside as Raggedy Ann Week, during which time a lobby display, a window display, an attention-getting street ballyhoo and plenty of newspaper publicity served to remind Utica kiddiedom that "Raggedy Ann" was com-

ing to the Avon and don't think they forgot!

The week culminated in a Special Raggedy Ann and Raggedy Andy matinee on Saturday, which was attended by hundreds of boys and girls.

The Playworld Toy Shop, largest store of its kind in Utica, not only devoted an entire window to a display of the toys, but also took a number of tie-up ads in the local newspapers.

Directly above is the lobby display of toys, all promoted gratis from eleven firms, which Manager Arnold Stoltz of the Avon Theatre, Utica, N. Y., used to plug the engagement of Paramount's two-reel Technicolor cartoon, "Raggedy Ann." In the center are two members of the house staff dressed as dolls in

costumes furnished by the manufacturer. They received lots of attention as they paraded the streets. At the right above is a window display of toys, promoted from the town's largest toy store. These displays were just a part of the excellent campaign launched by Showman Stoltz. Business was great.

This is an example of the kind of marketing individual theaters did to attract audiences. A two-reel Technicolor short such as this one would be promoted just as prominently as many features.

# Chapter Three

## *Paramount shows its cards*

I've tried to organize the information in this book in a roughly chronological order so information flows from one series of cartoons to another. With this brief chapter placed here it will give readers greater context for the business politics that happened at the studio.

Author and film historian Justin Humphreys has revealed in his new book about animator and film producer George Pal – "George Pal: Man of Tomorrow" – that Paramount's efforts to control the studio began in 1939.

Pal, who came to the United States as war raged through Europe, was known for his successful Puppetoons advertising shorts. Paramount had taken interest in them and had contacted Pal to see what his plans were and offered him two places to have a new studio for him: New York City or at the new Fleischer Studio in Miami.

Humphreys noted Pal and his family had already settled in Los Angeles when this offer was made. He wanted to stay there. Pal established distribution ties with Paramount and opened his studio in Los Angeles.

Subsequently, his animated shorts became popular, but by the end of the 1940s, with rising production costs, Pal discontinued the shorts and successfully went into feature film production with such films as "The War of the Worlds," "Destination Moon," "The Seven Faces of Dr. Lao" and many more.

My point in noting this is that the Miami studio was filled to capacity in 1939 due to the fact of a feature film production. When veteran animator Grim Natwick arrived from Los Angeles there was no room for him and a desk. He did his work on "Gulliver's Travels" in Dave's office.

For Paramount to make that offer to Pal meant the studio's execs believed they had the right to tell Max to make room for another animation studio. Clearly, they thought they already controlled the Miami studio.

The worst was yet to come, though.

In this photo from February 1939, Paramount president Barney Balaban visits Max at the new studio. In 15 months, he would be taking over Max's studio.

Richard Fleischer noted in his memoir about his father that on May 29, 1941, Dick Murray, who acted as a liaison between Paramount and the studio, hand-delivered an unexpected contract to Max.

The contact was dated May 24, 1941, and in it, Paramount called the note for the money lent to Max to build the studio, a loan that supposedly had 10 years to repay. The contract was 65 pages long.

The contract essentially stated that Max and Dave had to hand over everything to Paramount and for the next 26 weeks the studio would run as normal except Paramount would own it.

According to his son, Max was told to read it and sign it. Dave was to do the same. Murray could offer no other details. If Max didn't sign it, he couldn't have met the payroll that week and he would have had to declare bankruptcy.

Max signed it, as did Dave.

The contract was very specific about how the studio would now work. For the time being, it would retain the name "Fleischer," but Paramount would rename the studio in 1942 as "Famous Studio." The company had a music publishing division called Famous Music.

One clause stated:

"The Producer [Max] shall during the period of one year commenting May 24, 1941, produce the following motion pictures cartoons and such other motion picture cartoons of features, two-reel, one-reel and other length in black and white or color, all as Paramount may from time to time designate or request upon and subject to terms, provisions and conditions in this agreement provided:

"The feature motion picture cartoon in three-color Technicolor tentatively titled 'Mr. Big Goes to Town,' now in the course of production, but which will not be released until after Aug. 3, 1941

"The two-reel motion picture cartoon in three-color Technicolor, tentatively entitled 'The Raven,' now in the course of the production, but which will not be released until after Aug. 31, 1942.

"Twelve one-reel Superman motion picture cartoons in three-color Technicolor, the first of which is in the course of production, but none of which will be released until after Aug. 31, 1941.

"Twelve black and white one-reel Popeye motion picture cartoons, the production of the first has been completed or will be shortly completed and the next four or five of which Popeye one-reelers are in the course of production, but none of which will be released until after Aug. 31, 1941.

All at such places and studios using such equipment and material that Paramount may from time to time designate."

The production schedule was established and Max and Dave would continue to be Paramount employees for 26 weeks. Richard Fleischer added that both men had to submit a letter of resignation to be implemented at Paramount's discretion. The contract called the letters "collateral security."

The contract also stipulated that if Max or Dave were planning to work on a project on their own time, Paramount has first rights to purchase that film.

Paramount established content control under this agreement stating that each new cartoon's script would have to be approved before production. It could also recut and retitle any cartoon submitted to them.

Max and Dave were no longer in charge of their employees. "The Producer [Max] shall not in any event make any changes in or discharge any of its present employees or make any changes in any its present contracts with any artists, animators or any others or make any changes in any moneys or compensation paid or payable to any employees whatsoever, whether or not under contract or engage any new employees or enter into any new contracts with artists, animators, or others without in each instance first obtaining written consent thereto of Paramount."

The costs of each production are also listed in the contract. According to the contract, "Mr. Bug Goes to Town" was given a budget of $60,000; "The Raven" had $54,000; The first Superman cartoon had $50,000, while the remaining 11 had a budget of $30,000; and each Popeye was $16,500. If Max needed more money, he would have to ask Paramount in writing.

Any patent developed at the studio would become Paramount property and all of the cartoons produced by the studio would become Paramount property, with any future revenue going to Paramount. Max had to supply Paramount with a detailed report about costs associated with each cartoon when it was delivered to Paramount.

If Max or Dave decided to break the terms of the contact neither of them would be able to use the phrases "Max Fleischer Studio," "Dave Fleischer Studio" or "Fleischer Studios" for a year.

As will be noted in detail in a later chapter, Max was forced to resign on Dec. 28, 1941. In a meeting with Paramount President Barney Balaban in New York City. Richard said his father asked why and was never given an answer.

The question remains unanswered. It's purely speculative but I think it's fair to write Paramount saw an opportunity of continuing to produce cartoons and to streamline costs by eliminated Max and Dave and controlling animation studio directly. The advantage they employed was the fact that Max was in debt to them.

It was not uncommon in the word of animation to have the kind of arrangement Max had with Paramount. Walter Lantz supplied cartoons to Universal as an outside producer. Leon Schlesinger had an arrangement with Warner Bros. as an outside producer and sold the studio his operation in 1944 when he retired. MGM initially had an arrangement with producers Hugh Harmon and Rudy Isling, but in 1937 that studio decided to make animation an in-house activity. Interestingly enough, MGM then rehired the pair to work on cartoons. Paul Terry distributed his sound cartoons first through Educational Pictures and then had a long-standing deal with 20th Century Fox.

Post Mickey Mouse's debut, Disney went through a number of studios: Columbia, United Artists and RKO. In 1953, he founded his own distribution arm, Buena Vista.

Max, though, clearly felt comfortable enough with his 14-year association with Paramount to go into debt to Paramount. He obviously trusted the management.

The arrangement of working with a distributor was what Max had tried to escape when he headed Red Seal in the mid-1920. He produced his own cartoons and other short subjects and acquired other productions for distribution. He opened exchanges throughout the country to ensure theater owners would have access to prints and heavily advertised in the trades. But he grew the company too fast and wound up with debt and a receiver.

Cutting a distribution deal with Paramount and setting up a new corporation allowed Max to get from underneath his receiver and start fresh.

At the risk of amateur psychology, I believe that Max having gone through the public indignation of court proceedings with Red Seal – covered by the trade press – and was convinced in the security of his business relationship with Paramount. According to his son, Max had never a problem with Paramount until this fateful day in 1941.

I think the knowledge of what was happening behind the scenes – no one told me that anyone outside of the closest circle of Max or Dave knew about the takeover – makes the studio's accomplishments even more impressive: The Superman shorts, the continuing quality of the Popeye cartoons and the artistic triumph of "Mr. Bug Goes to Town."

During this 26-week period though, one can only imagine the stress that Max and Dave were under. Their personal differences had reportedly become worse. As noted in my first book, Max was more of an introvert while Dave was definitely an extrovert. Myron Waldman said to me, "Max was soft and quiet, very well spoken. Dave was more flamboyant. His nature was entirely different."

Max liked going home and relaxed by playing his mandolin or by reading. Dave was a gambler and partier.

They were not speaking. Dave's affair with studio employee Mae Schwartz continued after the move to Miami. She was apparently living in New York City still and Dave would take the train to see her. Dave had accused Max of having an affair with his secretary Vera Coleman and reportedly said his brother was a hypocrite.

Richard Fleischer noted in his book that his mother was known to be jealous and even attempted suicide once in reaction to an alleged infidelity committed by Max. If there had been something between Max and Coleman, Richard didn't mention it in his book. One thing is for sure, Coleman was amazingly loyal to Max and followed him to his post-studio jobs.

I spoke briefly to Coleman in the late 1970s and wanted to interview her but couldn't make that happen. Richard had given me her phone number and she was very gracious to me on the phone.

The top management of the studio now faced their termination as well as their deep-seated personal conflict. This all happened as production on the Popeye and Superman shorts as well as a new feature were unabated.

# Chapter Four

## *Hoppity comes to Town*

The second and last feature produced by Max is one of the most completely realized productions the studio ever presented and its most misunderstood. Everything in it works: a solid and original plot, intriguing characters, accomplished animation, wonderful songs, as well as great scenics and backgrounds. In many, many ways, it succeeds as a film far better than "Gulliver's Travels."

It has the urban New York Fleischer feel to it. Its music definitely reflects the pop music of the 1940s. It opens with a beautiful 3-D set that screams of the studio's touch. It takes better advantage of Technicolor than its predecessor.

Yet the financial failure of the film coupled with the long-assumption that Paramount sabotaged the release to obtain the studio has given the film an undeserved negative reputation.

To be clear: Paramount did not sabotage the release to get the studio, as it already owned the Fleischer Studio. The trade papers show there was advertising and promotion behind the film. Perhaps it was not the same push given "Gulliver's Travels," but a considerable effort was made. And remember, Paramount execs had approved the subject of the film.

Despite the marketing campaign, the movie did not find its audience in the earliest days of World War II and much of the foreign markets were not available because of the war. It was very well-reviewed by the trades indicating that at least within the industry, the film should have been a hit.

The widest audience the film has received undoubtedly came when National Telefilm Associates (NTA) bought distribution rights and sold it to TV stations as well as having a theatrical re-release with a new title "Hoppity Goes to Town" in the 1950s.

How "Mr. Bug" came about is a fascinating story of a 180-degree turn, as initially the studio announced its follow-up feature to "Gulliver's Travels" and it was not a story about insects.

Almost immediately after the release of "Gulliver's Travels," Paramount authorized Max to undertake a second feature. *Variety* reported on Jan. 10, 1940, "Paramount execs are trying to decide what subject the next Fleischer cartoon feature would be; having the field of subjects reduced from 20 to four … Getting the right story is said by Paramount's story department is made difficult by the demands of the company's heads that it not be scary, yet have suspense."

There had been a backlash from some people who believed Disney's "Snow White and the Seven Dwarves" had been too horrific in some scenes and clearly Paramount wanted to avoid that criticism.

A film based on the myth of Pandora's Box was initially announced. On Jan. 20, 1940, *Motion Picture Herald* reported that "Pandora" "will run seven or eight reels to be ready for Paramount release by Christmas of this year."

*The Film Daily*, April 2, 1940, then reported, "Max Fleischer will start second feature 'Pandora' starting about June 1. Screenplay by Edmund Seward. Dan Gordon will direct. Pix will cost about $1.5 million."

There are several significant statements here with someone other than Dave receiving director credit. Dan Gordon was both an artist and story man who had worked in animation starting at Van Buren in 1933 and moved on to Paul Terry's studio, according to a detailed profile by animation historian Devon Baxter. After a short stint at MGM, Gordon found employment at the Fleischer Studios around 1938, where he worked in the story department.

Gordon could both draw and write and seemed to be considered an up-and-coming talent at the studio. Baxter quotes James Davis, an animator on "Mr. Bug," saying, "Dan could do it all, and do it better. His problem was that it all came so easy for him, if that's a problem. We were always amazed at his skills."

This film though, did not happen and was replaced by a wildly different concept.

The most common part of the "Mr. Bug" story held by many is that Paramount did not promote the film and sabotaged it. In reality, the studio did promote the film, although not as much as it did "Gulliver's Travels." Here are some examples: a two-page full color trade ad. There were ads aimed at the South and Latin American market as well as an ad in French and one seen in popular American magazines.

# CINE - MUNDIAL

### REVISTA MENSUAL ILUSTRADA
### 516 FIFTH AVENUE, NEW YORK

Director: F. García Ortega

Jefe de Redacción: Francisco J. Ariza

Gerente de Anuncios: Ervin L. Hall

Administrador: J. M. Escuder

Vol. XXVI     Junio, 1941     Núm. 6

Qui donc en France ne connaît Mathurin, le fameux marin mangeur d'épinards, créé par Dave Fleischer?... Qui ne connaît de ce même magicien du dessin et de la couleur les inoubliables "*VOYAGES DE GULLIVER*" qui ont ravi des millions et des millions de spectateurs dans le monde entier?...

Or, voici qu'aujourd'hui, Dave Fleischer nous offre une nouvelle création, et qui l'emporte de loin sur les précédentes : "*DOUCE ET CRIQUET S'AIMAIENT*

*D'AMOUR TENDRE*", le plus DROLE des grands dessins animés qui enchantera les enfants et les parents de ces enfants, et les grands-parents de ces parents...

Réalisé en Technicolor, c'est un véritable éblouissement pour les yeux : les couleurs les plus vives, les plus ensoleillées, y sont prodiguées comme sur la palette d'un peintre.

\*

Votre public sera dans la joie en

suivant les extravagantes aventures de Douce la blonde, de Criquet son maigre amoureux, de Monsieur Bourdon, solennel et disert, du piquant Moustique et du méchant Scarabée qui voudrait bien épouser la jolie Douce mais qui verra échouer ses noirs projets. Que de situations comiques! Que de gags! Que d'irrésistibles images croquées par le pinceau génial de Dave Fleischer!...

"*DOUCE ET CRIQUET S'AIMAIENT D'AMOUR TENDRE*", avec son rythme tourbillonnant, sa folle gaieté, ses mélodies ensorceleuses est le type même du film qui va au succès tambour battant, et battant tous les records...

On June 26, 1940, *Variety* announced, "Norman Corwin, CBS staff director-writer, has a deal with Max Fleischer to direct the dialogue for a Paramount cartoon feature in the fall. Using legit [theater actors] and radio actors, he will add the dialog in New York after the film is made in the Fleischer Studio in Florida. Voices will be selected by Fleischer from test records made in New York."

This is also significant as Dave Fleischer usually directed the voice actors. Corwin was a very well-known writer who had a huge output on radio and other media and, ultimately, was celebrated for that work with a One World Award, two Peabody Medals, an Emmy Award, a Golden Globe Award, and a duPont-Columbia Award. He was nominated for an Academy Award for Writing Adapted Screenplay for "Lust for Life."

On the surface, getting a talent such as Corwin involved for an animated feature is fairly astonishing.

Broadcasting reported on Sept. 1, 1940, that Corwin had left Hollywood on Aug. 27 to travel to Miami to "fulfill commitments at Max Fleischer Cartoon Studios."

Variety then reported on Sept. 11, 1940, that RKO had bought the contract for his services from Max Fleischer.

However, was this all just public relations? In 1977, I asked Corwin about his involvement and he wrote, "I'm afraid your information is inaccurate. I never worked with the Fleischer Studio. For a time, he [Max] was interested in a radio play I had written, ('My Client Curley' – about a dancing caterpillar) but there was never any deal made. If indeed he made a film called 'Mr. Bug Goes to Town,' and it bore any resemblance to 'My Client Curley' that would be news to me of special interest."

Or was Corwin's memory incorrect? It's difficult for me to believe there was nothing behind these various announcements.

To make this more confusing, "My Client Curley" was indeed made into a movie in 1944 starring Cary Grant and released by Columbia.

There have been reports that Maurice Maeterlinck's "The Life of the Bee," was being considered but the rights could not be obtained.

On Nov. 27, 1940, *Variety* noted, "The basis for the story of the second Max Fleischer feature-length cartoon for Paramount is the Karel Capek fantasy 'World We Live In.' It has been adapted by unrevealed writers with considerable freedom to suit the requirements for the picture, Norman Corwin did some work on the yarn. Hoagy Carmichael has written all the music for the cartoon, production on which will begin to roll, under plans, around the first of the year."

Capek was a writer and satirist best known for his science fiction book "War with the Newts," as well as his play "R.U.R.," which coined the word "robot." His play, known under the titles "The Insect Play," "The Life of the Insects," "The Insect Comedy," "The World We Live In" and "From Insect Life," was written with his brother Josef and was first performed in 1922. In the play, a tramp falls asleep in the forest and dreams of seeing insects and their lives as representing human traits. The play was a commentary on life in post-World War One Czechoslovakia.

If you have seen "Mr. Bug," then you know the story is indeed about insects with human characteristics, but the finished screenplay is not a darkly satiric look at human behavior through their lives.

There was no mention of Capek in the credits, nor was Corwin credited. Instead, the story is credited to Dave Fleischer, Dan Gordon, Tedd Pierce and Isadore Sparber. The screenplay was written by Dan Gordon, Tedd Pierce, Isadore Sparber, Graham Place, Bob Wickersham, William Turner, Carl Meyer and Cal Howard.

The songs for "Mr. Bug" were largely written by a red-hot composter and performer, Hoagy Carmichael with Frank Loesser. Carmichael was the rarest of Tin Pan Alley song writers as his songs were not only hits at the time but have become American standards: "Stardust," "Georgia on My Mind, "The Nearness of You" and "Heart and Soul," among others. He also was a character actor who appeared in "Have or Have Not" with Humphrey Bogart and "The Best of Years of Our Lives."

Getting an artist with the popularity of Carmichael was a real coup for Max and Dave. It ensured ancillary publicity for the film's release. The songs included "We're the Couple in the Castle," "Katy Did, Katy Didn't," and "I'll Dance at Your Wedding (Honey Dear)" by Carmichael and Loesser.  One song, "Boy Oh Boy," was written by Sammy Timburg. All are accomplished 1940s pop songs.

The infamous Hearst newspaper Hollywood gossip columnist Louella Parsons placed the following item in his column on Feb. 7, 1941: "I am greatly intrigued with the description sent me by Max Fleischer of 'Mr. Bug Goes to Town,' the first cartoon to tell a story. Fleischer has spent over a year making these drawings, which are neither fable or fantasy, but the story of a town of insects 45 inches from Broadway who are menaced by steel, cement and the human race."

She continued, "Fleischer's idea is a radical departure form anything done in the cartoon world. Human beings appear only as heavies. An elaborate musical score has been written by Hoagy Carmichael and Frank Lester [sic]. The plot is as exciting as any feature movie."

The phrase "the first cartoon to tell a story" is an odd one, indeed.

In the Feb. 8, 1941, edition of the *Motion*

Like "Gulliver's Travels," Famous Music released sheet music of the movie's songs.

*Picture Herald*, Paramount publicity declared "Mr. Bug" as "a pioneering step in bringing to the screen the first solidly dramatic modern story of today in a feature cartoon form."

"Phil M. Daily," the anonymous columnist for *The Film Daily* wrote on Feb. 11, 1941, "That big title-line must, which tells the world that the events, characters and firms depicted in this photoplay are fictitious and 'any similarity to actual persons, living or dead is purely coincidental' is being knocked into a proverbial cocked hat by murmurings down Miami way. Rumor has it that (quite coincidentally, of course) the characterizations in Fleischer Studio' new million-dollar Technicolor production – 'Mr. Bug Goes to Town' – were patterned after Hollywood stars. Our scouts declare that Honey, the bee heroine, bears a striking resemblance (or stinging, if you prefer) resemblance to Denna Durbin, while Hoppity, the grasshopper, has characteristics a la Jimmy Stewart and that Beetle, the heavy, is astonishingly like Gene Lockhart. Max and Dave Fleischer may not seriously consider this suggestion but a world premiere in Washington's Department of Agriculture looms as a 'natural.'"

In the April 23, 1941, edition of *The Film Daily*, a front-page item noted, In the middle of production of "Mr. Bug," the Fleischers wrote to President Roosevelt to offer their services to produce "educational cartoons to assist in training U.S. troops."

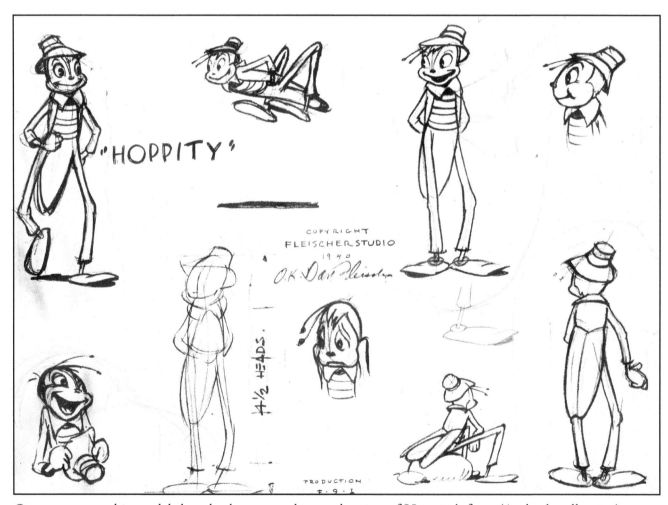

One can see on this model sheet both notes and a test drawing of Hoppity's foot. (Author's collection).

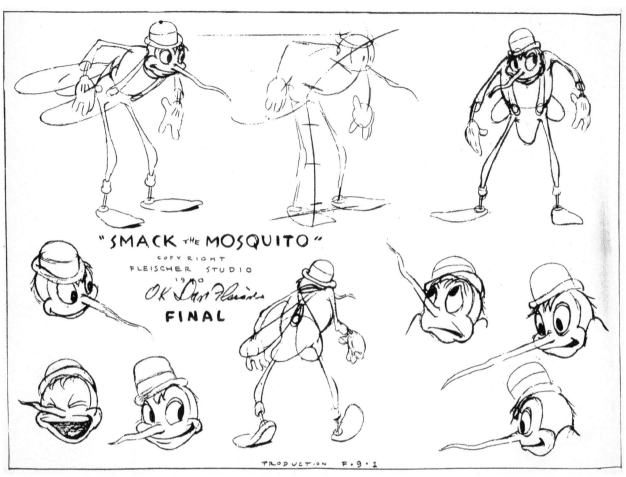

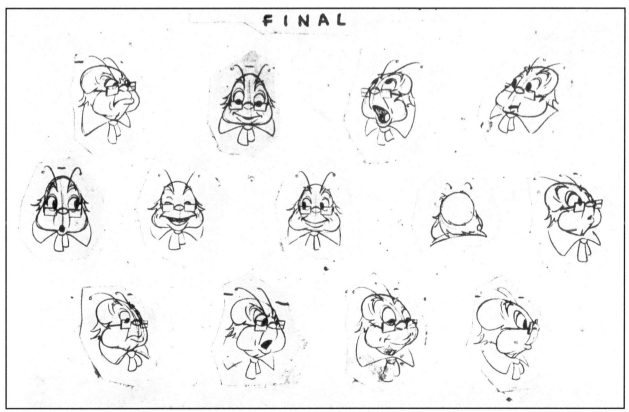

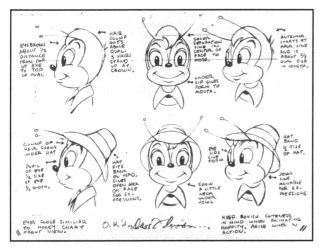
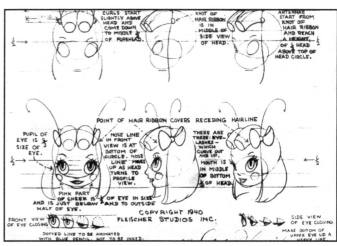

On May 5, 1941, *Broadcasting*, in a story about movies raiding radio for talent, reported Gleason's Royal Guards "popular radio sextette" will perform chorus number for "Mr. Bug."

On May 17, 1941, the *Motion Picture Herald* reported that Dave, Dan Gordon, Ted Pierce, Harvey Sparber and Cal Howard posed for butterfly characters in "Mr. Bug." In the same item, it was noted that Dave hired "Negroes to make vases for the artist the break" who need an outlet for "pent up emotions" during the production of "Mr. Bug." This is, I'm sure, press agent puffery.

In a story run on the *Miami Herald* on Aug. 11, 1941, the cost of "Mr. Bug" was discussed briefly as well as the story of the film. It was described as the first all-cartoon feature-length picture with a non-fantasy plot and "modern romantic comedy-drama – and instead of human actors, it has insects."

It would seem that everyone involved with the story realized "Mr. Bug" was breaking the mold that had been set with "Snow White" and "Gulliver's Travels." Those two films had used pre-sold well-known properties that many people would have described as fantasies or fairy tales. This message was being used as a sales point in it being something different than seen before.

In a department store advertisement in the *Miami Herald* on Nov. 20, 1941, for Burdine's end of the month clearance, it was noted, "Max Fleischer Originals, 79 cents. Actual drawings in color used at the Fleischer studios to guide cartoonists, juvenile subjects." One can only wonder what was being sold for less than a dollar.

In many ways, "Mr. Bug" was indeed a step forward from the animated features it preceded. It was an original story that was not pre-sold. It presented a story with an interesting theme that pretty obviously referenced the situation of a minority immigrant population. The bugs in the film simply want to live alongside "the human ones," but the benign neglect from the humans cause them many problems.

This is far different than "Gulliver's Travels" and shows a sophistication the previous film did not have.

The film opens with a beautiful tracking shot through space and then to Earth and to a city that is obviously New York, seen in a three-dimensional model. It's a neat visual reference that is underscored by the last line of the dialogue in the film: From the right distance we all look like tiny insects.

The camera leads us to a small older home surrounded by skyscrapers and to a yard that was once protected by a fence but has been broken down. The lack of fence creates a cut-though the "human ones" use, not knowing they are trampling through the homes of the insects.

The insect community is thrilled to learn that Hoppity is returning to the town, although one insect is less than happy – C. Bagley Beetle.

The characters are designed in a way to reflect archetypes that were found in movies of that time. Hoppity is a Frank Capra-style hero in the James Stewart vein. He is always trying to do the right thing, although he does fail occasionally. He is largely unaware that C. Bagley Beetle – who is strongly reminiscent of actor Edward Arnold – is acting against Hoppity and for that matter the entire bug community – in order to marry the much-desired Honey Bee.

Dave at the three-dimensional model seen at the start of the film (courtesy of JJ Sedelmaier).

Beetle is supported by two henchmen, Smack the Mosquito and Swat the Fly. Sticking to the way conventional movies handle such relationships, Beetle strives to be seen as affluent and a leader, while making sure his fellow insects have no idea that he is the boss of two thugs who do his bidding.

Both henchmen have New York accents and provide comic relief.

The plot of the film revolves around the bugs trying to find a safe place to live. As long as the fence is broken, they have no security.

Hoppity learns the couple living in the house are having problems of their own. The man, Dick Dickens, is a songwriter hoping to hit big. If his song, "We're the Couple in the Castle," is bought by the publisher – Famous Music, a Paramount subsidiary, no less – they will be all set and can repair their house and the fence. If not, they will have to leave.

An effort to relocate the insect community to the upper and protected yard fails when a garden sprinkler washes them back to the lower level.

Along with this relocation effort, Hoppity is deepening his relationship with Honey. They go on a date to a nightclub. In one of the movie's most inventive sequences, the nightclub is underneath a traffic light with the changing signals providing light. An old radio provides music.

Smack and Swat follow the couple to the club and are initially thrown out by the doorman. They do manage to sneak in with the intent of hurting Hoppity. Originally, Smack was going to hit Hoppity with a nail. Swat complains bitterly, "I never get to hit nobody on the head and things like that." So, the honors go to him.

They wait for the right moment to pounce and Swat fails, Smack takes over and the nail hits an exposed electrical wire from the radio. When Hoppity see this, he comes to help and then he is shocked by the wire. The result is a great sequence in which Hoppity is drawn to look like a neon light while performing a dance.

Beetle also learns about the royalty check and understands if he can hide it, the humans will be forced to leave, Hoppity will be discredited and he will wind up with Honey Bee. Hoppity overhears the plan and is overwhelmed by Smack and Swat and is sealed into the check's envelope.

Just as Beetle is getting ready to marry Honey, construction workers begin demolition. Beetle's plan has worked too well. The hidden check has indeed eliminated Hoppity and the married couple, but it hasn't stopped the destruction of the insects' habitat.

Hoppity is able to escape and the letter carrier finds the check, which eventually is delivered to the couple. Meantime, Hoppity convinces the insect community their future is to climb up the building as there will be a garden at the top.

The sequence of the construction with the insects is well handled.

Finally, by the time the building is built and the insects have arrived at the top, the composer and his wife have done what they said they would do if the song was a hit: build a penthouse with a large flower garden. Hoppity is vindicated.

At the conclusion of the film, one of the young bugs says to his brother, as he looks over the edge to the street far below, "Hey Murgatroyd, look at the 'humans ones' down there. They look just like a lot of little bugs."

As historian Keith Scott noted in his essential book, "Cartoon Voices of the Golden Years, 1930-1970," seeing voice credits on screen was a rarity in the animation industry at that time in general, much less at the Fleischer Studio. The voice actors largely consisted of Fleischer Studio employees, especially writers. Jack Mercer did Mr. Bumble and Swat. Writers Carl Meyer was Smack and Ted Pierce did C. Bagley Beetle. Artist Pauline Loth played Honey. Singer Kenny Gardner, who worked for years for bandleader Guy Lombardo, was Dick the composer and theater actress Gwen Williams as Mary. Stan Freed was a local Miami actor who brought a youthful optimism to the role of Hoppity.

Loth worked at the studio from 1939 and 1942 as an assistant animator. She later worked at Timely Comics as an artist.

Pierce is best known for his script work at Warner Bros. animation but was at the Fleischer Studio from 1939 to 1941. He worked in the story department and did the voice of King Bombo as well in "Gulliver's Travels."

Meyer was also a writer at the studio but supplied voices in several cartoons, as well.

Scott noted in his book the voice of the young "bee scout" was Mae Questel, who flew down to Miami to record. This is surprising to me as Margie Hines, who was initially known as a Helen Kane sound-alike and who was now performing Olive Oyl, would have been available. Perhaps nostalgia was in play at the studio.

This feature showed the evolution of style at the studio, but it was still the Fleischer style. Where "Gulliver's Travels" had issues with character development and plot, the story of "Mr. Bug" quickly establishes where it needs to go and goes there.

Both films used rotoscoping to denote the "human" characters and it was a very effective in "Mr. Bug."

If the Fleischers had been able to keep their studio and if the timing of the release had been different, "Mr. Bug" would have been the start of a new era at the studio, in my opinion. This feature and the Superman cartoons showed exactly what the studio was capable of doing and it was not copying Disney. "Mr. Bug" was an original.

Much has been said and written about the release of the film and that Paramount had

Stills from the film (author's collection).

**"HOPPITY GOES TO TOWN"** ("MR. BUG GOES TO TOWN") In TECHNICOLOR Produced by MAX FLEISCHER Directed by DAVE FLEISCHER An NTA PICTURES RELEASE R 59/110

**"HOPPITY GOES TO TOWN"** ("MR. BUG GOES TO TOWN") In TECHNICOLOR Produced by MAX FLEISCHER Directed by DAVE FLEISCHER An NTA PICTURES RELEASE R 59/110

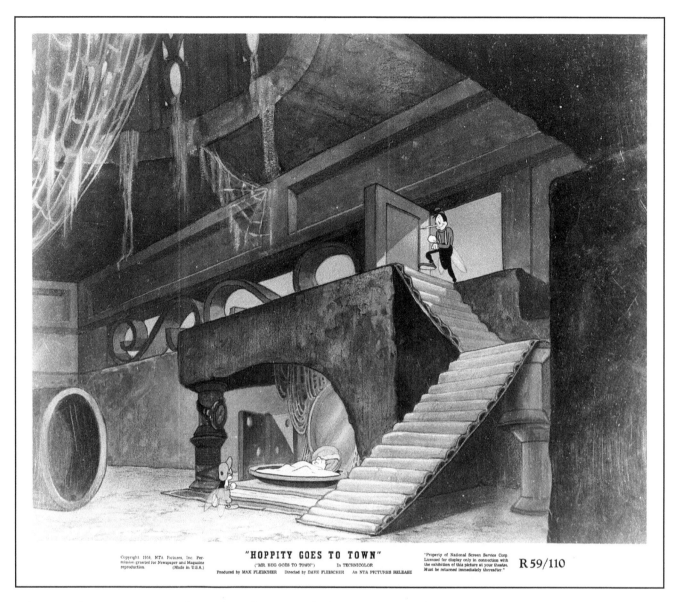

sabotaged it. Knowing they already owned the studio at the time of the release, there is no reason why Paramount would want to lose on its investment.

One trade ad had a theme of Christmas presents from Paramount to exhibitor. "Ooh Daddy! Look how Paramount has fixed me up for Christmas!"

Another ad read "Go to Town with … it will lead you to box office sugar!" A different trade ad read, "the whole industry's buzzing about Paramount's new kind of full-length cartoon feature, "Mr. Bug Goes to Town!' Solid adult entertainment packed with laughs, excitement, swingable tunes!"

Paramount was clearly saying this isn't Disney, it's different.

Spanish-language movie magazine Cine-Mundial had a feature about the film and a French release was promoted in French publications.

Paramount also bought ads in popular magazines. Some of the ad copy challenged readers to "play the latest movie game" – "Is Hoppity Bob Hope? Honey Madeline Carroll?"

Fleischer artist Polly Loth was the voice of Honey Bee.
(courtesy of JJ Sedelmaier)

The popular movie magazine, *Photoplay*, ran a full-page photo essay about the film.

Animated features were not seen as sure things in the industry. Disney lost money on "Pinocchio" and on "Fantasia." "Dumbo" had been released in September of 1941 and was a financial hit due to good reviews and the fact the 64-minute feature deliberately cost far less than its predecessors.

On the east coast alone, trade screenings of "Mr. Bug" were presented in Albany, NY, Boston, MA, Buffalo, NY, New Haven, CT, New York City, Philadelphia, PA, and Washington, D.C.

*Showman's Trade Review* on Jan. 10, 1942, reported, "Something new in movie preview audiences was established during the holiday season when Paramount showed 'Mr. Bug Goes to Town,' its new full-length Technicolor cartoon feature from the Fleischer Studios to selected groups of children in a number of large cities. Thousands of youngsters, chosen from among theater official's, and newspapermen's children, members of boys' clubs, orphanages and settlement houses saw the screen's first cartoon feature with a present-day metropolitan theme, at a special screening several weeks in advance of its showing at their local theatre.

"Largest of the showings took place in Pittsburgh at the Schenley Theatre for an audience of orphans and settlement kids, and in New Haven at the Paramount when the New Haven Register played host to guests from local orphanages, young tenants of New Haven housing projects and members of boy's clubs and newsboys' groups. Each of these two showings drew an audience of 1,500."

The story goes on to report screenings of this sort were also presented in Philadelphia, PA, Boston, MA, Albany, NY, Chicago, IL, Cleveland, OH, Milwaukee, WI, and Minneapolis, MN. The goal was clearly to start word-of-mouth messaging about the film.

By the time "Mr. Bug" was released, animated features were no longer a novelty, however the trade reviews were mostly in favor of the film.

*The National Board of Review Magazine* declared in its January 1942 edition, "Like all Technicolor feature cartoons, this one is delightful and should prove a natural for juvenile audiences. It is about a community of assorted bugs living on the last patch of ground left in a busy city. Finally, that property is torn up for a skyscraper to be erected and things look black indeed for Hoppity Bug and his girl Honey Bee. But a penthouse proves the saving of all. It is perhaps a little slow, but it has the warmly amusing insect parallels to human life that are found in 'The Wind and the Willows.' The musical scoring is effective and numerous sub-plots are full of charm."

*Showman's Trade Review*, Dec. 6, 1941, called "Mr. Bug," "an appealing story, skillful animation and catchy songs help make this a delightful and engaging cartoon feature for family audiences. *Box Office* slant: Ingenious showmanship and word of mouth comment should create above-average grosses ... Skillful and adroit animation coupled with an appealing and neatly contrived story make this Technicolor feature a delightful and engaging fantasy for family audiences. Children and adults will sympathize with Hoppity, Honey and Mr. Bumble and the other insects seeking safe and happy homes and will rejoice when the goal is achieved. The cartoon is enhanced by a fitting musical score and the songs, which include 'We're the Couple in the Castle,' 'Katy Did, Katy Didn't,' 'I'll Dance at Your Wedding' and 'Boy, Oh Boy,' have catchy melodies that should carry them far in popularity. A program headed by this cartoon feature and including a careful selection of short subjects should provide a couple of hours of grand entertainment for any audience. Exhibitors will have the benefit of national tie-ups now in preparation and plugging the songs should be part of the promotion."

*Motion Picture Daily*, Dec. 5, 1941, noted. "The feature-length cartoon in Technicolor brings its new world of make believe, a fantasy depicting a community of bugs and their problems of life. It is an amusing fable that affords pleasant and amusing diversion for the young and old alike.

"Technically, is a splendid work and it attests to the advancement of the animated cartoon art. That great care and skill are exercised in materializing the imaginative idea is evident. The animation and color work are consistently superior and are bound to draw praise from the technical observer. The character creations, particularly 'Honey Bee,' 'Hoppity Grasshopper,' 'C. Bagley Beetle' and 'Mr. Bumble' are quite charming.

"'Mr. Bug' is endowed further with a musical score of merit. The three songs by the Hoagy Carmichael-Frank Loesser combination titled "I'll" Dance at your Wedding,' "We're' the Couple in the Castle,' and 'Katy Did, Kathy Didn't' are the type that usually has the customer humming as he's leaving the theater.

"The fable has an amusing plot whose central character is 'Hoppity,' the hero who seeks to provide the bug race with a refuge from 'the humans' who trample through the community. 'Beetle' who has designs on 'Honey' and is jealous of 'Hoppity,' hampers with the latter. After many shortcomings by which he loses favor with the community, 'Hoppity' eventually finds the refuge in a penthouse garden atop a skyscraper. This all worked out with comedy effects."

The reviewer for the *Motion Picture Reviews* in March 1942 wrote, "It is possible that this

eighty-minute color cartoon could be divided into two or three perfectly delightful shorts; in the present form it needs drastic cutting to maintain interest. The film lacks the matchless rhythm and the emphasis on certain characters and events which put Disney features in a class by themselves… The color work is beautiful and the cartoon is often fascinating."
The reviewer seems a little conflicted.

*Motion Picture Herald,* (Dec. 13, 1941,) said, "For exhibitors who have found previous feature cartoons successful at the box-office, this Fleisher-Paramount production, properly exploited, should attract consistent cartoon fans and also bring new patrons of all ages to the theater. The Fleischer Brothers in this have hit a new high in their animated cartoons. Previewed at the Twentieth Century-Fox exchange in New York where Paramount held the screening. The audience, comprising many exhibitors and a few representatives of the trade press, found the picture entertaining."

*Independent Exhibitors Film Bulletin,* (Dec. 15, 1941,) wrote, "This Max Fleischer feature cartoon in Technicolor is extremely clever and should prove entertaining for adults as well as children. Chief problem lies in the fact that it has not been drawn from some popular fable with familiar characters. Your reviewer feels that this will prove a handicap at the box-office and that "Mr." Bug' will require feature support to attract substantial grosses.

"The drawing, most of it in odd angle perspective to point out the smallness of the insects is imaginative and artistic. It will draw comment. The cartoon characters have been humanized to such an extent that they almost lose their bug identities. The voices are well-matched. The Technicolor is outstanding, Songs by Hoagy Carmichael, Sammy Timburg and others are fair to good.

"The smoothness of the entire production indicates that producer Fleischer poured considerable time and money into it."

There were additional favorable reviews in fan magazines such as *Screenland* and *Modern Screen.*

*The Showman's Trade Review* noted in its positive review, "Audience slant: (Family) An appealing story, skillful animation and catchy songs help make this a delightful and engaging cartoon-feature for family audiences.

"Box-office slant: Ingenious showmanship and word of mouth comment should create above-average grosses."

*Variety's* reviewer, Wear, didn't care for the film. He wrote, "This second feature from the Max Fleischer Studio is better than 'Gulliver's Travel,' his initial effort. While it looks like a money-maker for the distributor, hitting the finish line with an overall cost of $60,000 or thereabouts, 'Mr. Bug Goes to Town' does not loom as a top grosser.

"Picture will be best received in smaller city spots and neighborhood theatres due to it family appeal. Film will take plenty of selling and Paramount already has a sweeping publicity campaign topped by vast syndicate coverage in full swing.

"Fleischer's fable of the struggle by a community of insects against the chiseling by members of its own group and against the encroachments of the human race fails to measure up to its potentialities. It lags because no great amount of interest or sympathy is created for a single character. Nobody cares particularly whether Hoppity, the poor but enterprising cricket, wins Honey, his youthful bee sweetheart or whether he is successful in finding a safe home for the always-threatened bug village populace. In fact, Bagley Beetle, the extremely obvious villain, is made more of a character than either one of the youngsters, while his two stooges Swat and Smack are favored by the two most likely voices in the production."

Wear called the vocal performances "colorless" and wasn't impressed how the film used the Hoagy Carmichael songs, as well.

*The Exhibitor* also expressed doubts about the success of the film. In its Dec. 10, 1941, review it noted, "This doesn't rank with its predecessors "Snow White," "Gulliver's Travels," "Pinocchio." It has been well produced and from the drawing and animation angle it is aces, But the theme in which children will not find particularly attractive and the story, while adults, will probably not appeal to grown-ups. Naturally, any cartoon feature is a novelty but this will need plenty of work to get into the better money, of at all…There is a lot of effort in this, but it will need lots of exploitation."

Animator Al Eugster had come back to the studio to work on "Gulliver's Travels" and stayed to work on "Mr. Bug." He described the film to me as "an impressive production." He worked in the group led by head animator Tom Johnson and noted that each group had its own room.

He said, "It was a better picture technically than 'Gulliver's Travels.'" Eugster worked on Smack and Swat, as well as the dance sequence for Beetle.

He used one sequence as an example of the improvement in animation. When Mr. Bumble and Hoppity are in a watering can, Eugster pointed out the galvanized surface of the metal can had been reproduced. "I thought that was outstanding," he said.

Noting the changes, he said, "It wasn't the same routine we did when we were doing the shorts in 1930. I didn't see too much of Dave, really." There were pencil tests on this picture, though and that's when Dave would be seen, reviewing the tests.

The formal release date was Dec. 9, 1941, two days after the attack on Pearl Harbor and the start of America's involvement in World

Studio staffers Ethel Livingston and Marguerite Trupp look over the character designs of "Mr. Bug." (courtesy of JJ Sedelmaier)

War II. Much has been speculated about that event and its effect on "Mr. Bug." Paramount had promoted the film in the trades and in mass market magazines, although not at the level of "Gulliver's Travels."

For whatever reason, the film did not click with audiences. Disney's "Dumbo" was released several months previous and it was a financial hit for that studio.

There were notices in the trades of theaters playing up the feature, as well as one report of a large department store in Minneapolis presenting the film in its Christmas window display. But apparently, none of this worked to give the film the traction it needed.

Paramount ran a four-page full color ad in the *Motion Picture Herald* advertising the film on Feb. 21, 1942, in an effort to build bookings.

Influential radio and newspaper columnist Walter Winchell praised the film in his column published on Feb. 24, 1942.

"Hollywood Is On the Air," a series of 15 minute clips promoting new releases, featured "Mr. Bug." The program featured several excerpts of the film's songs. To listen to it go to https://archive.org/details/otr_hollywoodisontheair/Hollywood_is_on_the_Air_-_Mr._Bugs_Goes_to_Town_1941.mp3.

*Variety* reported on the film's reception at the Carleton Theater in London on March 4, 1942. "Mr. Bug Goes to Town, retitled 'Hoppity Goes to Town,' (second week). First stanza around $7,000, fair. Looks like picking up with word-of-mouth advertising, but unlikely to duplicate 18 weeks' run of 'Gulliver's Travels' in this house last year."

In a story about Dave's departure from the studio in *The Miami Herald* on Jan. 14, 1942, the reporter noted, "Dave Fleischer has resigned his position as producer and director at the Fleischer Studio it was announced Tuesday [the day before] by General Manager Sam Buchwald. In disassociating himself with the business with the production end of the business Dave retains his stock interest along with his brother Max, who will carry on as president of the concern.

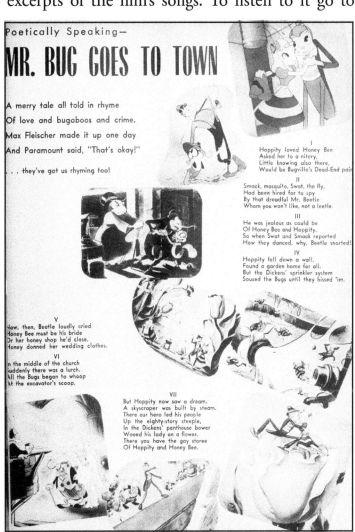

*Photoplay* was one of the best-known movie fan magazines of the 1930s and '40s. It featured this full page spread on "Mr. Bug."

"Future productions, including 24 cartoon shorts already entrusted to a board of three, composed of Dan Gordon, Isidore Sparber and Seymour Kneitel. No other changes in personnel are involved.

"At present he [Dave] is in Hollywood preparing for the release of his latest million dollar 'Mr. Bug Goes to Town,' which is expected in the early part of next month, with a good chance that Miami will get the world premiere. This, however, is up to Paramount, which will release the picture."

There was no premiere of the film in Miami as there had been for "Gulliver's Travels." The feature didn't make it to its hometown, so to speak, until March 8, 1942. It received positive local reviews and appeared at another theater on April 10, followed by books at other theaters in November,

In 1943, there were still bookings as a photo from a theater in Canada showed in *The Motion Picture Herald.* An exhibitor had a huge cardboard standee made of Hoppity for his lobby. The picture grossed just over $200,000 and was deemed a financial failure.

With the acquisition of the film by National Telefilm Associates (NTA) – along with "Gulliver's Travels" – in the mid-1950s, both films experienced a new life in theaters and on television.

As noted in the chapter about "Gulliver's Travels," NTA bought the rights to several Paramount films. New posters and other promotional aids were designed for both films, although NTA made the decision to re-name the movie to "Hoppity Goes to Town."

Into the 1960s, it was common for theaters to have "kiddie matinees" and special programming for children. Often times, old serials and cartoons were part of those shows, as well as contemporary features. For instance, I saw the 1943 "Batman" serial at a theater in Alabama in 1962, almost 20 years after its initial release.

*Box Office* reported that "Mr. Bug" and "Gulliver's Travels" rights were sold to Exclusive International Films Corp. for additional theatrical release in January 1961. The film was being booked theatrically into the 1960s, as a story in Boxoffice published Aug. 26, 1963, noted.

Whereas NTA bungled the copyright renewal for "Gulliver's Travels," it apparently successfully renewed the protection for "Mr. Bug." For years, the NTA VHS was the only way to see the film.

In 2007, a DVD of the film was released by the British company, Cornerstone Media. It is available only in the Region 2 format and requires an all-region player. The DVD titled "Bugville" was released in 2008 by Legend Films in this country. By all reports it is not a restoration of the film and shows the disrespect of giving the film a new title.

Animation historian and journalist Jerry Beck reported the following on Cartoon Brew website about an interesting release of the film: "In 2009, we reported on the Ghibli Museum exhibit devoted to Max Fleischer's 'Mr. Bug Goes To Town' (1941). I believe this was somewhat tied into Studio Ghibli's "Areitty" (2010). Ghibli and Disney have since teamed to release 'Mr. Bug' (aka 'Hoppity Goes To Town') on home video in Japan.

"Brew reader Rick Nodal sent us this report about the DVD (and supplied the images in this post): "Hoppity Goes to Town (Mr. Bug Goes to Town) was released on DVD (region 2) in Japan back in 2010 by Studio Ghibli through Walt Disney Studios Home Entertainment Japan. I just received the copy I purchased online and it's fantastic. The audio & video quality is excellent, and although the disc defaults to Japanese subtitles when it begins, you can change the setting to 'no subtitles.' I've attached a few screen shots/grabs including the end title Paramount logo."

"As Mr. Bug is still protected by copyright, does this mean Ghibli, Disney or Pony Canyon (their Japanese video distributor) sub-licensed the film from Paramount Pictures? If so, that's very interesting! Disney presenting a Fleischer cartoon?!"

Steve Stanchfield of Thunderbean Animation has brought out many collections of classic animation restored on first VHS and then on DVD and Blu-ray. He is one of premiere animation restorers in the nation. He worked on planning to restore and release "Mr. Bug," but posted the following in his column on Cartoon Research in January 2018, "The project that is in limbo at the moment is 'Mr. Bug Goes to Town.' We have a tentative license deal that got muddied up in the business office. Until Thunderbean is a bit bigger (and can offer more substantial guarantee money) it looks like this project is staying in a holding pattern. One of the reasons to have so many titles in a short period of time is to get 'Hoppity' further along. Let's see what happens…"

To this date, nothing has yet happened.

Beck confirmed the status of the film in 2023. He noted to this writer, "Still under copyright. Restored, but unreleased legally. NTA/Republic was absorbed (bought by Paramount via the acquisition of Blockbuster) so Paramount has the copyright (again.)"

There is a certain irony that Paramount has the rights but is not doing anything with the film.

For this chapter I watched the print of the film that is on YouTube, which is in very good condition.

Few movies deserve more than this one for a real restoration and release.

Theaters owners who had booked the film in its re-release would receive a press book that outlined ways to promote and market the film. (Author's collection)

## ADVERTISING

Mat 301—3 cols. x 100 lines

Mat 101—1 col. x 27 lines

Mat 201—2 cols. x 25 lines

# PUBLICITY

Mat 2B

Biggest social event in Bugville threatens to be a bust. One of the high spots of NTA's Technicolor full-length cartoon production, "Hoppity Goes to Town," which comes .............................. to the .................. Theatre, is the wedding of C. Bagley Beetle and the beautiful Honey Bee whose heart belongs to her grasshopper sweetheart, Hoppity. "Hoppity Goes to Town," created by Fleischer Studios, is chock-full of fun, action, romance and music—a treat for young and old.

## 'Hoppity' a Delight with Song and Story

You may not be aware of it at this moment, but there's a world at your feet. Yes, indeed, a busy little world of fascinating people, more commonly known as insects. They have a wonderful life of their own that parallels ours in highly amusing, and amazing, ways.

For instance, right in that little patch of grass outside your door—or in your back yard, if you have one—live the most exciting and enchanting little folk imaginable. They love and laugh and quarrel as they flit out of the way of your careless feet. They are products of the brilliant imagination of the Fleischer Studio artists who have created a new feature-length cartoon picture in Technicolor called "Hoppity Goes to Town" which comes............ to the ..............Theatre.

The stars of the film are Honey, a beautiful little bee; Hoppity, her grasshopper boy-friend; C. Bagley Beetle, the no-good number one villain of the piece, aided and abetted in his nefarious schemes by Swat, the Fly, and Smack, the Mosquito. Then there are Honey's father, Mr. Bumble, a kindly soul, and Mrs. Lady Bug with her two children, Ambrose and Murgatroyd. The story of "Hoppity Goes to Town" is a modern tale of what happens to this little community when their existence is threatened from without by the construction of a skyscraper and from within by the treachery of Mr. Beetle.

Five song hits—"We're the Couple in the Castle," "Be My Little Baby Bumble Bee," "Katy-Did, Katy Didn't," "I'll Dance at Your Wedding" and "Boy, Oh Boy!"—add to the enjoyment of this thoroughly delightful picture.

## Bugtalk Cussin'

A custom-made cussin' vocabulary, tailored to the diminutive needs of a group of little insects, is one of the innovations of NTA's "Hoppity Goes to Town," the Technicolor cartoon feature produced by the Fleischer Studios, which opens .................. at the .................. Theatre.

"Hoppity Goes to Town" is the happy adventure in song and story of a group of little people whom human beings call insects. Among them you'll recognize the folks you know so well in your own human neighborhood.

"Whistle a thistle," "By Bug" and "Sufferin' snapdragons" are a few of the insect-sized expletives indulged in, as well as "Aw Gnats" and "Gee Weeds!"

## New Cartoon Gay, Original Musical Treat

Entirely off the beaten track of movie entertainment is NTA's full-length feature Technicolor cartoon, "Hoppity Goes to Town," which opened yesterday at the ..................Theatre. It is full of the most amazing flights of fancy ever seen on any screen, and this reviewer heartily endorses it as one of the most delightful and original contributions to feature cartoon film-making.

It is not the usual type of cartoon in that it tells a modern story and not a fairy tale. "Hoppity Goes to Town" describes the adventures of a little community of people, known to ordinary mortals as insects, who live on a patch of land just forty-five inches from Broadway. They are surrounded by towering skyscrapers, and while human passersby and their lighted cigarettes are a constant menace to them, their entire existence is threatened when a new skyscraper is to be built right on their homeland.

Hoppity, the grasshopper hero, goes out into the world to seek a Shangri-La for his people. He is spurred on by Honey Bee, the girl he loves. C. Bagley Beetle, local tycoon of Bugville, a no-good villain, who owns the fairly safe "Highlands," wants to marry Honey himself and is determined to do so, no matter by what foul means. He offers the community the safety of his land if Honey will say "yes."

The desperate hunt for a safe place to live and the tug-of-love for Honey are the basis for some remarkable cartoon animation. The characters are as nearly human as any ever seen. They're practically real people and you'll love them and hate them—and remember them, because they'll remind you of people you know.

Among them are "We're the Couple in the Castle," "Be My Little Baby Bumble Bee," "Katy-Did, Katy Didn't," "I'll Dance at Your Wedding" and "Boy, Oh Boy!"

## Here Comes 'Hoppity'—A Whiz-Bang Film

You might think you're the kind of person who wouldn't hurt a fly, but until you see NTA's new full-length Technicolor cartoon, "Hoppity Goes to Town," you just don't know your own strength.

"Hoppity Goes to Town" is due at the.............Theatre next ................ and when it buzzes into town with its hilarious low-down of life among the little people we call insects, you'll be amazed at the bug's-eye view of yourself it contains.

Advance reports have it that "Hoppity Goes to Town" is the best of the feature-length cartoons. It isn't a fairy tale; it's a modern story of life in Bugville, a community of fascinating, humanized insects. They live in the shadow of towering skyscrapers just a few inches from Broadway, and we humans constitute a constant danger to their fragile lives. They quarrel and kiss, love and laugh, sing and dance. They have their problems, too, and the very urgent one of the impending construction of a new skyscraper which will dispossess them from their homeland is one of the high spots of the film.

Hoppity, the grasshopper hero, returns to his home town to find his fellow citizens in a stew about the necessity for vacating their carefully built, compact little village. Spurred on by Honey Bee, his lady love, Hoppity goes out into the world to seek a safe place to which his people can move. But there is dirty work on the ant-hill. C. Bagley Beetle, the villain, wants to marry Honey himself and he comes near to destroying the entire town to do so.

There is much excitement, comedy, action and suspense before Hoppity and his Honey are reunited and Bugville is once again safely established. All of it is set to delightful music which you'll be humming and whistling for a long time to come.

## Match-Box City Built for 'Hoppity'

One of the most novel settings ever used in motion picture work was constructed at the Fleischer Studios in Miami, Florida, for NTA's new full-length Technicolor musical comedy cartoon, "Hoppity Goes to Town," now at the .................. Theatre.

The set is an entire city and a city such as the human eye has never witnessed before. It is a city, just 45 inches from Broadway, where dwells a community of little people whom we call insects. These insects have been amusingly humanized for their roles in "Hoppity Goes to Town," the highly imaginative comic melodrama with music.

The entire set was constructed in miniature so that it could be used for long shots in the picture to obtain a perfect third dimensional effect. There is a palatial kodak box villa with a bottle cap swimming pool overlooking a very modest match folder dwelling. There are cigarette carton skyscrapers, gum package apartment houses and match-box tenements. Materials to build the insect city included only those articles which might be found in a patch of earth which our Bugville friends might convert into homes.

## Dry Tidal Wave Floods 'Hoppity'

A flood that lasted five full months beginning with a sprinkle and swelling to a tidal wave, ended recently in Miami, Florida.

It was a strange inundation involving not a single accident, death or property damage—in fact, not even one drop of water. It was a bone dry flood and it took place exclusively in a series of animated cartoon drawings for a special sequence in NTA's "Hoppity Goes to Town," the full-length Technicolor musical comedy cartoon now at the .............. Theatre.

"Hoppity Goes to Town," in which the pictorial flood occurs, is a merry story with a gay, musical score, about the little people of the insect world. They are cleverly drawn to resemble people we all know and it is very amusing to recognize counterparts of the folks next door in Honey, the cute little heroine; Hoppity, her grasshopper sweetheart; Mr. Bumble, Honey's kind-hearted father; C. Bagley Beetle, the greedy, pompous villain and all the other equally interesting characters.

In the film the flood is the bursting of a garden hose, but to the tiny people of the insect kingdom it seems like a deluge.

## 'Hoppity Goes to Town' in Happy Feature Cartoon

Feature-length cartoon films are all set to give the live-star-movies some really stiff competition. Gone are the days when they were simply fairy tales, planned primarily for the entertainment of children. Today the trend is toward modern, more adult stories—stories which are unhampered in their telling by the lack of flesh-and-blood actors.

The first full-length cartoon production to tell a realistic, modern story is NTA's "Hoppity Goes to Town," which is due ............at the ............ Theatre. It is the gay and adventurous account of a community of little people (called insects by humans) who live in a weedy patch of earth just 45 inches from Broadway, entirely surrounded by the cement-and-steel world created by the menace they fear most of all — the human race. It tells of their love affairs, their hates, their petty jealousies, the good and the bad among them.

The plot concerns the love story of Hoppity, grasshopper hero, and Honey Bee, the heroine, and the machinations of the villainous C. Bagley Beetle to separate them and win the fair Honey for himself. Including as it does romance and skulduggery, laughter and tears, action and music—five new hit songs, "We're the Couple in the Castle," "Be My Little Baby Bumble Bee," "Katy-Did, Katy Didn't," "I'll Dance at Your Wedding" and "Boy, Oh Boy!" —it is safe to say that "Hoppity Goes to Town" will make many a live-movie Academy Award winner look to its laurels.

## New Cartoon Film Buzzes with Pesky Trio of Villains

One of the major problems of cartoon picture-making, just as in "live" picture making, is type-casting.

When plans were made to produce NTA's feature-length Technicolor cartoon, "Hoppity Goes to Town," which is now at the .............. Theatre, it was necessary to create a villain with a dictator complex and two subordinate stooge villains. Because "Hoppity Goes to Town" tells a story about humanized insects, it was necessary to nd prototypes of humans among the millions of little people of the animal kingdom.

So the artists at the Fleischer Studios scouted around and selected what critics agree is a perfect trio of villains.

C. Bagley Beetle was cast as the chief heavy. The beetle, in real life, is a would-be dictator and the personification of greed. He literally keeps rolling his pile of food, keeps destroying far more than he can ever use himself, and hiding it away.

Swat, the Fly, and Smack, the Mosquito, were found more more than adequate to do the bidding of the master-mind. The fly and the mosquito are plain pests. Together with the beetle, the brains of the outfit, they form perfect partners in crime.

## Honey and Hoppity Star

"Hoppity Goes to Town" is a modern story about humanized insects and their life on a little patch of land just forty-five inches from Broadway. They have their homes, their shops and even a night-club. They have their loves, their hates, their good bugs and bad ones. It is highly amusing to see ourselves in bug-form—for in these cleverly animated insect figures we see ourselves, the things we do and the things we feel.

Honey Bee, the unwilling object of Mr. Beetle's affections, is bugs over Hoppity, her grasshopper sweetheart. Beetle, who lives in the "Highlands," which he owns, is comparatively safe from passing human beings and their carelessly dropped, lighted cigarettes. Together with his henchmen, Swat and Smack, Beetle rolls a lighted cigar into the "Lowlands" where Honey lives, setting the community grounds on fire. Then he unctuously offers the community the safety of his "Highlands," provided Honey will marry him.

Plot communications develop when the construction of a skyscraper threatens Bugville, but you must see for yourselves how ingeniously the little people work out their destiny.

Mat 2A

Love bugs in the throes of a great romance. Honey Bee and Hoppity, her grasshopper sweetheart, are the stars of the NTA's full-length cartoon production in Technicolor, "Hoppity Goes to Town," which opens .................... at the ............................................ Theatre. They live just forty-five inches from Broadway, and their delightful story is told against a background of exceptional beauty and originality. Gay new songs are an added entertainment feature.

# EXPLOITATIONS

## RADIO ANNOUNCEMENTS

## EXPLOITATION SUGGESTIONS

## ACCESSORIES

22" x 28" LOBBY *IN FULL COLOR*

11" x 14" LOBBIES (SET OF 4) *IN FULL COLOR*

14" x 36" INSERT CARD *IN FULL COLOR*

ONE SHEET *IN FULL COLOR*
40" x 60"

ORDER YOUR
ADVANCE TRAILER
FROM NATIONAL SCREEN

AVAILABLE FROM
NATIONAL SCREEN SERVICE

# Chapter Five

## Max meets Walt

When I interviewed Edith Vernick in the late 1970s, I had been warned.

Edith, I was told, was a little eccentric.

There was a story about her, in the 1920s, when she first started working at the studio. She managed to get her dress wet during a rain storm. Her solution at work was to strip down to her slip and dry her dress near a heat source. Max didn't know this and was quite surprised when he was guiding a visitor through the studio to see the scantily clad (at least for that time) Edith.

I was also told how she romantically pursued a Paramount official in New York and wound up dying her hair green by accident in an effort to attract his attention.

She had done different jobs at the studio and had wanted to animate. Myron Waldman gave her the chance on "The Fresh Vegetable Mystery," and he told me that Edith had talent but she was too slow.

Edith later worked on the Bozo and the Clown cartoons, produced by Larry Harmon for television. She declared him a "schmuck."

When I spoke to her, it was in her small apartment in a former hotel in Atlantic City, NJ. She offered me, by her own admission, stale Doritos and flat soda as a snack. I ate the offering as I could tell this is what she had on hand for a guest. She was friendly and eager to speak candidly. She spoke of the negative attention Dave's affair and divorce received in Miami, for instance.

She also said something which I report here with a caveat: I have not been able to completely confirm this story.

Generally, as a journalist I would avoid repeating gossip, but in this case, the date on which this incident took place does align with fact. So please consider the following in that context.

Edith said that one day Max asked her to accompany him to the Miami airport, which she did. Once there, Edith was surprised to see Walt Disney.

Disney was at the Miami airport in August 1941. He had been asked by the Roosevelt Administration to fly with a small party of artists to South America. The goal, as described by the book, "South of the Border with Disney: Walt Disney and the Good Neighbor Program," was for Disney to meet with a number of people in Brazil and other countries to gather material for a series of films that could be used to strength ties with those countries.

Although the United States had not yet entered the war, it was clear Nazi Germany was taking steps to have friendly relations with nations in the southern hemisphere.

There had been other efforts before Disney's that had not produced films or experiences that effectively built bridges.

So, Disney and his party were on its way to Brazil and were in Miami. He wanted to see Max.

Edith said the two men spoke and Disney asked Max if he would be interested in investing in the Disney Studio.

That's a mind-boggling concept that Disney would seek help from Max.

Disney was coping with a serious financial loss from 1940. As *The Motion Picture Herald* reported Dec. 28, 1940, "Walt Disney's enterprises lost $1,259,798 during the year past, stockholders were informed on Monday from Hollywood in Walt Disney Productions' first annual report to the public. Stock in the company was first offered the public in April.

"The loss is attributed both to the company's inability this far to realize production costs on its feature 'Pinocchio' and by the war situations aboard.

"The total production cost on that film was $2,595,370, Mr. Disney told stockholders in a letter complementing the report. Up to Sept. 28th the film has grossed $71,673,956 of which the company's share was $976,211. It will probably gross $619,167 more for the company, Mr. Disney anticipates."

Disney's studio was in trouble. Interestingly enough, the article did not list "Fantasia," which had started its roadshow run in November 1940. "Fantasia" may be seen today as a triumph in music and animation and a bold innovate effort from Disney, but the film was not money maker.

When Disney was in Miami to fly to Brazil, "Fantasia" was still in a limited roadshow run set up by Disney. The film would not be generally distributed until January 1942 in a shortened version by RKO, Disney's distributor.

It must have been a true act of desperation for Disney to ask Max for investment money.

What Disney did not know is that by August 1941, Max was in the 26-week period in which he was a Paramount employee with little power. Max no longer had any ownership of his own studio.

Edith did not share how long the conversation was or if Max admitted to Disney that he was in a worse position than his most significant rival.

It does not surprise me that this incident has stayed hidden. I think it's fair to say that Max was in shock and embarrassed about losing the studio in the manner that he did. He had trusted his long relationship with Paramount and they had betrayed him. Certainly, while Disney's financial status had been reported, I think it's also fair that Disney would not have wanted this story circulating either. Both men were facing huge financial problems.

If Max had not lost his studio, would he have considered such an alliance? Who knows?

# Chapter Six

## *Faster than a Speeding Bullet*

In looking at the Fleischer Superman cartoons, one must take a step back and understand exactly how big a deal these cartoons really were.

Pop culture enthusiasts today see the comic book character as an institution. In 1940, Superman was seen as a genuine phenomenon coming out of a new medium, comic books.

There were masked heroes in popular culture previous to Superman, such as Zorro, The Phantom and the Lone Ranger, as well as crimefighters such as The Shadow with superhuman powers in the pulp magazines and the incredibly popular Popeye the Sailor with clearly super powers, but there wasn't anything quite like Superman, an alien immigrant to this planet.

Looking at stories in the motion picture trade publications, one sees references to the Superman comic strip, but the writers didn't reference his appearance in best-selling comic books, because at the time they didn't understand the popularity of Superman was creating a whole new industry.

While comic books existed before Superman's appearance in 1938, the popularity of Superman drew many more readers to comics and much more attention from publishers seeking to cash in on the trend.

To see how the film industry treated comic strips in comparison to comic books, consider for the moment that comic strips were seen as a legitimate art form. Comic strips were serious business and recognized as a means by which newspapers could build loyal readerships. Hollywood frequently turned to comic strips for material starting in the silent era.

Aside from many adaptations into animation, the movie industry also turned to comic strips for live action features.

Consider "Blondie" for a moment. The comic strip by Chic Young was the basis for 28 live action comedies released by Columbia Pictures from 1938 to 1950. "Bringing up Father" inspired one silent film in 1928 and then five features from 1946 to 1950. There were four "Dick Tracy" features from RKO as well as four Republic serials based on the crime fighter. "Joe Palooka" was the basis for 12 features.

In 1931, "Skippy," based on the comic strip by Percy Crosby, was made into a movie starring Jackie Cooper. It was so well regarded that it won director Norman Taurog the Academy Award for Best Director

And these are just a few.

While many of these films were considered "B" films, they were aimed at general audiences, not just children.

With the advent of Superman, comic books were seen as a children's medium. Superheroes were considered by many as too fantastic to be taken seriously as entertainment for adults, at least by Hollywood. Look at the way comic book heroes were handled by the film industry – they were made into serials.

While, again, many adults watched chapterplays, if one can go by the reviews offered by theater managers, the serial was aimed squarely at juvenile audiences. Republic Pictures made "The Adventures of Captain Marvel" and "Spy Smasher," both based on best-selling comics published by Fawcett. Columbia made a deal with the publishers of Superman for serials based on Batman and The Vigilante, before then producing two Superman serials. After the first Superman serial, the Congo Bill character from DC was made into a serial.

There is a clear distinction in the minds of film executives between comic strip and comic book properties.

In 1940, though, that distinction had not yet been fully drawn, in part at least to the sudden success of Superman. As David Hajdu noted in his book "The Ten Cent Plague: the Great Comic-Book Scare and How it Changed America," Superman represented big business.

Introduced in 1938, Hajdu wrote, "Superman caught on fast. After a few months a survey by National Periodicals (later known as DC, as in Detective Comics) found children asking news sellers for its Superman character by name and the editors started promoting him on every issue of Action; by its 19th issue, Action was selling some 500,000 copies per month, more than four times as much as any other comic. In 1939, National started publishing a comic book named Superman, and the company spun off a syndicated Superman strip. By 1940, Superman comics were selling 1,250,000 copies per month and the daily strip was appearing in 300 cities. Newspapers were following the comic book's lead."

Superman was more than just another comic book character. He was the comic book character that was being adapted onto different media platforms. And he was a merchandising bonanza.

In Jim Harmon's seminal book, "The Great Radio Heroes," he wrote that Superman became the star of a syndicated radio series in 1938, shortly after his appearance. That syndicated series was picked up by the Mutual Radio Network and ran from 1942 to 1951.

It should be noted that until the Superman series, theatrical animation was seen as a medium for telling stories with humor and/or sentimentality. While Winsor McCay showed animation could also be used for drama with his "Sinking of the Lusitania" in 1918, there was little interest in using animation for anything else.

As the late animation historian Jim Korkis noted in his essay on the Cartoon Research website, animator and director Bob Clampett did attempt to bring adventure and science fiction to animation when he produced a demonstration film based on the John Carter of Mars character created by Edgar Rice Burroughs in 1936.

The Mars books were a popular series by the author who created Tarzan of the Apes, and Burroughs heartily approved of Clampett's proposal. Clampett produced several minutes of finished animation in color to show the potential of the storytelling.

MGM was initially interested in it, but as Korkis reported, "The local MGM sales representatives, who were primarily from the Mid-West and the South, expressed their concerns to MGM that the project would be a 'tough sale.' They felt audiences would not be able to understand nor accept the concept of an Earth man having adventures on Mars. It all just seemed too strange. The first Flash Gordon movie serial had not yet been released. They pushed for a Burroughs cartoon series featuring Tarzan who was already well-known and well-loved by the public. Clampett was heartbroken."

Some of Clampett's footage is on You-Tube.

There should be little wonder that other people in the entertainment industry were looking at Superman. Republic Pictures might have been a small studio, making mostly low-budget films, but it had quickly earned a reputation in the movie business for its filmmaking prowess. Republic was the home of Gene Autry and Roy Rogers, among other cowboy stars, as well as John Wayne in action roles. Republic's films were noted in the industry for having the production sheen of any "A" movie from the larger studios.

Known for its "B" westerns and serials, the studio clearly saw in Superman another hit property. Republic had made its most successful serial of the 1930s when it adapted The Lone Ranger from radio. It should be noted that Republic's treatment of the character strayed from the storyline of the radio show, something the studio tended to do with characters from other mediums.

Republic altered the origin story of The Lone Ranger into a guessing game for audiences and had the character working with other Texas Rangers. The alterations in the story treatment caused friction between the studio and the owner of The Lone Ranger, George Trendle. He went to Universal for the serial adaptation of his Green Hornet character would ensure a more authentic adaptation.

Reported in *Film Daily*, April 29, 1940, "Although formal contract had not been signed between Republic Pictures and Superman Inc., calling for the production by the former of a 13-chapter serial based on the comic strip character, 'Superman,' it was learned at the weekend that the deal has been agreed upon in principle.

"Republic, reportedly in competition with Universal and Columbia for the screen rights, will make the Superman serial as part of its 1940-41 lineup. An unusual contractual clause is reported to reserve to Superman, Inc., the right to cancel if, after the release of the first series, it is found that the serial detracts from the popularity of the Superman radio program or the Superman comic strip appearing in Action Comics Monthly and via syndicates.

"Deal was engineered by Paul Kohner, coast agent, and is said to involve one of the highest prices for a comic strip's film rights. A representative of Superman, Inc., is to have the right to be present on the Republic lot and to play script and production."

Kohner is an important name in cinema. In the silent era, he worked at Universal and was a producer on "The Hunchback of Notre Dame," among others.  He founded his agency in 1938 and represented stars such as Ingrid Bergman, Maurice Chevalier, Greta Garbo and directors including Billy Wilder and John Huston. It speaks to the dollar potential of the red-hot character that a powerhouse Hollywood agent would become involved in the deal.

*Variety,* May 1, 1940, also noted that Superman would be a Republic serial in 15 chapters.

*Hollywood* fan magazine reported in 1940 that Republic was interested in actor Victor McLagen's son Andrew for the role of Superman. He was 19 years old. After World War II, he started working at Republic in various capacities eventually becoming a director, often working with his father's friend John Wayne.

*Motion Picture Herald,* June 1, 1940, said that Republic announced its 1940-1941 schedule and noted that "Superman" had its "Super Serial" designation, meaning it would be a 15-episode serial.

But then something happened. *Motion Picture Daily,* Aug. 16, 1940, noted under "Late News Flashes from the Coast" that "Republic today shelved its 'Superman' serial because of restrictions imposed by the copyright owners. 'Dr. Satan' in 15 episodes will be substituted."

Let's go back to one key phrase in the initial announcement story – "A representative of Superman, Inc., is to have the right to be present on the Republic lot and to play script and production."

The book "Men of Tomorrow: Geeks, Gangsters and the Birth of the Comic Book" by Gerard Jones expertly recounts how Superman came about, but also how the owners of National Periodicals understood how to capitalize on its star property. It can be assumed the production of a live-action version of the character had to be in line with all of the character's origin story and personality. It's not surprising to learn that National Periodicals would have wanted to protect Superman.

In its Sept. 7, 1940, edition the *Motion Picture Herald* reported that Paramount "had completed negotiations with Harry Donenfeld, president of Superman, Inc., for the production of a series of short subject cartoons which would be produced by the Fleischer Studios, Russell Holman, head of the short subject department, said this week."

Less than after a month of the deal with Republic failing, Paramount was able to obtain the rights to the comic book hero.

The next month (Oct. 11, 1940) the *Motion Picture Herald* discussed how Hollywood was raiding radio programs and stars for movies. The story noted Superman and reported, "Paramount is paying a royalty fee of $7,500 to $10,000 a month" for the character.

The story continued, "Manny Reiner, sales manager for shorts for Paramount, estimates that the entire production cost for the 12 shorts will be more than $850,000, which includes the cost of advertising, promotion and exploitation. Thirteen comic book magazines will carry a Paramount ad announcement about the release of the short at neighborhood theatres. Other promotional items include a national 'Super Boy and Super Girl' contest held through the combined tie-in of radio programs, newspaper strips and motion picture theatres."

Generally, there has been reporting the Superman shorts were budgeted at about four times the cost of a typical Fleischer black-and-white short. According to Richard Fleischer, the budget proposed by his father and his uncle was $100,000 per cartoon. This tactic was an effort to avoid doing the series.

Let's put this into some perspective. At Republic Pictures, a full-length western in its lowest budget class, called "Jubilee," could cost as much as $50,000, according to the essay by Charles Flynn and Todd McCarthy in the essential book "King of the Bs."

In other words, a 70-80-minute live action film could cost less than a single seven-minute Superman cartoon.

The Fleischers, again according to Richard, agreed to do the series because of their financial obligations to Paramount. Paramount execs okayed the budget.

*Film Daily*, on Jan. 15, 1941, reported, "Shift of plans to make the series pictures, 'The Adventures of Superman,' in Technicolor instead of the originally planned black and white, has necessitated the postponement of the production's release until the spring, it was learned yesterday from sources close to the situation. Originally, the release was announced for December or the present month.

"The film is currently before the color cameras at the Fleischer Studios in Miami, Fla., with the staff there concentrating on the initial 'chapter' of which there will be 12 when the entire series of completed.

"Production is based on the comic strip character, 'Superman,' and the first chapter will deal with his advent on Earth from the fictitious planet, Krypton."

Technicolor added greatly to the budget of the films, but also added something exhibitors were almost demanding: cartoons in color.

There was growing excitement for the new series as "Phil M. Daly" noted in his column in the *Film Daily* on May 1, 1941. "Particularly conservative [in a Paramount sales document] was the paragraph about the 12 Superman cartoons in Technicolor. The first of which is completed (all but the scoring) in the Fleischer Studios. These reels will have a huge pre-sold audience value resulting from the sensationally popular comic strip. Here's a celluloid article for Paramount to shout about and outlets to get excited about."

This Paramount trade ad shows what it expects from Superman.

A tease about the new cartoons was in the May 3, 1941, edition of *The Showman's Trade Review*. Dave Fleischer supposedly sent a memo reading, "After the credit titles dissolve to long shot of the universe, have planets moving about in their orbits and stars twinkling."

The fight between Republic and National Periodicals/Superman, Inc. continued, though.

"Suit for $50,000 damages was filed yesterday in the New York Supreme Court by Republic Productions, Inc., against Detective & Superman, Inc., owner of the comic strip 'Superman.' Republic claims that in April 1940, it made a contract with the defendant which gave it the right to make a film serial based on the 'Superman' cartoon. Subsequently, according to the complaint, the defendant breached the contract and gave the film rights to Fleischer Studios (*Film Daily*, June 27, 1941)."

The interesting part of this terse report is the fact that Paramount's involvement in securing the rights to Superman was not included in this story nor was any mention of the clause that assured Superman Inc. the right to okay the script.

National Periodicals moved in another direction to try to protect its dominance in the superhero world in light of Republic turning to Fawcett Publications and securing the rights to Captain Marvel for a serial. *Motion Picture Daily*, Sept. 10, 1941, reported that Republic and Fawcett Publications were named defendants yesterday in a copyright infringement suit filed by Superman, Inc., and Detective Comics, Inc. "The plaintiffs as copyright holder of the action comic strip 'Superman' charge the defendants with creating a character 'Captain Marvel' which is allegedly a copy of the plaintiff's character, Superman."

National Periodicals were not about to stop their efforts to maintain the status of its star character, especially in light that Republic turned to Fawcett for its Captain Marvel property. It should be noted that later in the 1940s, the Captain Marvel comics were outselling Superman.

Republic started filming its Captain Marvel serial on Dec. 23, 1940, and released the serial on March 28, 1941, according to Republic historian Jack Mathis. Even with a pending lawsuit, Republic forged ahead. It beat the first Superman cartoon to the screen and became the first comic book superhero adaptation in the movies.

The Superman shorts became the second superhero on the big screen.

(An aside: the Captain Marvel serial received good notices at the time of its release and is generally believed to be among the very best serials ever produced. It showcases the work of stuntman David Sharpe, the special effects of the Lydecker Brothers and fine performances by Frank Coghlan Jr. as Billy Batson and Tom Tyler as Captain Marvel. It is also wildly different than the comic books with the good Captain actually killing people – from turning a machine gun onto fleeing combatants to tossing an engine block at the head of a thug.)

With the release date drawing closer, Paramount issued a press book to theater owners. Press books were essentially a collection of pre-written stories a theater owners could release to newspapers and radio, as well as potential advertising/exploitation angles and which kind of posters, ad slicks and banner were available.

*The Exhibitor,* Sept. 17, 1941, noted that Paramount issued the previous week a 20-page full color campaign book for the Superman cartoons with an emphasis on "tie-ups" by listing the newspapers, comic books, radio shows in which the character appeared. *The Showman's Trade Review,* (Oct. 4, 1941) also had a story about the campaign book and reported "a special feature is the pocket envelop attached to the back page in which the exhibitor can keep the synopsis of the 12 issues of the Superman series together with supplementary material that may be furnished him from time to time."

The story continued, "There is every reason to believe that any showman fortified with the wealth of suggestions contained in this merchandising manual can boost his business to high levels when he plays Superman."

It should be noted that this kind of effort for an animated short subject series was unusual, but then, the Superman series was greatly unusual.

A five-foot tall standee of the Man of Steel would cost theaters owners $2.50, while the trailer cost them $3.50.

Using the kind of language frequently seen in the movie trade papers, *Film Daily,* Oct. 16, 1941, noted, "Paramount has the two-page center spread of *Click Magazine* on the noozestands yes'day) in full color, 'cause that publication selected the first of the 'Superman' shorts as the best fab reel of the month (the reel, by-the-by, goes into the Broadway Paramount on Oct. 22)."

This was followed up by an amazing development: a trailer. In the *Film Daily,* Oct. 31, 1941, edition was "One of the few trailers ever made for a short subject has been prepared by Paramount for 'Superman,' its series of 12 Technicolor cartoons, produced by Fleischer Studios. Trailer, a combination of Technicolor and peach blow film, is available to theaters for outright purchase. Second trailer for the series features the Superman of America Club."

The trailer is about 18 seconds long and features scenes from the first cartoon. It can be seen on YouTube.

The Superman depicted in the cartoons is not the character we are used to seeing today. He is not as god-like in his abilities. While bullet-proof, he can certainly be stopped or slowed down by cannon fire or high-voltage electricity. He leaps rather than flies. While his strength is far greater than an ordinary man, it's clear he can't do something like reverse the orbit of the earth and manipulate time as seen in the first Christopher Reeves film, for example.

Paramount boasts of its powerhouse combination of Superman and Popeye in this trade ad from May 1941.

There's isn't any Kryptonite in the series as there was no such thing in the comics books at the time. Reportedly, co-creator Jerry Siegel did write a story in 1940 that introduced a prototype of the element but the story was not published. The deadly remanent of the planet Krypton wasn't introduced to Superman fans until the radio series did so in 1943.

There was no "Smallville" in which he grew up and no Ma and Pa Kent, either. In the brief origin sequence opening the first cartoon, Superman was raised in an orphanage. He acquired his powers as he grew older.

The Fleischers designed the character to have a black background on his costume's "S" crest. Looking at the early comics, the "S" design varied. Apparently, no one at National Periodicals was worried about the studio's design change. It is a dramatic look with the red "S" popping from the black background and one that was unique to the cartoon series. Most recently, the CW TV series "Superman and Lois" used the black crest in a flashback sequence.

Today Superman fans recognize the use of the black background as a homage to the cartoons. The collected collection of Superman daily comic strips has a beautiful rendition of the Joe Shuster Superman by Peter Poplaski with the black background on his chest.

The opening of "Faster than a speeding bullet! More powerful than a locomotive! Able to leap tall buildings in a single bound!" is also from the Fleischer shorts. And the studio made a transition in which Superman flew more than he leapt.

The early comic books and the comic strip place Superman in a series of crime-related story lines. The Fleischers obviously saw the potential in stories with more cinematic plots and the first 12 shorts definitely went in a more science fiction direction.

In a 1983 interview published by Nemo magazine, Joe Shuster was asked what influence he and Jerry Siegel had, if any on the cartoons.

Shuster replied, "It was purely accidental. I was just in Miami for a visit and someone who knew me said, 'How would you like to come down and visit the studios?' I said, 'Yeah, I'd love to see them doing Superman.' They were just

Joe Shuster and Jerry Siegel appeared at the Loew's State theater in their home town of Cleveland, OH, for two days of personal appearances to support the showing of the Superman cartoons in October 1941.

starting on it. I went down there and I was fascinated by it. And I suggested, I wouldn't mind drawing some shots for you showing how Superman looks in side view, front view, three-quarter view; how Clark Kent would look and Lois Lane would look. They said fine; they'd love to have me do it. So, I just sat down and spent a couple of days there drawing model sheets. I loved doing it and I loved being involved in it. And we were lucky enough to receive a credit line on the cartoons afterwards."

The first Superman short received a trade screening months before its general release. *Film Daily,* Aug. 1, 1941, noted "Cartoon newcomer is a super-duper. Latest entry in the animated cartoon field is the well-known comic strip character Superman. He makes his bow under auspicious circumstances. All he does is save a city from destruction by a mad scientist. Possibilities for the new series catching on are very good. Superman here as in the strip certainly taxes the imagination but that should make for more fun. It is a Fleischer Technicolor cartoon."

In *The Showman's Trade Review,* (Aug. 2, 1941) the word was also positive. "A Cinch to Sell – The first of the Superman cartoons from the Fleischer studios show how easy it will be to sell this entire series. The action follows exactly the pattern of the comic strip which runs in hundreds of newspapers throughout the country. Done in Technicolor it should be a knockout for the kids. Tie up with newspapers running the strip. You should be able to get a line on the page with it or opposite.

There will also be many merchandising tie-ups made on this series, so be sure to get the dealers who handle these items to cooperate. It's rarely you've such a ready-made audience for any cartoon subject, so go to town on your sales campaign."

# SUPERMAN

©FLEISCHER STUDIOS AUG. 1941

Details of a Superman model sheet shows the Shuster style is maintained.

In the October 1941 edition of the *National Board of Review Magazine*, the first cartoon received this review: "The marvelous methods that characterize Superman's approach to dealing with villains are displayed with vigor and crackling color. The film follows the line of the comic strip stories and all the characters are presented by normal voices."

Another theater owner reported to the *Motion Picture Herald* on Dec. 6, 1941, "This rings true to the form with the comic strips and with a little plugging will bring in the young'uns. Wonderful cartooning and sure-fire box office for kids. Don't play on preferred time but build up the weak days with this extra. It's worth the extra dough."

On the other hand, one exhibitor expressed his disapproval in a review he submitted to the *Motion Picture Herald* on March 21, 1942. "There is no excuse for pictures like this. My son is standing beside me as I write this and he said there aren't enough bad words to describe this short and he is a Superman fan."

There was a great emphasis in these trade reviews on the pre-sold quality of the Superman property. Theater owners, in an era when movies were actually marketed, took advantage of the fact that Superman was on the radio, in the newspapers and on the newsstands in a comic book.

*The Showman's Trade Review* noted in its Aug. 1, 1942, edition of a theater chain in St. Louis

This full page is interesting as it has article detailing the release of the cartoon series, as well as a trade ad for it.

This original still is from the first Superman cartoon (Author's collection).

that used advertising in newspapers that carried the comic strip to present a list of theaters where the cartoon would be shown. In turn, the theaters ran a special trailer that listed the newspapers in which the comics strip ran.

The company that distributed the comic book put posters about the theaters on its delivery trucks and window displays in the stores that sold the comic book. Every theater in the chain had "a giant standee" in its lobby and special one-sheet posters. To top off their effort, the chain stamped "Superman is coming" on all of its outgoing mail.

This kind of marketing activity underscores first the competitive nature of the business in the 1940s and what theaters owners believed they must do to maximize their attendance and profit.

The reviews from both the trades and the ones submitted from theater owners show that despite the popularity of the character for some people the very nature of the superhero – still a very new concept – as well as the "fantastic" nature of the stories was off-putting. It's clear some exhibitors embraced the cartoons and made money with them but others didn't know quite what to do with them.

*The Mad Scientist* (Sept. 26, 1941) opens with a brief origin story. The Fleischers wanted to introduce the

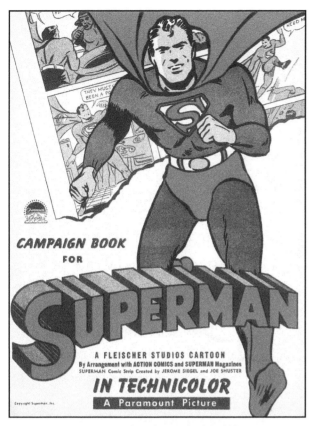

The Superman pressbook guided exhibitors in their efforts to promote the cartoons.

character but clearly didn't want to dwell on it, instead moving quickly to the story itself.

The way that story was presented was very much in line with a fast-moving action picture and in many ways, it would seem that someone at the studio had studied either the style of Warner Bros. movies or the action films from Republic.

The story is told with as little dialogue as possible, with the action carrying the story forward. Look at how the short opens: after the brief origin sequence, the camera zooms into the newspaper building; cut to a shot of a door with the title "Managing Editor" on it; fade to an intercom on a desk where we see a hand flip a switch and we hear the editor calling in Clark Kent and Lois Lane to brief them about the latest note from a scientist who is threatening the city with destruction unless they pay him.

The camera pulls back to show the three newspaper staffers. The editor reads the threat and the scene cuts to a close-up of Clark and then a pan to Lois who asks to cover the story on her own. Lois exits the medium shot, leaving the editor and Clark, who asks if this too dangerous an assignment for her.

All of this exposition is presented quickly and concisely. With about seven minutes to tell the story, it's clear the Fleischer staff understood the need for a different kind of storytelling.

The next scene shows Lois getting ready to fly to the headquarters of the scientist. Cut to the mad scientist who has been waiting until midnight to let his ray weapon decimate the city. Lois has just arrived at this lab and the scientist is tipped off by his bird. It was the first and last Superman short that had a bad guy with a remotely humorous sidekick – in this case, the raven-like bird.

Lois is captured, and after hearing a radio

report about the scientist, Clark utters the words the audiences would learn to associate with the character, "This looks like a job for Superman." He changes in a stock room and then leaps out of a window.

The scientist unleashes his ray weapon onto the city specifically on a building which starts to bend. Superman manages to right it and then starts beating back the ray. The scientist increases the strength of the weapon which pushes Superman back to the ground.

He recovers and literally punches the ray back to the lab. Tying the barrel of the ray weapon in a knot causes the apparatus to explode, but not before he rescues Lois and grabs the villain.

There is a beautiful panning shot of the ground – clearly Superman's perspective as he is flying – followed by a quick scene of the scientist getting thrown into a jail cell. Lois is congratulated by her editor, to which Lois adds, "Thanks to Superman." The camera pans to Clark at a nearby desk, who breaks the fourth wall by winking at the audience.

The first short sets the tone for the series: a minimum of dialogue, many short fast scenes edited like a live action film and fantastic plots. We understand Lois views Clark as a rival and a bit of a wimp while there are hints of a relationship between Superman and Lois, the point is not always prominent.

The cartoon wisely used the voices of Bud Collyer and Joan Alexander from the radio series as Clark Kent and Lois Lane, as historian Keith Scott noted in his landmark book,

This trade ad from Dec. 6, 1941 touts the success of the Superman cartoons.

This interesting trade ad is actually from the publishers of Superman congratulating Paramount on its anniversary, as well as the success of the cartoons while pointing out that Superman, Inc. has other properties such as Batman and Robin, as well as Hop Harrigan

"Cartoon Voices, of the Golden Age, 1930-1970."

Jack Mercer did a variety of supporting voices in the series.

The first Superman short was nominated for the 1941 Academy Award for Best Short Subject: Cartoons. It lost to "Lend a Paw," a Pluto cartoon from Walt Disney.

Aiding the on-screen action perfectly was a beautiful dynamic score by Sammy Timburg. What he did for the Superman series shows that he has been a woefully under-rated composer. His theme is magnificently rousing and his scores set the tone for the action.

In this era of making sure comic book creators get proper credit it should be noted that Seigel and Shuster did get the credit as the character's creators.

"The Mechanical Monsters" *(Nov. 28, 1941)*

Again, the action starts almost immediately with a robot breaking into a jewelry store and stealing the contents. We see it is being controlled by its creator, another villainous scientist. I love how when the power to the robot is turned off, the device slumps onto the wall. The Superman shorts are full of these little touches.

The series makes great use of scenes with a newspaper providing exposition. It's quick and certainly appropriate since the heroes are reporters. There is an opulent gem exhibit coming to the city – so far not identified as Metropolis – and Clark and Lois are assigned to cover it. One of the robots turns up to rob the exhibit and the police can't stop it with machine guns. The robot scoops up the gems and Lois hoists herself into the cargo area of the robot.

Clark changes into Superman and follows the robot. This cartoon marks the first time Superman uses his x-ray vision when he tries to rescue Lois, he is flipped off of the robot and falls into high tension wires.

We are learning – apparently along with Superman himself – the limits of his power.

He recovers and traces the robot to the lab where the villain uses all of his robots to try to kill Superman in a superbly animated fight scene.

There are two continuity mistakes in the short. The first is all of the robots are numbered and the numbers switch on one of the robots. The second occurs as Superman is about to save Lois from being burned alive by molten metal in the villain's lab. The background color of his crest changes from black to a light blue. These kinds of bloopers are rare in animation at this level.

*Film Daily,* Dec. 19, 1941 "Top Flight Cartoon" "Fleischer Studios, Director Dave Fleischer and Paramount offer herewith the second of the Superman shorts in Technicolor. The reel is well delineated, highly imaginative, and crammed with all those exciting elements which have made the character of Superman a byword among the current generation of Americans and a 'buy' word among all exhibitors seriously interested in adding something new and colorful to their screens as well as profitable to their box-offices…Short is highly exploitable and every bit as engaging and novel as its predecessor."

*Motion Picture Herald,* May 9, 1942

A theater manager from Alberta, Canada said about the first cartoon, "I made a mistake when I did not run this 'Superman' first; it explains 'how he got that way' and isn't so much of a shock. Anyway, Superman is catching on here", from gta theater manager from Alberta, Canada.

"Billion Dollar Limited" *(Jan. 9, 1942)*

Myron Waldman was the head animator of this short and he told me that to get a true sense of weight – essential to a more realistic form of animation – additional drawings had to be done for the scenes.

Again, a newspaper front page sets the story and again one can see the live action conventions being used. We see the newspaper and then a shadow of a man's head falls on it. The camera pulls back and then pans showing a group of heavily armed policeman guarding the loading of gold onto a special train. The camera pans to the right to show that Lois is boarding the train to cover this shipment of gold to a federal mint.

A group of thugs in a modified car follows the train. Several jump aboard and separate the cars with the guards. In a struggle in the engine, several of the robbers are pushed over the side of the moving train along with the engineer and a guard. Lois makes her way to the engine, exchanges machine gun fire with the robbers in the car and discovers she is on a runaway train. Clark discovers what is happening and Superman is now chasing the train. In an effort to stop the train, the crooks blow up a bridge, but Superman is able to hoist the train back onto the tracks.

A bomb destroys the engine and now Superman is the engine. Slowly at first, but quickly gaining speed, he hauls the cars with the gold back up a sharp incline only to have the robbers throw tear gas at him. He falters and while coughing nearly loses his grip on the train. It is a bravura piece of animation.

In the *Motion Picture Herald*, (March 28, 1942), a theater manager wrote, "Poorest of this series, so far. Even the kids didn't like this one. Just

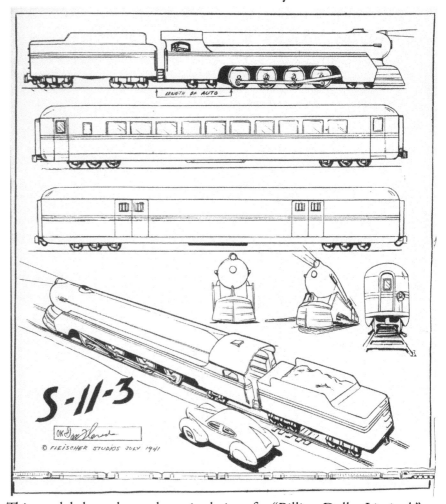

This model sheet shows the train designs for "Billion Dollar Limited."

too extreme to get by. The other two we have shown got by pretty well."

### "Arctic Giant" *(Feb. 27, 1942)*

This plot is straight out of a science fiction pulp magazine. Scientists discover a frozen dinosaur in the Arctic, which they bring back to Superman's city to be put on display at a museum. The creature remains frozen until an accident stops the dynamo that runs the refrigeration unit keeping the dino on ice. While workmen feverously work to repair the unit, the creature thaws out and is alive once more.

Looking like a tubby Godzilla, the dinosaur roams the streets of the city destroying buildings. Naturally, Superman saves Lois at the museum, only to have her pursue the dino again. "Miss the best story in years. No chance!" she declares.

The beast is wading in a reservoir overlooking the city where he breaks a dam. Superman manages to fill the hole. He finally catches up to the dinosaur outside a stadium where he is able to capture the dino, but not before he has to rescue Lois again.

There is almost a comic element in the design of the dinosaur. The threat of the character would have probably been heightened if it looked more like a Tyrannosaurus Rex.

One theater manager wrote in *Motion Picture Herald* (April 2, 1942), "The old folks said it was corny, but the kids ate it up."

### "The Bulleteers" *(March 27, 1942)*

Another group of thugs with advanced technology use a missile shaped flying car to destroy the city's Police Headquarters and then threaten to do the same to all municipal buildings unless they are paid off with the city's treasury.

There is an incredible shot in which the camera "dollies" through a crowd of people standing outside of city hall after the gang has made it ultimatum. The camera goes through the doors of the city hall, through a hallway and into the mayor's office, where Lois is interviewing him. The camera keeps moving forward through the mayor's window showing how the police are making preparations to protect the treasury building. With barely a cut, we now see a quickly edited montage of the work the cops are doing: putting machine guns into place, constructing a sand bag barrier, etc.

It's a brilliant sequence.

This ad points out the business synergy of the popularity of the radio show, the animated cartoons, the newspaper strip and the comic books. It cannot be underestimated what a sensation this property quickly became.

The gang destroys the city's electrical generation plant and then robs the treasury with Lois attempting to the wreck the bullet car. Superman saves her and the day.

*Film Daily*, April 20, 1942 "Fast moving"

"This time a bullet-shaped missile shoots out of nowhere and leaves destruction in its wake. The gang responsible for the wreckage threatens the mayor of the city and, infuriated by his refusal to heed the warning, proceeds to do considerable damage until Superman comes in and gets everything under control. Sure-fire thriller for the kids."

**"The Magnetic Telescope,"** *(April 24, 1942)*

A scientist has developed a means of magnetically attracting a comet to bring it close to earth for examination. After his initial public display fails, he is ordered to stop, but doesn't, as any slightly mad scientist would do. The police wreck his generator which means the scientist has no control over the comet, which will come crashing to earth.

Superman cannot push the comet back into space and must restart the generator to supply power again to the scientist's device. Holding the cut wires, Superman is able to direct power back to the magnetic telescope and ,with Lois' help, push the comet back into the space.

This short uses some great special effects animation as well as wonderful use of shadows.

May 2, 1942, Review of "Magnetic Telescope" *For the Fans*

"Here's Superman again this time fighting not men from Mars or some other planet, but an inhabitant of earth who has invented a method of attracting other planets to earth. It looks as though the earth is in for a bad time of it until Superman gets busy with his super-human powers and pushes the planets back into the sky where they belong. Max Fleischer produced."

**"Electric Earthquake"** *(May 15, 1942)*

A Native American has invented and installed a giant underwater device that can create an earthquake in

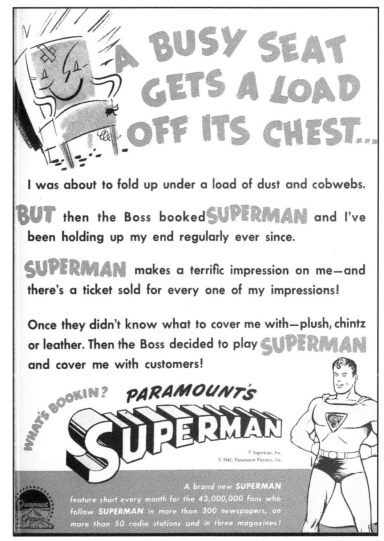

This trade ad from June 1942 shows the continued sales push for the Superman cartoons.

the city. He goes to the Daily Planet hoping to gain its support in his effort to reclaim Manhattan for native people. When he is rebuffed, he leaves, issuing a veiled threat.

Once again, Lois follows him and stows away in his motor boat only to be discovered and brought down into the bay to his lab. There, he shows her how his electrical device causes the city to suffer an earthquake. Underwater, Superman tries to disconnect the device so it can do no harm. Lois is trapped and Superman goes back to rescue her, unaware the villain has sent a bomb down into the underwater chamber. He manages to rescue Lois and capture the villain.

The interesting thing about the short is that identifies Superman/Clark as living in New York City.

The *Motion Picture Herald's* reviewer wrote in its May 16, 1942, edition "The Magnetic Telescope" was "another good Superman cartoon."

### "Volcano" *(July 10, 1942)*

This cartoon doesn't have a villain per se, but instead has a natural phenomenon that Superman must address. Clark and Lois are supposed to work together on the story but arriving on the island with a volcano about to blow, Lois steals his press pass, putting her on site of the volcano when it begins erupting. Superman must save the island's city from the flowing lava, as well as rescue Lois. He uses explosives to disrupt the flow of the lava and successfully diverts its away from the city.

I was impressed with the special effects animation of the flowing lava and the explosion of this short and liked the fact it didn't involve a human villain.

### "Terror of the Midway" *(August. 28, 1942)*

As an old reporter, I can feel the pain of Lois assigned to cover a circus, but something happens she could not anticipate: the accidental escape of one of the circus' chief attractions, a huge gorilla.

This cartoon again emphasizes the decision of the studio to treat it as a live action production. The introduction of the gorilla into the performance tent is expertly done with a combination of visuals and the use of music and sound effect, or rather when the circus band stops playing realizing what has happened.

The animals in the carton are realistically rendered and the gorilla was conceived by studying footage of a live gorilla as the existing model sheet reveals.

Clark is back at the Daily Planet when all hell breaks loose. In a neat, almost throw-away bit of animation, he turns to the street when hearing sirens and the headlights fall on him. He jumps into a cab and tells the driver to "see what's cooking."

Lois is able to save a little girl from the gorilla, but now is the center of his attention. Superman, unaware of her plight, is rounding up other animals that have escaped.

Seeing the threat to Lois, he tries to save her, but the gorilla is a formidable opponent, especially since Superman is trying not to kill it. While they fight, a fire in the big top breaks out.

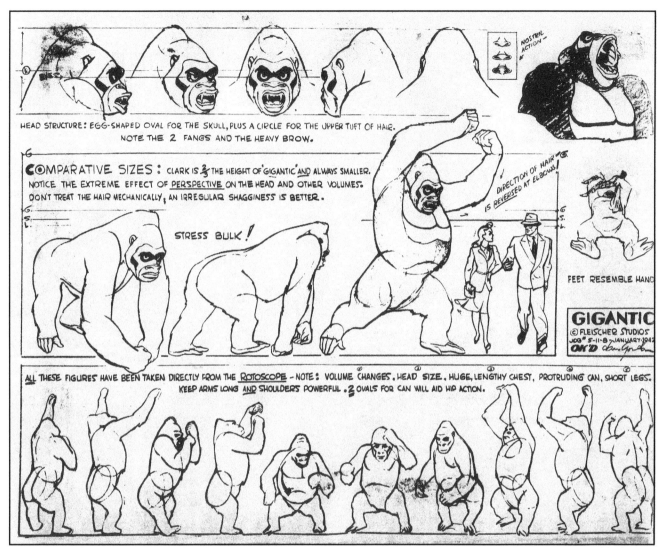

"Terror on the Midway" model sheet.

During their fight, the framing of the action is quite unusual as the standard was to show the full figures in action. Instead, the action is conveyed by partial figures and in one shot extreme close-ups of the gorilla and Superman. It's a very dynamic approach to the action.

This is one of my favorite Superman shorts.

In the *Motion Picture Herald*, (July 3, 1943), a theater manager from Austin, TX, wrote, "We think these cartoons are very poor, but seem to draw in extra business. We plug them with extra trailer we bought from National Screen. Always gets in extra business. Why is a mystery."

Another manager review noted of the short, "These are nuts – we are tiring of them and they're definitely not worth the rental we are paying for them."

## "Japoteurs" *(Sept. 18, 1942)*

The first Superman cartoon without the Max Fleischer credit, the short showed the new emphasis on stories that reflected the war effort. A new very large bomber has been completed,

# EXPLOITATION IN PICTURES

The Gallo Studios

Ed Fisher, publicity director of Loew's Cleveland theatres, arranged for this window in the Terminal Tower.

Lillian V. Pennell, owner and manager of the Heart theatre, Hartford, Mich., in the heart of the fruit belt, gets a chance each year to put a display at the Van Buren County Fair. Shown above is this year's display. She worked and pulled the crepe paper into tubes of about ten different colors. Photos were used on about a dozen features. The Fair lasted for six days and 5,000 tickets were sold a day, making the display valuable to the theatre.

Howard Pettengill put this animated display (right) in the lobby of the Beach, Miami Beach. Globe and cameraman turn.

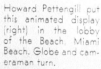

"THE EYES AND EARS OF THE WORLD"

Ray King Photo

Members of the Superman Club in the Utah theatre, Salt Lake City, compare a super Superman erected by Charlie Pincus, manager, with the one in the *Deseret News*.

This feller was hired by Bill Elder of Loew's, Indianapolis.

Above display in the window of Norwich, Conn., store is devoted to records from every musical picture playing the Broadway theatre. Joe Boyle really has a "record" tieup there.

"Mr. Bug" at the Bugg. The theatre is in Chicago. Clarence Wagner sent the photo.

This page of photos shows how individual theater owners promoted films. There is a huge Superman standee in a Salt lake City, UT theater, as well as a theater called The Bugg in Chicago running "Mr. Bug Goes to Town."

attracting the attention of a Japanese spy. Lois and Clark are sent to cover the plane's debut. True to form, Lois hides in the plane when the tour is concluded so she can fly in the bomber for her story.

There is another stowaway, as well: the Japanese spy and several accomplices, who are trying to steal the plane. Lois manages to alert the military, but the spy turns the plane around and bombs the airfield. Clark changes into Superman and follows the plane. The spy thinks he has foiled Superman by threatening to eject Lois though the bomb bay. Naturally, he saves Lois, and after the spy has wrecked the control of the plane Superman manages to control its descent to Earth.

I first saw this cartoon at Myron Waldman's house. He was the head animator on this short, and pulling a 16mm print of the cartoon from a shelf, he asked me with a smile on his face, "Do you want to see a half-assed Superman cartoon?" Apparently, he wasn't impressed with the short, although I think it has a lot of small flourishes that speaks of the care the studio put into the cartoons – as Superman's hair fluttering in the wind is something that shows the attention to detail.

The Japanese spy is, of course, a borderline racist character, which is unacceptable today. A theater manager declared in the Motion Picture Herald (Feb. 6, 1943), "Japoteurs – Superman is still a class by himself as far as our audience is concerned. It is the only cartoon series which gets an instant reaction from our people."

## "Showdown" *(Oct. 16, 1942)*

This short is the first with the Famous Studio named attached to it and opens with a new introduction, "Faster than a streak of lightening, more powerful than the pounding surf, mightier than a roaring hurricane."

A thug in a Superman costume, employed by a gangster, has been committing a series of robberies which are blamed on the hero. The thief turns up at an opera performance to steal the jewels of the rich, which Clark and Lois have been assigned to cover. "My double is in for some trouble," Clark says as he changes into his costume. He captures the thug who brings him to his boss, clearly patterned after Edgar G. Robinson. The two criminals think they have escaped, but Superman persists and clears his name.

The idea that someone is impersonating a hero has popped up in many forms and the treatment of that trope is well done. It is, though, far less spectacular than Superman's other adventures.

*Film Daily* Oct. 26, 1942, noted, "Nothing Super – The latest chapter in Superman adventures is strictly for the comic-loving kids. It is much too dull and unoriginal to be of any interest to older fans. This time Superman occupies himself with the capture of a gangster who carries on his nefarious activities under the guise of our hero. Superman pulls some amazing stunts in tracking down the phony impersonating him. Done in Technicolor, this cartoon hasn't much to offer."

On the other hand, *Motion Picture Daily* declared (Oct. 21,1942) declared "Children of all ages will love this."

### "The Eleventh Hour" *(Nov. 20, 1943)*

The cartoon opens with a reprise of the origin story that was presented in the first cartoon. The story is set in a fortified Yokohama, Japan, where a new naval ship is sunk by Superman. The hero then returns to an apartment that is clearly acting as a jail cell. Lois is in the apartment next door. In response the Japanese officials beef up security, but that doesn't prevent Superman from wrecking another ship. More acts of sabotage follow, all committed at 11 p.m. Realizing it is Superman, Lois tries to talk to Clark through the wall but is caught by a guard. The Japanese then put-up posters saying any more sabotage would result in her death. He ignores the warning, destroys another ship but is caught underneath a pile of falling girders. He escapes in time to save Lois from a firing squad and gets her back to safety behind Allied lines. She tells reporters that Clark was not saved, but Superman would keep him safe. The short ends with a clock tower noting 11 p.m.

This is a great example of a solidly animated cartoon that has a frustrating story. How and why were Clark and Lois captured? How did Lois not realize that Clark is Superman? Why is she so nonchalant about Clark being left behind as a prisoner of war?

The writing is sloppy, but it's classic wish fulfillment. I'm sure that all Superman fans wished their hero was real and could end the war. Max had pledged to support the war effort in the cartoons, and although Max was gone, the pledge was still in place.

The *Motion Picture Daily* noted in its review on Dec. 14, 1942, "Youthful America's hero is interned in a Tokio [sic] hotel but makes nocturnal visits to centers of Japanese industry in a one-man sabotage campaign, Since most of the scenes are at night there is little opportunity for the usual brilliant colors, which are characteristic of this series."

A theater manager wrote in the March 27, 1944, *Motion Picture Herald*, "[Eleventh Hour] this isn't the best in this series, but it gets the reaction from the audience just the same, Superman is a 'money man' here as we always get extra trade when we have him on the bill."
*Variety* reported in its Dec. 2, 1942, edition in a story about USO shows for the troops, "Aside from Bob Hope, the big clicks with the troops were the Superman shorts."

### "Destruction, Inc." *(Dec. 25, 1942)*

A guard at the Metropolis Munitions Works is murdered and Lois is on the story. She meets a new guard, an elderly man at the plant. She gets a job at the plant where she uncovers a sabotage ring but is discovered. Caught, she is put inside a torpedo. The new guard tries to save her but is buried under a pile of metal. Her torpedo is selected for a demonstration for Naval officials. Superman recovers the torpedo and saves Lois. The leader of the sabotage group drives a truck filled with TNT towards the plant but is thwarted by the hero. At the end, Lois shows she recognized Clark under the old man disguise, but yet, she still hasn't figured out who Clark really is.

The war theme continues in this short, which is competently done.

*Film Daily* wrote of this short on Jan. 21, 1943, "Rather Flat – Strictly for the most infantile mentalities. There really isn't much to this latest Superman release. This time our hero foils an enemy plot to blow up a munitions plant. The guy has to work doubly fast because also at stake is the life of a girl reporter who has been caught snooping on the saboteurs. Again, the incidents are utterly beyond credibility and on the foolish side."

### "The Mummy Strikes" *(Feb. 19, 1943)*

A scientist is found dead at a museum and his young assistant is convicted for his murder. Clark receives a tip about the case and goes to the museum to discover that the dead scientist was killed when he attempted to open the coffin of a boy pharaoh. When the director of the museum and Clark open the coffin, the king's giant bodyguards, mummified along with him, come back to life to protect their sovereign. Superman manages to subdue them under a pile stone. Clark gets the scoop as Lois was injured and can't type.

One of the few Superman cartoons with a fair amount of dialogue. One wonders if the studio took inspiration from the on-going series of horror films from Universal Pictures featuring Kharis the mummy for this cartoon. There were several similarities in the plot.

The review in Film Daily (March 31, 1943), noted, "Okay for Kids – the kids will probably find the latest Superman dainty to their liking. The short in Technicolor, has enough action to hold their interest. The story has to do with the mystery surrounding the murder of a scientist connected with an Egyptian museum. Some of the mummies come to life and assault those trying to solve the crime. It is Superman who comes to the rescue in true heroic style. Like the others in the series, the current entry is too fantastic for grownups."

### "Jungle Drums" *(March 25, 1943)*

We are back with another wartime cartoon, this time set in Africa where Nazis have set up a secret base in a temple in the jungle to manipulate the native population and be able to attack the Allies.

There is an American convoy coming and the secret base is supposed to relay information to a group of Nazi subs. Lois is captured by the Nazis when her plane crashes. She is given Allied plans to destroy, but being Lois, she keeps them only to have them discovered. The Nazis are going to burn her alive.

Luckily, Clark, who is flying to meet Lois, gets there in time to save her and she is able to get a message to the Allies who destroy the subs.

The end scene has Hitler disgustedly listening to an American radio broadcast describing the Nazi loss.

The origin sequence is repeated again in this short. There are some very arresting images in the short, especially with the use of primary colors and shadows, but the insensitive depiction of African natives cannot be ignored.

A theater manager, *Motion Picture Herald*, (Sept. 11, 1943), "This lacks cartoon appeal – a little too serious to win the audience. Let's keep cartoons for what they are intended – to keep our audience laughing."

## "Underground World'" *(June 18, 1943)*

Perhaps the most unusual of the Famous shorts, this short sees Clark and Lois accompanying a scientist who proposes an expedition to explore a series of caverns.

Lois goes first with the scientist but they manage to lose their boat on which dynamite was stored. Clark comes in a second boat and searches for them.

What he doesn't know is they have been captured by a race of bird men who live deep in the cave.

Seeing the scientist and Lois being slowly lowered in lava, Superman beats the bird men back, manages to save them and seal them in the cavern. Perry White tells Lois it is a great story but burns her manuscript as "no one would ever believe it."

"Underground World" is a very off-beat short with a horror edge. More explanation of what we are seeing is certainly needed. By the way, this is the only cartoon in which the name of the Daily Planet editor is seen, "Mr. White."

*The Exhibitor*, (June 2, 1943) judged the short as "fair." The reviewer for the *Motion Picture Daily*, (June 2, 1943) wrote, "The colors employed for the underground scenes are beautiful, The story is on the familiar melodramatic side."

*The Showman's Trade Review*, (May 29, 1943) noted, "It's a good 'Superman' Technicolor cartoon, however for "Superman' fans."

## "Secret Agent" *(July 30, 1943)*

Clark is in a drug store making a phone call to his editor when a car crashes into the store. Armed men get out of a second car and there is a race joined by the police. Clark is clinging to the trunk of one car as the bullets fly.

One car escapes the other and a blonde woman clutching a brief case, gets out saying she must go to the police.

Clark has been taken prisoner by the men in the other car who are Nazi spies.

The blonde makes it to the cops who escort her to the airport so she can bring her information on the spies to Washington but is attacked by the spies enroute.

The spies stop her on a draw bridge and she falls to the gears in the bridge's mechanism where she is about to die.

Clark becomes Superman, and captures the spies and saves the woman and her info. He flies her to Washington, D.C., himself and as he flies off, he salutes an American flag.

Once again, there was great care taken in the animation and editing, especially in the car chases and gunfights, to create the kind of cinematic action seen in live action films. The story is a bit pedestrian, though.

A theater manager in Oklahoma wrote, "Average Superman cartoon." *Motion Picture Herald,* (Oct. 9, 1943)

And with that war-time short the Superman series came to a close. While the shorts were popular, they were also expensive to make and the higher rental fees were a continual subject of comment among exhibitors in their reviews. It's clear the licensing fees to Superman, Inc. were also hefty, which added to the production expense.

It's also important to note, that despite the popularity of the character, many theater owners implied the shorts were too fantastic for the public to accept. Science fiction had not been a strong movie genre for adults – there were plenty of science fiction elements in serials, a medium largely design for children – and the fans that enjoyed contemporary science fiction in the 1930s and '40s were limited to a half-dozen pulp magazines.

Although Superman remained the most recognized superhero in popular culture, by the mid-forties two things had happened: The Captain Marvel series

was often out-selling Superman and the glut of superhero titles certainly shows the character was not as unique has he has been in 1940.

With the ouster of the Fleischers and the return of the new Famous Studio to New York City, there was clearly an interest in producing more economical animation.

The success of the Superman shorts was not repeated in the animation industry. No other studio attempted to produce one-reel action/adventure shorts. In an exchange with former Fleischer animator James "Shamus" Culhane, he challenged the concept that the series was an important moment in animation because it had not inspired other studios to produce their own superhero cartoons.

His point is faulty. He confused economic realities with artistic aspirations.

The only studio that was inspired was Terry-toons, which released in 1942 a short called "The Mouse of Tomorrow," which is clearly a parody of Superman and led to the successful Mighty Mouse series.

If there was an entity that did benefit from the cartoons it was DC and Superman, Inc. Undoubtedly, the success of the cartoons is what allowed DC to strike a deal with Columbia Pictures for a 15-chapter movies serial, released in July 1943, based on Bob Kane's and Bill Finger's Batman character. DC had both a live action adaptation as well as an animated one.

Two Superman series, starring Kirk Allyn, were produced by Sam Katzman for Columbia, the first in 1948 and the second in 1950. For the flying sequences, an ani-

mated cartoon Superman would be shown. Many critics have cited this is one of the weakest parts of the productions.

The serials gave way to a feature film "Superman and the Mole Men" in 1951 with George Reeves as the Man of Steel, followed in 1952 with the successful TV series.

And the 1950s saw the return of the Fleischer Superman cartoons, not to theaters, but to television as cartoon packages sold to local stations.

Still, it should be noted that superheroes were considered the province of children's entertainment until 1970s with the success of the Superman films starring Christopher Reeve, followed by the surprise success of the 1989 Batman film starring Michael Keaton. It was the Batman film that had audiences truly seeing superheroes differently.

I started seeing Superman cartoons in 1970s at comic book conventions. In 1977, a nationally distributed compilation film, "The Fantastic Animation Festival" included "Mechanical Monsters." In the 1980s, I made a trip to DC Comics in New York City to see several of the company's 16mm prints. A projector was set up in a conference room and I was joined by artist Bob Layton.

With the VHS revolution, the Superman cartoons were now everywhere in poor dupey transfers. Believe it or not, DC Comics had neglected to renew the copyright on the shorts.

It wasn't until 2009 that Warner Bros. decided to collect all the shorts and present them in a DVD. Although the shorts were not restored, the prints generally were sharp.

A recent Blu-ray release has been criticized for not restoring the films to their 1940s sheen.

The Superman shorts continue to stand a true highpoint in theatrical animation and they continue to impress people today. The artists of the Fleischer Studio should be revered for this work.

# Chapter Seven

## *Max & Dave*

Animator Al Eugster was still at the studio when the change of leadership took place. He said, "There was a sort of rumble before it happened. The transition went very smoothly since we knew all the people."

Speaking of the conflict between Max and Dave, he said, "There was some talk over the watercooler. It wasn't anything definite."

According to Richard Fleischer's book (and in some correspondence with me) Dave's affair with Mae Schwartz and his gambling habit angered Max and alienated the brothers from one another. Edith Vernick told me that Dave's issues with his wife became the subject of controversy in the Miami area.

*The Miami Herald* noted on Nov. 7, 1939, that Ida Fleischer said a hearing will be sought in Circuit Court this week in her separate maintenance suit against Dave Fleischer. Her attorney, John Murrell, said Fleischer had been notified in Hollywood of the action to force him to give his wife temporary alimony.

*The Miami Herald* noted on March 1, 1942, that a court ordered Dave to $250 a week in alimony to his wife, Ida.

Turning down his appeal for a reduction in payments, the court said Dave had "totally failed" to show how much he was able to pay and that his proof in support of inability to pay the described amount is not sufficiently strong to warrant a reversal in appeal."

"At time of separation several years ago, Fleischer's petition said his assets were $500,000 and his income was $650 a week plus an expense account of $100, but now his assets are only $18,000 and his salary only $100 a week."

Ida Fleischer stayed in the news and in Miami in 1942 for her charity work in the American Legion Auxiliary.

Clearly though, in documents by Joe Fleischer, there was additional tension between the other brothers and Max.

I've yet to find a trade story about Max's departure. It may have been known within circles of the motion picture industry, but I'm assuming Paramount did not want to look bad in firing one of the most prominent figures in animation, especially considering there was no particular reason for the dismissal.

*Film Daily* reported on Jan. 2, 1942, that Dave had resigned, "but will retain his interest in the cartoon producing organization." The paper reports unconfirmed rumors about Paramount taking over.

*Variety* reported on April 29, 1942, that Dave had joined the Screen Gems animation unit at Columbia as its head.

*Motion Picture Daily* on April 17, 1942, had a story mentioned the Fleischer Studio in Miami under "the guidance of General Manager Sam Buchwald."

A story in *Motion Picture Herald* on May 23,1942 detailed how the war has made an impact on the "Max Fleischer studio," with Sam Buchwald making comments about availability of supplies. The story also noted several films have been made for the Navy and putting Popeye in the Navy is part of the war effort.

*Film Daily* (July 3, 1942) reported more details about the change. "Under a change in the corporate set-up, Fleischer Studios Inc. will be known as Famous Studios, operating under the ownership of Isador Sparber, Seymour Kneitel and S. Buchwald. Studio will continue to produce cartoon subjects for Paramount release, concentrating on Popeye and Superman, same staff of approximately 275 persons is retained."

*Film Daily* on Oct. 6, 1942, announced that Paramount may shift production and the studio, now identified as Famous, back to New York City, which it did.

*The Motion Picture Herald* on Jan. 9, 1943, reported Famous Studios will "establish a branch at 24 West 45th St." The story continued, "The vocal and musical talent shortage because of the Army personnel in Miami was said to be the reason for the shift, although the Miami studios will operate as before, but on a reduced basis."

It should be noted that Max and Dave tried to stay active in the motion pictures/animation business until they retired. Their brothers chose other pursuits.

## *Dave in Hollywood*

In his book, "The Boy who Loved Batman," comic book historian, writer and movie producer Michael Uslan reproduces a letter from Dave that he uncovered while he worked at DC Comics. Uslan had been charged with going through material that was in a storage closet and the letter was among what he found.

The letter is dated Jan. 25, 1942, and is written on hotel stationary from "Peyton Hall, Hollywood California." It was addressed to Jack Liebowitz of Superman, Inc. (DC Comics). It reads, "In reference to the 'The Bat Man' subject we discussed in New York, I am sending you a budget which will give you an idea of what it would cost to film it.

"This budget is based on the presumption that our shorts will be made at one time thus lessening the cost considerably. As a result, each one-reel subject will cost about $5,500. This will be 'live' pictures rather than cartoons and will be done in black and white.

"These figures represent the actual cost of production, excluding my own interest, which can be discussed later. At this price the 'Bat Man' could be a real money maker, especially if the 'Superman' series should depreciate in quality after the fifth or sixth one.

"I feel that you will be happy in knowing these facts and I will be pleased to hear from you soon.

"Regards to Harry Donnenfield and the boys."

This is pretty remarkable as Dave did not have a job as yet in Hollywood but was clearly trying to come up with something of his own. It is also interesting that he was not proposing an animated one-reeler, but a live-action one instead.

Although today, when most people think of short subjects from the 1920-1950s, the animated cartoons and live action two-reel comedies come immediately to mind, the one-reel live action subject was most definitely part of the picture. There were travelogues, comedies and musical one-reelers.

It's quite possible, since Dave had the experience of working on the Superman shorts that he believed the public would accept a series featuring Batman, even though that character wasn't exactly the phenomena that Superman was.

It would appear that Dave wanted to seal the deal with DC Comics before he shopped it around. There was no follow-up letter discovered but since the series never happened, either DC turned it down or Dave couldn't find a studio willing to take it on.

It is also curious that Dave thought there was a chance the Superman shorts might lost their level of quality. Perhaps it's a bit of ego on his part, thinking without him the series would decline.


At Screen Gems, Dave brought in a series based on the highly popular "Lil Abner" comic strip. The "Lil Abner" shorts didn't click with audiences. The shorts didn't capture the sly satire and sex appeal of Capp's popular strip and instead had a re-occurring theme in which Mammy Yokum rescues Lil' Abner from a perilous situation. There were striking similarities with the formula of having Popeye rescuing Olive.

The series only lasted for five cartoons and, according to author Jeff Lenburg, the comic strips creator, Al Capp, was not pleased with the shorts.

Dave's stay with the company was only about two years. Columbia opted to close their animation unit in favor of releasing shorts produced by UPA.

Dave also appeared as himself in one movie made in the mid-1940s – the low-budget Republic Pictures musical revue "Trocadero" (1944) and was the associate producer of "That's My Baby," another musical revue at Republic, set at a comic book publishing house.

In "Trocadero," a love story plays out as a new nightclub is getting started. One after another singers and variety acts are trotted out for the audience's amusement.

Dave's appearance in "Trocadero" was interesting as he was presented as a household name, something his brother may have been, but he was not. Dave created a new animated character who appears briefly in the film, named Snippy, that struck a strong resemblance in appearance and behavior to Ko-Ko the Clown, the brothers' first star.

*Showman's Trade Review*, (April 8, 1944), said about "Trocadero," "This film is heavy on story value and light on production. In other words, it could have been really big had it been accorded some heavier star power and more elaborate setting. The talent of the entertainers it boasts are entirely adequate and the basic idea is splendid, but the handling and acting just doesn't measure up…a brief animated sequence involving Dave Fleischer will go over well…" There was another animated sequence he supervised for the conclusion of the second film, "That's My Baby." It too was a low-budget review movie about a comic book publisher who finds nothing funny. His daughter and her artist boyfriend organized a series of novelty vaudeville acts to try to get him out of his slump. When the artist discovers the publisher had come up with a character of his own and an animated film was made of the character, the publisher finally laughs.

Both films are available on YouTube. Neither is very good.

For the rest of his time in the film industry, Dave maintained a very busy multi-year attempt to stage some sort of comeback. His time with Universal was perhaps the most successful period following his departure from Fleischer Studios.

Historian Don Yowp detailed Dave's post-Fleischer Studios career by a list of clippings from trade publications on his blog "Tralfaz." Yowp shows a series of false starts and attempts at comebacks in the entertainment industry. My additions are in brackets. Among the media reports were the following:

*May 4, 1944, Hollywood Reporter*

Dave Fleischer, for many years a producer of Paramount cartoons with Max Fleischer, and who has been at Columbia in charge of its cartoon output since completion of "Mr. Bug Goes to Town," was signed to a ticket yesterday by Walter Colmes, under which he will function as associate producer on the features Colmes is making for his Republic release.

*May 11, 1944, Miami Herald*

Alleging that Dave Fleischer, movie producer and head of the former Fleischer Animated Cartoon studios, is $6,600 in arrears in separate maintenance payments his wife, Mrs. Ida Fleischer, 4459 Sheridan Ave., Miami Beach, filed a motion for contempt of circuit court Wednesday. She says that a court decree of Dec. 29, 1939, for $250 a week was reduced to $100 a week when Fleischer represented considerable shrinkage of his former $50,000 annual income and that up to April 14, when he sent $100, he was behind $6,200. Since that date $400 more became due, according to the motion. They were married 21 years.

*June 1, 1944, Hollywood Reporter*

Dave Fleischer is drawing a special cartoon character known as "Baby" for the Walter Colmes production, "Anything for a Laugh," which will be released by Republic. The character is part of the basis of the story. Fleischer is associate producer of the picture. [The feature was released later in the year as "That's My Baby" starring Richard Arlen and Ellen Drew. *Variety*, Oct. 25: "Dave Fleischer, vet of the animated cartoon field, worked on this pic, and it is his cartoon handiwork which is a key to the yarn." It ran only 68 minutes.]

*July 14, 1944, Hollywood Reporter*

Dave Fleischer will start producing early this fall a cartoon feature based on Greek mythology, depicting the adventures of Ulysses from the classical Odyssey. It will be in color. Walter Colmes will be associated with Fleischer. [The film was never made.]

*Oct. 2, 1944, Hollywood Reporter*

Walter Colmes is organizing Film Education, Inc., as a post-war activity for the purpose of making educational films in 16mm. The company will function with an advisory board of heads of departments of various universities who will set the program of subjects to be taught and plan general treatment. Cartoon technique, under Dave Fleischer, will be used extensively.

*March 3, 1945,* Louella Parsons column

Well, flip my lid, as the jive kids say. They are going to swing a $500,000 Technicolor version of "Cinderella," and by "they" I mean Lou Levy, manager of the Andrews Sisters, the gals themselves, and Dave Fleischer, who made "Gulliver's Travels" for Paramount. Not only will the Andrews jive the vocals but Count Basie will furnish the boogie-woogie for the big ball scene when Cinderella meets the Prince. [The film was never made.]

*March 23, 1945, AP*

Dave Fleischer, 49, producer of animated cartoons, and his secretary, Mae Miriam Schwartz, 32, obtained a marriage license today. It is Fleischer's second marriage and Miss Schwartz's first.

*June 14, 1945, Hollywood Reporter*

Dave Fleischer has purchased a financial interest in the recently formed Sebastian Productions, Inc., it was announced yesterday by Dave Sebastian, head of the new company. Details of the transaction were handled by attorney Nathan L. Freedman, who is also negotiating a release for the proposed "Simon Lash" pictures. Exact amount of Fleischer's interest was not disclosed. It is believed he will not take an active part in the organization.

*Aug. 30, 1945, Hollywood Reporter*

Financed by Harold A. Baker, of Chicago, Peter Tinturin, song writer, and Dave Fleischer have merged their film companies into one organization, Advanced Pictures, Inc., to produce two musical films. Fleischer is the cartoon producer whose Popeye and Superman shorts and the feature-length "Gulliver's Travels," have been released by Paramount. The Tinturin-Fleischer product will start with the film of two musicals, one of which is "Heaven Only Knows," recently purchased from David Boehm for $60,000. The second Tinturin-Fleischer production will be based on the life of Paganini. [Peter Tinturin was a composer who had contributed songs to many B-Westerns made in the 1930s and '40s. There was a 1947 comic western called "Heaven Only Knows," but that is apparently not the same production with which Dave was involved.]

*Dec. 17, 1945,*

A device to be known as the Fleischergraph has been patented in Washington by Dave Fleischer, who, with Peter Tinturin, will produce "Heaven Only Knows" for Advanced Pictures. It is described as a scientific story plan in chart form. Basis of plan is a large graph, divided into 85 minutes of running time and broken down into fractions of seconds, designed to take guesswork out of producing motion pictures, Fleischer, who has already invented and patented number of mediums for accelerating efficiency in making pictures, originated graph from a study of hundreds of best pictures used as samples of motion picture art, and it is a means whereby it is possible to tell if screenplay has any empty spots. "Heaven Only Knows" will be first picture on which Fleischergraph will be tried.

*Dec. 26, 1945,*

Peter Tinturin and Dave Fleischer plan a music publishing firm with eight songs from the score of "Heaven Only Knows." Tinturin wrote the score and will co-produce the film with Fleischer. Harold A. Baker, who is backing the film, will also put up the coin for the music house.

*Dec. 5, 1946, Hollywood Reporter*

Jack Schwarz will produce "Jack and the Beanstalk," color feature based upon the famous children's story, in association with Dave Fleischer, cartoonist. The picture will combine "live action" with cartoon. [The film was never made.]

*Feb. 1, 1947, Billboard*

Burke Meyer & Associates, Inc., has purchased masters for six kiddie albums from Cartoon Records. The Dave Fleischer wax production will be released retaining the Cartoon label. [At least one album was released.]

*Feb. 7, 1947,*

Dave Fleischer reviving "bouncing ball" musical film shorts.

*Aug. 4, 1948, Hollywood Reporter*

Dave Fleischer, who for many years did the "Bouncing Ball" shorts at Paramount, has been commissioned by Universal-International to do the cartoon sequences for a series of eight "Sing and Be Happy" community-sing short subjects. The group, all to be made here under U-I's new shorts program, will be produced-directed by Will Cowan. Formerly made by U-I's Eastern office, it was announced recently that production of the series had been transferred to Hollywood, along with the production of Cowan's regular two-reel musical western miniatures. Another single-reel series titled "It's Your Life," featuring astrology, is also on Cowan's plate. Fleischer's first chore at U-I, under his new deal there, is "Choo Choo Swing," which has just been completed. [Cowan was a busy producer at Universal producing and directing a long list of short subjects, mostly musicals and westerns, as well as being an associate producer on a number of low-budget feature films. This was Dave's entry into Universal, which would later be his home for years.]

*Aug. 4, 1948,*

New video firm, "Television Clearing House," has been formed by Dave Fleischer, Lou Notarius and Walter Bowman. Firm will make animated telepix, the first of which will be "This Amazing World," and will employ the old motion picture bouncing ball in filming commercials. Fleischer asserted that company would make TV reels on order only.

*Jan. 14, 1950, Box Office*

Universal - International has introduced something new into a trailer—a cartoon character called Preview Pete. The animated figure will be used in the "Francis" trailer for the first time and will be introduced into trailers for future features. Arthur Lubin, director of "Francis," directed the trailer sequence, in which Don Wilson and a cast of 28 appear. Voices of two announcers, Art Gilmore and Frank Graham, are heard. Dave Fleischer created the cartoon character and the animated cartoon sequence. U-I used animated cartoon teaser trailers for "The Egg and I" and "Family Honeymoon" and decided they were successful, but this will be the first use of an animated sequence along with live talent.

*Aug. 18, 1950, Hollywood Reporter*

Preview Pete, cartoon character employed with good results in the trailer on Universal-International's "Francis" and "Louisa," appears again in the animated cartoon sequence made by Dave Fleischer for the trailer on "The Milkman." Other promotional uses of the Fleischer character are now being planned.

*Sept. 8, 1951, Box Office*

A new one-minute cartoon film, publicizing Fire Prevention Week, is now available from Filmack Trailers. The trailer, produced for the National Board of Fire Underwriters by Dave Fleischer studios in Hollywood, points at all of the fire hazards in the home and how to correct them.

*Feb. 17, 1951, Box Office*

Dave Fleischer, who formerly produced cartoons for Paramount release, has been booked to supervise the artwork and animation on a new series of eight one-reel "Cartoon Melody" shorts being produced by U-I. [These shorts were directed by Will Cowan, with Dave in charge of the animation. It's interesting to note that Famous Studios had revived the original Screen Song series starting in 1947 and continued with the series until 1951 when it was forced to rename the series "Kartunes" because it had lost the rights to the name. The last series ran until 1953.]

*Nov. 15, 1952, Box Office*

Toasts of Song Univ.-Int'l (Cartoon Melody) 10 Mins.

Good. This is the last in the series offering popular old-time songs for audience participation. The selections are "After the Ball," "My Gal Sal" and "Little Annie Rooney." The Kings Men are again featured. Will Cowan directed and the humorous animation was supervised by Dave Fleischer. The distributing company did not know if the series will be resumed.

*Oct. 17, 1957, Hollywood Reporter*

Paramount and others are named as defendants in a suit for an injunction filed in Federal Court yesterday by Dave Fleischer, individually and as co-trustee of the Fleischer Studios of Florida, a dissolved corporation, to restrain selling, leasing or booking the new "Popeye" and "Superman" series to TV. Other defendants are AAP, PRM Productions, UM&M TV, WPIX, Flamingo Films, DuMont Broadcasting, Fleischer Studios of New York, and Max Fleischer, individually and as trustee of the dissolved corporation.

*Dec. 25, 1957, Variety*

Variety quotes Don Hillary of Local 839, Motion Picture Screen Cartoonists, IATSE, is quoted to signing with "new Dave Fleischer tele-blurbery, engaged in making Chevy commercials."

*June 2, 1958, Broadcasting*

Stereotoons, a new company specializing in the production of three-dimen-

"The Snow Queen" was a Soviet-produced animated feature bought by Universal for release in this country. Dave supervised the re-recoding of the dialogue.

sional animated motion pictures for TV and theatres, has been formed by Don Hillary, retiring business agent for Motion Picture Screen Cartoonists, IATSE Local 839, Hollywood. Stereotoons is at 1546 No. Highland Ave., Hollywood; telephone: Hollywood 3-2326. Associated with Mr. Hillary in the new company are Dave Fleischer, veteran producer-director of such animated films as the Betty Boop and Popeye series, and Jack Paar [Parr], a Disney animator for 19 years. The company's first production, a 20-second public service TV film, is now being distributed to TV stations by mental health groups across the country. A theatrical short film, "Li'l Pedro and Tasty Taco," will be premiered in June in 36 Arizona theatres.

During Dave's lengthy association with Universal, he mainly worked on story construction and special effects. One of his innovations of which he seemed most proud was a story chart (mentioned above), which he claimed could analyze the script of a movie or play and determine its audience appeal. Dave said that he had used it to show how the "Francis the Talking Mule" films would be a hit.

His last completed job in animation was in 1959 while he was at Universal on the company's release of a Russian animated feature "The Snow Queen." The U.S. State Department had been trying to arrange for a Soviet-made film to be released as part of a foreign policy to ease the Cold War. Universal had bought the American rights to the film, which was an adaptation of the Hans Christian Andersen's fairy tale and brought to the screen by Soyuzmultifilm Productions in 1957.

Universal shot a prologue starring TV personality Art Linkletter and recorded a new English soundtrack featured then-teen favorites Sandra Dee, Tommy Kirk and Patty McCormack. According to the film's press materials, "Universal-International engaged Dave Fleischer, one of Hollywood's foremost animation experts, to supervise the matching of dialogue and sound effects to the picture."

The press book also has a short story that the film uses "a new process," "Rotomotion," which is, of course, rotoscoping.

Universal promoted the film heavily and received the following review from the *Film Daily*, "A delight for all, a beautiful orchestration of sight, sound and color has been achieved in this feature-length cartoon…includes the voices of some top-drawing names…by every indication this bright presentation looks like a thorough winner for audiences of very age."

*Box Office* reported (July 8, 1963) that Dave was working on "The Enchanted World of Mother Goose" for independent producer R.T.G. Burdge and Trend International. As far as I can tell, nothing came of the announcement.

Dave stayed at Universal until 1967, when he retired. In a note to this writer, he declined a request for an interview with me in 1976 stating he was too busy preparing a new feature film based on the myth of Pandora's Box, which at one point had been planned as the Fleischer's second feature film. The feature never was realized.

In 1969 Dave consented to a lengthy interview with historian Joe Adamson for an Oral History sponsored by UCLA. It is pretty wide-ranging, with the general tone being Dave was behind most of the innovations and successes of the studio. While he did praise brothers Lou, Charlie and Joe in the discussion, Max was not discussed all that much. Adamson noted there were 15 pages of the transcript that Dave requested not be included in the interview until after his death. Adamson noted that while he though Dave's memories were accurate in some instances, he had doubts about others.

Adamson wrote, "When discussing his brother. Max, a fair amount of a degree of bitterness crept into his tone and the dispute as to the proper share of credits may go on for some time." Dave Fleischer died in 1979. He is buried with the epitaph, "Beloved Husband and Uncle" in Mount Sinai memorial park in Hollywood Hills, CA.

# Max's life after the studio

According to Richard Fleischer, Max joined the Jam Handy organization, which made industrial films in Detroit in the first half of 1942. He stayed with the company until 1953, first living in Detroit and then commuting from New York. Here, he worked on a variety of projects, the best known being the first animated version of "Rudolph the Red-Nosed Reindeer" in 1948. Jam Handy promoted Fleischer as an animation expert in trade ads.

"Mr. Bug" was scheduled to run in Detroit according to a writer in the *Detroit Free Press* (April 1, 1942). This is an example of the lengthy release period for the film.

*Detroit Free Press* reviewer, Charles Gentry, didn't care for the film and wrote, "This is a clever animated cartoon, but Max Fleischer hasn't the Disney touch. We think these studios should confine themselves to short subjects and comedies and leave the full-length features to the master hand."

During his time in Detroit, Max appeared at several speaking engagements under the title of advisor on televisual and animated cartoons for Jam Handy.

On Aug. 11, 1943, *Film Daily* ran a column by "Phil M. Daly" noted a mistake made by the New York Times about Max working for Terry-toons. The story was about Max inventing a calculator "obviously useful in horse races." It also mentions that working on "war effort pix" but doesn't say where or what.

The *Detroit Free Press* published a column by Anthony Weitzel on May 6, 1944, that included Max. "Gentle soft-spoken Max Fleischer, who started drawing 'Out of the Inkwell' movie cartoons years ago and worked through a long list to the 'Popeye' shorts, dined with friends in Detroit the other night. Between the meat course and the dessert, he got into a discussion of unions with some of the gals around the table and the argument waxed so hot that one of the males present grew a bit alarmed, 'You can't convert these girls,' he warned Fleischer, 'their opinions are set in concrete!' Fleischer smiled. 'Maybe I'm like a salesman who grew despondent over business and decided to jump in the river. Just as he was crawling over the parapet, a policeman came along, hauled him back and demanded 'What's the idea?' The salesman began telling the cop his troubles and the sad state of the worlds in general, He talked for half an hour and then they BOTH jumped into the river!'"

Was Max talking about his opposition to unions? Again, not to play amateur analyst but in a city dominated by the auto makers and the UAW ,it seemed not to be the wisest argument in which to enter while in public.

# Noah's Shoes

While in Detroit, Max wrote a book titled "Noah's Shoes." A fairly difficult book to find today. Max assumes the role of Noah in assembling all of the world's animals into the ark and looks at the event through 20th century eyes. This concept gives Max the opportunity to recount numerous facts about the number of species and their characteristics.

Max clearly did a lot of research about the characteristics of animals, even explaining for a page about the reproduction cycle of tapeworms.

Max also presents information including as how much food Noah would need to take on to last a year, such as 65,000 pounds of fish and 575,000 pounds of hay. Max wrote, "How much each animal will eat is something I didn't give much thought in my eagerness to pilot the Ark. But now we face the problem and it must be solved. Frankly, my idea was to corral the animals, shoo them into the Ark and slams that door. But it isn't that simple. Not if we expect them to walk out at the end of the trip by their own power."

The book, whether intended or not, actually debunks the story of Noah through presenting just how overwhelming such an enterprise would have been and the many issues it presents in the preservation of every species on Earth.

After a lengthy passage about stoats, a member of the weasel family, and what they can do to the rabbits they hunt, Max wrote, "Perhaps I'm not the right man for the job. I've been suspecting this all along. I'll speak up: I don't want to pilot the Ark if stoats are to be saved. Anyway, this isn't the kind of a job I thought it would be.

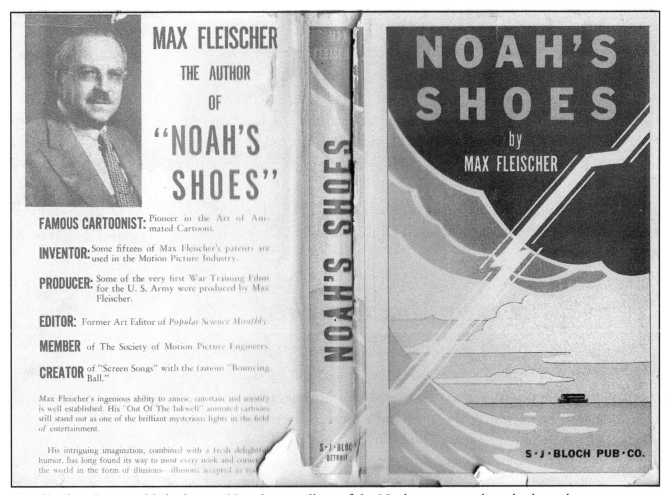

"Noah's Shoes" was published in 1944 and is re-telling of the Noah story in realistic biological terms.

"There's too much to worry about. Think of it: not an animal must be crippled, starved or set down on terra-firma in a run-down condition or poor health; for they are to be the parents of the new world."

Max/Noah declares the five billion pounds of food needed for the animals would fill 20 more arks, but he doesn't have the time to build them or finds pilots. Yet they fit the animals and food into one ark.

Max/Noah also does something oddly unscientific as he loads dinosaurs into the ark.

Some people have assigned a psychological value to the book in that Noah as played by Max is not a confident person and was initially ready to stay behind and not be part of the world after the flood. He does decide to come in, though.

He seems defeated, as I'm sure Max felt when this book was published.

Max/Noah stays in the dark with the animals learning about them but leaves the care and feeding of the animals to his assistants. The book often has an odd tone. "Hunger does not trouble me. My assistants slap food into my mouth in passing in the same manner the other animals are being fed. When feeding time arrives, I open my mouth and keep it open until food is thrown in. Mastication proceeds instinctively. More and more do I realize the significance of feeding from the animal point of view."

Another odd passage from the book: "Unfortunately, the last six months of my life on the Ark are not even a memory. My mind became blank when – let me see now: yes, when an assistant in total darkness attempted to force scrambled centipedes down my throat. An error no doubt, but in my weakened condition from my experience with the blue rainbow, my conscious existence was effectively blacked out for nearly half a year. At least my beard seems to indicate that length of time … In fact, everything on the Ark seems to be alive, but I wonder how long it will last? It all comes back to me now. We are actually captives – prisoners of a desperate hoard of blood-thirsty creatures."

In an ad run in the *Miami Herald* on Feb 24, 1946, by the publisher S.J. Bloch contained a quote from The Book of the Month Club that called the book, "a merry book with wild and high humor."

## *"New Sketches by Max Fleischer"*

Max produced an odd one-reel comedy in 1944, "News Sketches by Max Fleischer." The short featuring illustrated stories from the Associated Press using the style of the Inkwell cartoons with Max's photographed animated hand drawing out the gag images while a narrator reads out the description. There is no indication if there was a follow-up edition or if the film was actually distributed.

## *Max becomes a citizen*

According to the profile on www.thegermanway.com, Max did not become a citizen until July 20, 1948, when he received his naturalization card.

## *"Rudolph the Red-Nosed Reindeer"*

The most significant project during Max's tenure at Jam Handy was his production of an animated cartoon cased on the children's book "Rudolph the Red-Nose Reindeer."

Author Robert May created the story in 1939 as a give-away for the Montgomery Ward chain of department stores. The first mass market edition appeared in 1947.

The cartoon preceded the song which cowboy star Gene Autry made a hit in 1949.

The song The Motion Picture Herald (Aug. 7, 1948) reported, "Last week Jam Handy, one of the largest producers of business films, screened the one-reel subject, 'Rudolph the Red-Nosed Reindeer,' a Christmas cartoon made for Montgomery Ward. Except for the title credits, which carry the line 'Greetings from Montgomery Ward,' the picture contains no advertising or reference to the company."

The story went on to note the Motion Picture Association had decided the cartoon was not an advertising subject. The story said the short was to be shown in more than 1,500 theaters before Christmas "as part of the Montgomery Ward campaign in which the 'Rudolph' design is used on children's sweaters, toys, games, slippers, etc."

Jack Jackson, writing in his column in the *Showman's Trade Review,* (Nov. 20, 1948) said, "Among what's new on the horizon is a swell short subject that can be procured absolutely free in towns or cities where Montgomery Ward has a store or an order-taking establishment. The mail order

This page from the original book "Rudolph the Red-Nosed Reindeer" shows the design of the reindeer which Max carefully copied in his cartoon.

company has contracted with Jam Handy of Detroit for the distribution of a Fleischer cartoon entitled 'Rudolph the Red-Nosed Reindeer.' The reel is in color and runs nine-minutes. It's Jam Handy produced, and that means that the advertising is subordinated to entertainment. Handy's representative, John George, told me all about it and take my word for it, that it's very good plus. In addition is the fact that the big company stands to cooperate with theatres showing the subject by lending every possible support. Quarter, half and full-page newspaper ads, radio time, window cards, store displays, etc. are all available to the on-the-toes manager who gets busy and arranges his bookings NOW. Write Jam Handy, Detroit, about dates for your town."

Max used both former studio animator William Sturm on the film, as well as Charles Schettler, his long-time cinematographer. Schettler went back to the Out of the Inkwell silent

Photographer Charles Schettler (seen here shooting with a three-dimensional set) had been one of Max's first employees and stayed with the company until the Fleischer Studio had been disbanded. Max used him in the production of the Rudolph cartoon.

period with Max and after the close of the studio. He seems to have drifted out of movie work after this production although in the 1960s he did do some work for Terrytoons.

The short is solidly done and follows May's book in both story and design. Originally, the short opened with "Silent Night," but after the success of the song it was then re-edited to feature the song.

*The Exhibitor*, (Feb. 5, 1951) reported that Monogram was now distributing the cartoon and months (Oct. 15, 1952) later reported, "A host of tie-ups are available for 'Rudolph the Red-Nosed Reindeer,' the eight-minute Technicolor cartoon which will be available for Christmas booking, it was announced last week by Jam Handy, which produced the subject." *Motion Picture Herald* on Oct. 25, 1952, reported the J. Arthur Rank was distributing the film in Canada.

The next year (Dec. 3, 1952) *The Exhibitor* noted that Realart was distributing the film. Realart was a company that specialized in re-releasing movies from larger studios such as Universal.

Later in the 1950s, Jam Handy took out ads in the trades about booking the film.

## *Jam Handy and Beyond*

In *Business Screen Magazine,* Vol.3, Number 10, 1949, Max is credited as the "staff specialist in television and director of animated cartoons." The short story tells about a presentation about advertising in theaters and television.

Max was seen as a name brand asset by Jam Handy as seen in this ad that ran in Business Screen Magazine in 1948.

Business Screen Magazine in its third quarterly issue of 1949, reported that Max and Russ Robins of Jam Handy Organization met at the Dayton (OH) Ad Club to discuss "the uses, problems and potentialities of screen advertising, televised as well as theatrical."

In a column with the headline "Pioneer Sees Video Taking Over the Movies," (*Detroit Free Press* on March 23, 1949) Helen Brower wrote, "Comes the revolution? 'The revolution in motion pictures is on now," says Max Fleischer of New York, the movie cartoon pioneer who now makes movie commercials for television.

"The future of movies is in television. In 10 or 15 years there will be video theaters instead of movie houses. If they don't realize this in Hollywood, it's because they would rather not."

"Fleischer, who produces industrial films for a Detroit organization, is in town to address the Junior Advertising Club of Detroit at the Hotel Fort Shelby Wednesday evening.

"Why should motion picture film be carted around the country when a picture can be thrown directly on a television screen?' he asks.

"Forty percent of the cost of an admission ticket to the movies today is in shipment of film.'

"Within three years, Fleischer predicts that video will be in color. Experiments in this are now being conducted.

"Part of the revolution will be technical.

"'Long shots in movies are not for video,' he says. 'Television is a more intimate medium mostly using close-ups.'"

After leaving Jam Handy, Max returned to New York where he worked with J.R. Bray until 1956. A 1955 listing of the personnel for Bray included Mas as "production manager of Max Fleischer Division of Bray Studios, Inc."

He then worked on inventions, a home course in animation and had the storyboards done for an animated Davey Crockett feature.

While Richard Fleischer was at Disney directing "20,000 Leagues Under the Sea," he arranged for his father to visit the Disney Studio. There were several photos taken, as noted by the *Independent Film Journal*, (Jan. 21, 1956) with one especially poignant. Max was the guest of honor of a luncheon with a number of people who had worked for him, including Dick Huemer.

There was a banner at the lunch, that read, "Inkwell Reunion or What Cartoons Can do to Cartoonists."

Richard recounted in his memoir, "Just Tell Me When to Cry," that his father and mother made a visit to California in December 1955 and on Jan. 5, 1956, his father visited the Disney Studio. Richard reported the visit went well but thought that Max in Disney's presence "was somewhat diminished and my heart broke for him. I had the feeling that Goliath had defeated David."


Broadcasting reported in its June 25, 1956, edition that Max had filed a suit seeking $2.75 million in New York State Supreme Court against Paramount Pictures Corp, Du Mont Broadcasting Corp. UM&M TV Corp, and Flamingo Films. He charged that his cartoons were bring shown on TV "unlawfully" and "without proper credit and authority."

"Mr. Fleischer asserted that his contracts specified that Paramount was to arrange for distribution and exhibition of his motion picture cartoons in connection with commercial advertising is wholly unlawful and unauthorized. He contended that his cartoons were being shown on Dumont Broadcasting Corp.'s WABD New York and elsewhere in a mutilated, altered and distorted fashion…with false and misleading screen credits inserted. Mr. Fleischer claimed that his professional reputation has been damaged by the manner of presentation of the presentation of the cartoons on TV."

This 1955 trade ad shows that eventually, Jam Handy handled the theatrical distribution of the cartoon.

His name had been eliminated from many of the cartoons struck on 16mm prints for TV. He unsuccessfully sued to have his name returned to prints of his cartoons. Paramount had removed his name when the shorts were sold to TV.

In 1959, Max regained the copyright for the Betty Boop character, setting the stage for the future merchandising of the character.

Max was also involved in a toy projector that pre-dated the Kenner Give-a-Show a prominent toy in the 1960s.

## *Koko returns*

In 1958, Max returned to animation when he formed Out of the Inkwell. Inc. in new York City and entered into a partnership with a former employee Hal Seeger. Seeger told me that he was successful in presenting an updated version to Max, something "the other boys" had attempted to do.

Seeger had done some animating at the studio in Miami and told me he had started as an office boy. After leaving the studio, Seeger had written screenplays for Cab Calloway's feature film "Hi-De-Ho" (1947) and the script for two other features aimed at Black audiences.

During the 1950s, Koko's silent cartoons were once more being seen as many had fallen into the public domain. Kids watching the blocks of cartoons on local TV stations had a chance to see them, some had added narration, while all had music tracks added.

With the alliance with Max, Seeger set up a studio operation to produce the new Inkwell shorts to be syndicated. Myron Waldman was to be the director of the 100 cartoons. He showed me the pilot for the shorts in which Max enters a room, sits down at a drawing board and draws a newly redesigned Koko for the 1960s. Waldman told me Max dyed his hair for the production.

Trade ad for the new Out of the Inkwell cartoons in *Broadcasting*, Feb. 19, 1962.

The pilot actually included a follow the bouncing ball segment which made the entire short nostalgic. The footage of Max's hand dipping a pen into the inkwell and closing the inkwell was used in later shorts.

The cartoons would open with an off camera "Uncle Max" drawing a background and giving Koko some instructions. That would launch the action. In some shorts, Uncle Max might return with a comment.

Actor and comic Larry Storch did many of the voices and was the only person to receive credit. The music seemed to come from a service, and ironies of ironies, in one episode "It's a Hap-Hap-Happy Day" is heard.

The important interplay between the artist and his creation of the silent cartoons is not used in the new series, as it was in the old. "Uncle Max" is a voice off camera and Koko is not the anarchist, as he was in the silent series. Instead, there was an apparent formula established in which Koko had a girlfriend, Kokette, and a villain, Mean Moe. Importantly, the cartoons were produced in color which gave them an edge with local programmers at a time.

Waldman did not direct all of the shorts, as Al Eugster and others did some. There are several examples of the shorts on YouTube. Waldman did tell me Max was disappointed with the limited animation budget that was assigned to the shorts.

Seeger was successful enough with the shorts to help launch more animated programs for children – "Milton the Monster," (1965-1968, ABC) and "Batfink" (1966, syndicated). Both series used animators from the Fleischer Studio, including Waldman, Graham Place and John Gentilella.

In 1972, Seeger produced "Popeye Meets the Man Who Hated Laughter," an animated feature for ABC featuring many comic strip characters from King Features.

Although "Milton the Monster" has been released on DVD, the Koko cartoons, aside from several on You Tube, are not available.

Richard Fleisher noted in his book on his father, "Out of the Inkwell: Max Fleischer and the Animation Revolution," that, much to his shock and concern, his mother and father were practically destitute by the 1960s. Max had spent much money in his legal proceedings against Paramount, which were not successful, and apparently Max and his wife were barely making do on Social Security payments.

Richard was able to move his parents into the Motion Picture Country Home, so the remainder of their lives were spent comfortably. He reports his father declined to dementia and Max died in 1972 after a long illness. *Time Magazine* called him "the dean of animated cartoonists."

# Personalities In The News

At a 20th-Fox two-day national sales conference called by distribution director Al Lichtman, plans for the national launching of CinemaScope 55 and "Carousel," and the merchandising and promotion of an amplified production and release program of 34 major C-S attractions were evolved. L to r: Lichtman; Buddy Adler, producer and aide to Darryl F. Zanuck; president Spyros P. Skouras; Murray Silverstone, president of 20th-Fox's International Corp.; and W. C. Gehring, exec. asst. gen. sales mgr.

Michael Todd (seated), United Artists president Arthur B. Krim (right), and board chairman Robert S. Benjamin sign an agreement setting worldwide distribution by UA of the multi-million dollar Todd-AO 65mm production, Jules Verne's "Around the World in Eighty Days."

Walt Disney and old associates host veteran animated motion picture producer Max Fleischer, creator of "Betty Boop" and "Popeye," at a luncheon in the Disney studio commissary. Now 72, Fleischer is still active as a producer of training films for the Armed Forces. Reading clockwise: Gerry Geronimi, Disney, Ben Sharpsteen, Ted Sears, Max Fleischer, Dick Huemer, George Stallings, director Richard Fleischer (Max's son), Andy Engman and Wilfred Jackson.

Leading industryites join Shirley Jones, star of Rodgers & Hammerstein's "Oklahoma!" in song as they celebrate the Mid-West premiere of the Todd-AO presentation at the McVickers Theatre. L to r: James Coston; John J. Jones, of Jones, Linick and Schaefer; Jack Kirsch, president, Allied Theatres of Illinois; Shirley Jones; John Balaban; George P. Skouras; and Arthur Wirtz, headman of the Chicago Stadium.

Plans for Variety Clubs International Convention, to be held at the Waldorf-Astoria May 9-12, get underway at a meeting held at New York's Tent 35. Seated, l to r: Ira Meinhardt, chmn. of operations; Martin Levine, general convention chmn.; and Harold Klein, chief barker of Tent 35; Rear, l to r: Edward Emanuel, international convention coordinator and Jerry Sager, publicity chmn.

The boards of directors of Theatre Equipment and Supply Manufacturers Assn. and TOA lunched together to discuss projected plans for the International Trade Show, Fair and Exposition to take place next September at the New York Coliseum. Among those present, (seated l to r): Larry Davee, M. H. Stevens, TESMA; Herman Levy, TOA general counsel; Walter Reade, Jr., former TOA president; Wm. A. Gedris, TESMA; Lee Jones, TESMA pres-ident; Myron Blank, TOA president; Merlin Lewis, TESMA executive secretary; Horace Denning, TOA vice-pres.; Robert Livingston, TOA sec'y.; Joe Alterman, TOA; (standing, l to r:) Carl Anderson; Albert Pickus, Pat McGee, and Julian Brylawski, TOA vice-presidents; George Gaughan, TOA field representative; Ernest Stellings and George Kerasotes, assistants to the TOA pres.; Tom La Vezzi, TESMA vice-pres.; V. J. Nolan and Joe Fetherston, TESMA.

The meeting of Max and Walt Disney was noted in this coverage in the *Independent Film Journal*, (Jan. 21, 1956).

# Chapter Eight
## *The Raven: One Last Special*

The last two-reeler produced by the studio can be seen as either a bold experiment or an inexplicable artifact. "The Raven" broke several of the molds at the studio.

First, its characters are all "funny animals," a style the studio never really embraced with the exception of Bimbo, Pudgey and background characters in the early Betty Boop cartoons. Second, the two-reelers were seen in the industry and by audiences as special events. They were unique in the marketplace, not just due to their extra running time, but by their execution.

"The Raven" could easily pass for simply a longer "funny animal" short.

The story was written by Carl Meyer and Pinto Colvig with an effective score by Sammy Timberg. Tom Johnson was the head animator for the cartoon.

The cartoon is described as "a cartoon travesty" of the Edgar Allen Poe poem, but other than a central character who is a raven and uses the word "nevermore" to punctuate the end of a statement, the film is not frightening or atmospheric in the least.

The short cannot be seen today in its original Technicolor glory. At this writing, the prints on YouTube are washed out television prints.

The film opens with a narrator quoting the Edgar Allen Poe poem, "Once upon a midnight dreary…" The camera pans through an apparently deserted house to the door which opens to reveal our hero, the Raven, voiced in verse by Jack Mercer.

The Raven tries to leave when he hears a sinister laugh, which is coming from a wolf character who obviously knows him. The Wolf is voiced by Colvig.

It seems the two were partners in a house-break years ago and The Raven explains his burglary days are over. He is now selling vacuum cleaners door-to-door and needs one more sale for the day.

The Wolf convinces his former partner-in-crime to join him the next morning at the Mc-Tavish castle. The Raven believes he can sell the owner a vacuum cleaner but the Wolf clearly has other ideas.

The reception the pair gets at the door is unexpected, as they press the doorbell designated for guests, and the reaction is several cannons shooting at them.

The Raven tells the Wolf, as he is scaling the castle walls, that he will not help him break into the castle. The Wolf responds that he knows how to get "that Scotchman" interested in letting them in so the Raven can demonstrate the vacuum cleaner. He takes a dime and bounces it in front of the locked door. Immediately the Scotchman opens the door. He is, course, a Scottish terrier dressed in a kilt and tam o'shanter.

The Raven takes the opportunity to make a sales pitch and although interested, the Scotchman says his bagpipes are fine for cleaning the floor and he demonstrates by playing them and blowing the dust.

The Wolf convinces the Scotchman to see a demonstration and manages to sneak off to case the castle.  He finds a safe.

Meanwhile, the Raven is vacuuming the carpet and interests the Scotchman when he manipulates the vacuum cleaner to sound like a bagpipe. The Wolf has found the Scotchman's safe and is intent to breaking into it.

The vacuum has sucked up a quality of Scotch, though and is now drunk – something not seen for a while in a Fleischer cartoon, an anthropomorphized machine.

Much to the amazement of the Scotchman and the Raven, the vacuum tears up a bunch of the carpet. The vacuum now can sew, and stiches the Scotchman to the carpet. The vacuum goes berserk, tearing around the castle.

The vacuum manages to stop the Wolf from stealing the Scotchman's money, and then the Scotchman gratefully buys the vacuum cleaner.

The film was released in time for an Easter 1942 release and was officially released on April 3. Paramount touted the film with trade ads.

The trade papers seemed to like the film. *Film Daily* reviewed the short in its April 20, 1942, edition. The reviewer wrote, "A Technicolor burlesque of the famous Edgar Allan Poe poem. It employs a few good gags but takes in some pretty old ones, too. The Raven in the person of a vacuum cleaner salesman, tries to sell an old Scotchman and gets all tangles up in the usual comic situation. The color and art work are excellent and the characters are new. Should take with cartoon fans."

*The Showman Trade Review's* reviewer called the production "excellent" in its May 2, 1942, edition.

*Motion Picture Daily*, in its April 15, 1942, edition also liked the short. "An amusing and cleverly animated takeoff of Poe's poem."

This trade ad shows the angle Paramount was using to sell the film.

The film is well animated and Sammy Timberg's use of classical music in the score is well done. It is simply a bit of a disappointment when compared to the previous specials with Popeye and Raggedy Ann. The use of original characters undoubtedly saved on licensing fees and perhaps the idea was to develop new characters the studio would own outright.

It is difficult, though, to really judge the film today in its faded shape.

Model sheets for the main characters have been collected at the Classic Animation Art Tumblr site.

# Chapter Nine

## *Brothers*

As I wrote in volume one, the Fleischer brothers all had talents, but they were not equal at the studio. Max and Dave were the president and vice president of the company, but Lou, Charles and Joe were employees – prominent employees, but employees none the less.

In her essay, "Cartoons in Paradise: How the Fleischer Brothers Moved to Miami and Lost Their Studio," published in *The Florida Historical Quarterly*, Winter 2000, author Donna Dial interviewed Dave's daughter. "'Only Max and Dave were partners,' Dave's daughter, Joyce Fleischer Weinberg recalled, 'They were all really geniuses, every one of them. All the other brothers worked for the studio, and they should have all been partners. I don't know why Dave and Max left them out.'"

Joe was the studio's electrician and had helped build the original Rotoscope. After the studio, he worked as an electrical contractor.

In a late in life undated essay titled "The Fleischer Follies," Joe wrote, "Fleischer Studios had a clown – 'Coo-Coo Max.'"

"I once had some business to talk to him about in his office. He looked at me, burst out laughing and said to Vera [Coleman, Max's long-time secretary], 'Ha, ha ha, Vera don't Joe look just like Mr. Zilch?' I felt like Mr. Zilch. [Zilch is a term meaning nothing.]

"Max had tremendous respect for Max.

"Max's brothers were only bothers.

"I had a breakdown in the studio due to overwork. Max became very sympathetic enough to have me go to the doctor, so that I would be back in shape for overwork.

"I became as Master Licensed Electrician to install a red light outside of Max's office door, so that he could exclude everyone, phone calls, employees, brothers, but included one female secretary, not for moments but for hours. Business can wait.

"On my own idea I made the very first portable illuminated animated drawing board in the world. Besides this board, I was making other novel items Max had patented and never told me about it.

"Max generously gave 51 percent of the Fleischers' lives to Paramount. Paramount consumed them.

"Max laughed me off to no end when I submitted upon his request for a new star, a mouse. As industry well knows instead Max introduced "Mr. Bug Goes to Town.' The bugs ate him out of the business.

"As far as I am concerned, the song in 'Gulliver's Travels' always rang out to me as 'Unfaithful Forever.'

"We Fleischers raised an empire – Max razed it.

"'I'm Cockeye the Sailor Man' – poo, poo. And I'm pooped Betty."

In another essay, designed to be presented to the public, Joe wrote that after Paramount took over the studio and moved back to New York, Paramount "kept me to again, set the business up in New York under the name of Famous Studios which I did, then left to go into the electrical contracting business in New York City."

This essay concluded with a poignant note. "Finally, this to me all seems like a passing dream, except to say that we remaining Fleischers [Dave and Lou were still alive at the time this was written] feel grateful for having the opportunity to bring laughter and happiness to people all over the word."

As I wrote in volume one, I've seen a letter from Dave written in the 1970s to Joe bitterly complaining about Max falsely taking full credit for the development of the Rotoscope.

Lou Fleischer who had been head of the music department, took a job as a lens grinder, a war effort position, after the brothers were ousted from the studio. He later re-settled to southern California. Despite the help of his son Bernie, Lou would not consent to an interview for this book. He died in 1985.

Charles, who was an inventor and had many patents, died in 1954.

# Chapter Ten

## *Popeye*

The move to Miami was a real gamer changer at the studio in many ways. One of those was the decision to eliminate the Betty Boop series and the Screen Songs, which meant the studio needed to fill the schedule with other shorts.

As noted in a previous chapter, the cartoons chosen to replace those series included the attempts to make Gabby a stand-alone star, as well as to establish the Stone Age series. Both missed the mark.

Popeye continued as a star, though, and certainly was still a success story at the box office. What would change with the character is the start of WWII, the end of Segar's influence and ultimately under Famous Studios, a standardization of story.

One thing to consider as the 1940s approached was the fact that Popeye's creator E.C. Segar died at the very young age of 43 in 1938. While there was no immediate change to the cartoons and successors were found to continue the comic strip, in a few years' time Popeye was a character that was seen differently in the two mediums. Segar's credit on the cartoons ended with "Never Sock a Baby" released in November 1940.

The successors to Segar in print carried on the characters and traditions that Segar had established.

The cartoons changed with the coming of World War II. Popeye entered the Navy as part of an effort to support the war effort. Gone was the familiar sailor outfit and now there were Navy whites. Also gone were standard characters such as Wimpy, Poopdeck Pappy and Sweet'pea.

The Fleischer Popeyes were still funny and inventive in the last years of the studio and showed innovation with story and use of characters. One of the issues noted in some of the reactions printed by the trade papers from exhibitors is that audiences did not want to see black-and-white cartoons any longer. The Fleischers used their color production funds for the Gabby cartoons, a decidedly less-than-popular series, and then for "Superman."

A theater owner on Kansas City, MO, wrote to the *Motion Picture Herald*, (June 15, 1940), "Popeye the Sailor – the Popeye cartoons used to be equal in popularity to the Disney product but have slipped. People expect to see cartoons in color and don't like the black and white."

"Cops is Right" was the first Popeye short produced at the Miami Studio and released in December, 1938. While the theme song is the same composition, the performance is not with a full orchestra as before, but rather a piccolo is emphasized. Margie Hines is now performing Olive and in this short it has far less of the Zasu Pitts tone.

Popeye is having a heck of a day. He accidentally runs into a cop with a sputtering car and gets a second ticket when he blows his horn. The tickets keep piling up when the cop sees that

Popeye has parked his car in front on a hydrant. All the while, he attempts to help Olive with her housework, to her growing irritation. Eventually, Popeye knocks out the cop, another accident, and locks himself in jail.

"Customers Wanted" (January, 1939) is a compilation of cartoons leaning on footage from two previous cartoons. Popeye and Bluto are running penny arcades with clips from the previous cartoons. Some sources list this as Pinto Colvig's first time as Bluto and it is certainly a far different voice than Gus Wickie. The best part of the cartoon are the scenes with Wimpy, who is in full moocher mode.

As Keith Ware noted in his essential book "Cartoon Voices of the Golden Age," Colvig's interpretation never quite made the impact as Wickie's.

In "Leave Well Enough Alone" (April, 1939) Popeye's love of animals is explored when he buys all of the dogs in Olive's pet shop and turns them loose. A parrot warns Popeye he should have left well enough alone, though, and the dogs Popeye has purchased are being scooped up by the dog catcher. He rescues them brings them back to the pet shop.

"Wotta Nightmare" (May, 1939) sees a departure of the sliding doors in the title. Popeye is dreaming he is heaven where he is wooing Olive, who is an angel. Bluto is the devil who wins her affections. The short has a real dream-like feel to it that quickly turns to a nightmare. Wimpy, the Jeep and Swee'pea make cameo appearances. This is an enjoyable short with some inventive imagery.

In "Ghosts is the Bunk" (June, 1939), Olive is reading ghost stories to Popeye and Bluto. Popeye declares there's no such thing as "ghosts and things." This gives Bluto an idea and he fixes up a haunted house to scare Popeye and Olive. After they discover Bluto is behind the hauntings, they find "invisible paint" and start torturing Bluto.

"Hello, How Am I?" (July, 1939) is one my favorites. Popeye and Wimpy are roommates. Olive calls and invites Popeye over for a hamburger dinner. On his way over, he is joined by his double – Wimpy in disguise. Wimpy does such a great job imitating Popeye that the one-eyed sailor staggers away from Olive's house defeated by Wimpy's logic and has an existential crisis. He says, "If I'm not me, who am I? And if I'm somebody else, why do I look like me?"

Jack Mercer does a great double duty vocal performance with the real and fake Popeyes.

*The Showman's Trade Review*, (July 29, 1939), said of the short, "it's a funny cartoon that both adults and children will enjoy."

"It's the Natural Thing to Do" (July, 1939) has a nice example of breaking the fourth wall when a brawling Popeye and Bluto are interrupted by a telegram that reads "Dear Olive, Popeye and Bluto, We like your pictures but wish you would cut out the rough stuff once in a while and act more refined. Be ladies and gentlemen. That's the natural thing to do. (signed) Popeye Fan Club. P.S. Now, go on with the picture."

Popeye and Bluto leave and come back dressed in tuxedos. Olive is in an evening gown. Needless to say, their best efforts to behave "refined" end in a fight.

Many of these photos, courtesy of JJ Sedelmaier, reflect shots found in the Popular Science short (https://www.youtube.com/watch?v=iy-Nwxugs-8) that featured work at the Miami studio in 1938. The footage gives a great overview of much of the animation process. Both Max and Dave are seen.

Assistant animator Ben Farrish works on an image from of the Superman cartoons. A "Bulleteers" model sheet is behind him on the wall.

Animator John Walworth is seen sketching Popeye.

Cameraman Bill Heins is seen here preparing for a zoom shot. The original caption reads, "This means that the camera may be used to photograph pix of Popeye coming into room with backgrounds behind him and then camera can 'zoom' up to take closeup using the same background."

Heins is seen in this photo lining up a cel in front of a background.

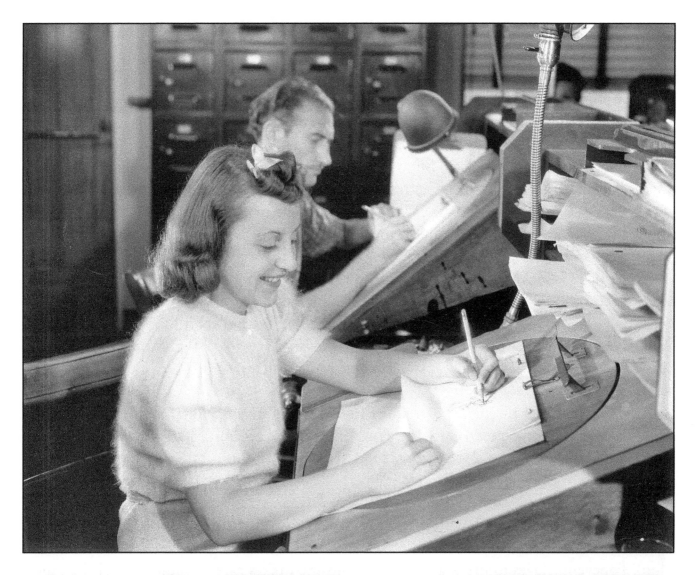

Studio artists are seen working on "Aladdin and his Wonderful Lamp.

What I liked is the cartoon's self-awareness of how the Popeye cartoons have a bit of formula and this is an effort to comment on it.

"Never Sock a Baby" (November 1940) sees the return of the sliding ship doors at the start of the cartoon. In the short, Popeye's spanks Swee'pea and then struggles with his decision. It's a sweet and sentimental short that is a showcase for Popeye's true literary characterization.

"Shakespearean Spinach" (January 1940) is a showcase for the vocal talents of Mercer, Colvig and Hines. Popeye replaces Bluto as Romeo in a production of "Romeo and Juliet" and Popeye sings Shakespearean dialogue. It's a lot of fun, although this exhibitor wouldn't agree with me – "What has happened to Popeye lately? He ain't what he used to be. This cartoon was liked about as much as people like spinach so at least its was named appropriately, (*Motion Picture Herald*, June 15, 1940).

In "Females is Fickle" (March 1940) the familiar sliding doors have new lettering. Popeye has to rescue Olive's "trained" goldfish when it escapes to the ocean. Olive implores Popeye to retrieve the fish. "Nothing doing! Do you think I should get wet for a fish?" he says in reply, but he does it when Olive accuses him of being a coward. The goldfish puts the sailor through his paces, especially when a jellyfish swallows the both of them. Colvig uses a modified Goofy laugh as the jellyfish.

As Keith Scott describes in his book, the studio had trouble settling for a new Bluto voice while in Miami. In the next short, "Stealin' Ain't Honest (March 1940) Bluto is played by writer Ted Pierce, who had a sound closer to Gus Wickie. Bluto is intent to beat Popeye and Olive to Olive's gold mine on a deserted island, but as always Popeye prevails. *Showman's Trade Review*, (May 4, 1940), wrote, "Judged by Popeye cartoon standards, this one is average."

Colvig, however, was back with the role for "Me Feelins is Hurt" (April 1940) Popeye gets a "Dear John" letter from Olive who has gone West and is dating cowboys now, specifically Bluto. Popeye manages to break a wild horse and then takes care of Bluto and all the ranch hands.

"Onion Pacific" (May 1940) marks the last time Wimpy appeared in a Fleischer Popeye. The cartoon is about a railroad race between Popeye and Bluto to determine which railroad gets the franchise. Naturally, Bluto cheats. With the help of spinach, Popeye rebuilds his wrecked locomotive and wins the race.

Popeye asks Olive to marry him in a scene played as a parody of romantic conventions. Olive tells him to wait until morning for her answer in "Wimmin is a Myskery." (June 1940) Olive then dreams of family life and their four kids Pip-eye, Pup-eye, Poop-eye and Peep-eye.

It's easy to see that the four versions of Popeye were a reaction to the introduction of Huey, Dewey and Louis, the three nephews of Donald Duck, first seen in "Donald's Nephews" in 1938. The Fleischer result is a decidedly unfunny cartoon with Olive tortured and beat up by her four sons. It is definitely a nightmare. This short is also one showing the studio tearing away from the Segar Popeye universe. Where's Swee'Pea?

"Nurse-Mates" (June 1940) sees a return of Swee'Pea. When Olive has to go to beauty salon to prepare for a date, Bluto and Popeye are left to take care of the baby and fulfill a list of chores with varying degrees of success. One of the best bits is that Swee'Pea is playing with a fountain pen splattering ink spots on his face. Popeye takes a spot removing liquid and seems to wipe the baby's features right off his face, but it's Swee'Pea playing with him. This is a cartoon in which the can of spinach never appears.

Popeye's and Bluto's relationship is further defined in "Fightin' Pals" (July 1940). "Dr. Bluto" is an explorer going to Africa, leaving his best friend Popeye. Popeye is pining for Bluto and when he is reportedly lost in the jungle, Popeye sets sail to finds him. Exhausted, Popeye imagines the worst but finally finds him. Bluto is being fanned in a hammock by three women. To revive him, Bluto feeds Popeye spinach and the two, with smiles on their faces, start fighting. Boxoffice, in its Aug. 17, 1940, edition called the short "very much worthwhile."

"Wimmin Hadn't Oughta Drive" (received, a positive review in *The Showman Trade Review*, (Aug. 24, 1940). Deemed as "excellent" the review noted, "It's an excellent subject and one of the best Popeyes in a long time. It should be easy to sell to all men who have ever tried to teach their wives or their girlfriends how to drive a car. And is there a man who hasn't cursed women drivers. The women will get a kick out of just the same."

Viewed today, it is just a series of gags based on the inappropriate idea that women can't drive.

"Doing Impossikble Stunts" (August 1940) is a compilation short with Popeye trying to get a job as a stunt man by showing clips from his previous cartoons." It's a bit of cheat, but the framing sequence is well done.

"Puttin' on the Act" (August 1940) reveals that Popeye and Olive were vaudeville performers and they rehearse their old act when a newspaper that says vaudeville is coming back. Once again Mercer shows his vocal skills as Popeye does impersonations, including ones of Jimmy Durante and Groucho Marx. The neat aspect of these vocal performances is that Mercer is performing them as if it is indeed Popeye is doing them. The short ends with Swee'Pea seeing the newspaper Olive had is from 1898. "Olive, we're too late!" Popeye says. It's a cute cartoon and again, one without the device of spinach.

In its review, *Showman's Trade Review*, (Aug. 24, 1940), noted "This is the final Popeye for the season, but a poor finish."

"Popeye Meets William Tell" (September 1940) features the work of Shamus Culhane and Al Eugster, two former Fleischer animators who had come back to work on "Gulliver's Travels." Popeye is in a foreign county where he meets William Tell and is forced to play the archer's son in order to placate the demands of the governor. It's a fast-moving short with some fun character animation.

In some ways, this short predicts the direction of many of the Famous cartoons a few years in the future, in which Popeye can appear almost anywhere or at any time. *Box Office*, (Oct. 5, 1940) said "in imagination, entertainment worth and execution [it] is considerably higher than usual cartoon offering."

"My Pop, My Pop" (October 1940) was described by the *Motion Picture Herald*, (Oct. 26, 1940) as "The father, son relation is amusing, if not riotously entertaining at times." The short opens with a funny introductory song sung by Poopdeck Pappy, another fun performance by Mercer. Popeye is working in a shipyard with his disreputable father. Popeye is building one side of the boat while Pappy is building the other. Pappy's efforts aren't successful and he falls asleep. Popeye finishes the boat and makes Pappy think he did it.

Poopdeck Pappy makes a return appearance in "With Poopdeck Pappy" (November 1940) Pappy wants to go out, but Popeye wants him to go to bed. Reminding him he is 99 years-old, Popeye says, "You've got to save your youth for your old age." Pappy manages to sneak out to a bar, where he manages to cause trouble while dancing. *Box Office* on Dec. 7, 1940, declared in its review, "Has the usual Popeye twists including a brawl and timely rescue by spinach."

This trade ad from September 1940 introduces Poopdeck Pappy to the Popeye series.

"Popeye presents Eugene, The Jeep" (December 1940) is unusual, as the studio had already introduced the Jeep in a previous cartoon. It also changes the Jeep's diet from orchids to everything else and ignores the Jeep's supernatural powers until the very last gag. It's well animated by Grim Natwick, but failing to present the Segar version of the character is a mistake. *Box Office*, (Dec. 7, 1940) called it "so-so."

"Problem Pappy" (January 1941) continues the little series. Popeye goes to Pappy's apartment only to find out he was out all night "My pappy's second childhood is making an old man out of me," he exclaims. He finds his father employed as flagpole sitter, balancing on a flagpole of a building, juggling, to draw a crowd. Popeye tries to get him down, but Pappy resists. It's only when a thunderstorm occurs that Pappy comes down with Popeye's help.

Using Pappy in the shorts added much to the series' appeal, which had put the Popeye/Olive/Bluto romantic format on vacation. The fun aspect of Pappy's character is he is everything Popeye isn't, but Popeye still cares for him.

In "Quiet! Pleeze," (February 1941) Pappy is waking up with a hangover from last night's partying. Popeye checks up on him and discovers Pappy is running a fever and needs rest and more importantly quiet, a difficult thing to do in the middle of the city. Popeye then addresses each source of noise. Of course, Pappy recovers to party on.

In one scene, Popeye punches a radio on which a singer is broadcasting. This footage is from a previous Popeye short. The difference in style is apparent, as is another moment in which Popeye brings down a building being constructed. It was clearly an economy move.

In "Olive's Sweepstakes Ticket," (March 1941) Olive wins first prize in a sweepstakes but can't find the ticket. The two then go through Olive's house looking for it. They find it, but Olive allows it to flutter out the window. Popeye pursues it as it carried by the breeze all over the town. Naturally, the prize is not worth the effort.

This run of cartoons without Bluto and with a minimal use of spinach shows a clear and successful effort to broaden the format and appeal of the shorts. It results in some very memorable cartoons.

Popeye is trying to take a nap when a group of flies congregate on his forehead in "Flies Ain't Human" (April 1941). While he gets rid of most of them, one fly decides to torture the sailor a bit. Popeye humanely gets him, but the fly finds an open can of spinach and then retaliates. The sailor succeeds in ruining his house, but not hurting the fly.

The idea that Popeye can appear in any time or place returns with "Popeye Meets Rip Van Winkle," (May 1941). The sailor encounters Van Winkle as the sleeping character is evicted from his house for lack of payment for the last 20 years. Popeye carries him to his house for his safety, but Van Winkle is a sleep walker who goes to where the elves are bowling, following the Washington Irving story. The elves fight Popeye, while Van Winkle sleeps, who only awakes when Popeye has brought him back safely to his house.

This Famous era model sheet shows the many changes to how Popeye would look.

This trade ad shows the new Famous lineup of cartoons.

The Segar character George Geezil, arch-enemy of Wimpy in the comic strip, makes a guest appearance in "Olive's Boithday Present" (June 1941). Popeye is looking for a present and is dragged into Geezil's fur coat store. When Geezil can't supply a genuine bear ski coat, Popeye goes hunting for a bear. Popeye finds a bear, corners him, but can't bear to shoot the bear when the bear's family comes to say it last goodbyes. "It just not in me nature to do it," he tells the bear. The bear decides to take advantage of Popeye's second thoughts and a fight ensues with a cute gag at the end.

"Child Psykolojiky" (July 1941) features three generations with Popeye, Pappy and Swee'Pea in the short. Popeye and Pappy are playing cards but are being interrupted by Swee'Pea's crying. Pappy just wants to hit him, but Popeye takes a more gentle approach by telling the baby about the importance of telling the truth. Pappy, of course, won't let the issue alone and Swee'Pea sets him straight.

This cartoon marks the final appearance of the iconic opening and shutting ship doors at the start of the cartoon.

Pappy ended his run in Popeye cartoons with "Pest Pilot," (August 1941). In this

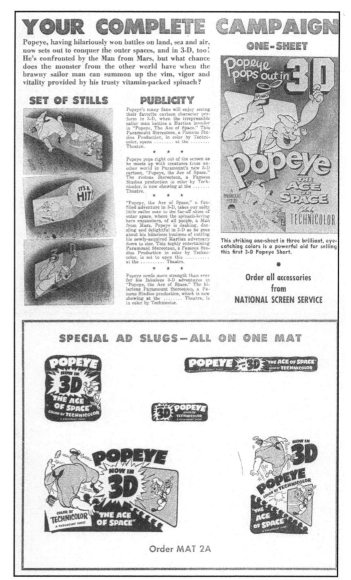

Famous jumped into the short-lived 3-D craze in the 1950s with a Popeye cartoon "Ace of Space" and with a 3-D Casper cartoon as well.

short, Popeye has taken to the air with a plane service, training pilots. Pappy wants to fly, insisting he can do it, but Popeye disagrees. Accidentally starting a plane, Pappy takes to the sky, causing havoc and crashes. Naturally, Pappy doesn't get hurt and Popeye reaches a solution, giving Pappy a flying helmet and his wings, so he can fly on a lawn mower.

"I'll Never Crow Again" (September 1941) is another short in which Popeye must deal with a bothersome animal or insect. Crows have raided Olive's garden and she calls Popeye to intervene. He tries scaring them away, putting up a scarecrow, but it doesn't work. Nothing seems to work and when Olive laughs at him, Popeye snaps, grabs Olive and makes her into a scarecrow that does frighten the birds off.

"The Mighty Navy" (October 1941) sees Popeye joining the Navy and appearing in Navy

SEPT. 1945    *Famous Studios*

whites. This cartoon certainly predicts how the series would change after world events on Dec. 7, 1941, and the country's entry in World War II. Popeye is on a Naval training ship and does not do so well, so badly that he winds up on KP in the galley. When the training ship is attacked by a group of ships – their flags simple say "Enemy Ship – Name Your Own" – Popeye goes into action. He sinks most of the ships and the planes and then, loading himself into a torpedo tube.

In "Nix on Hyponotricks" (December 1941) a would-be hypnotist picks Olive out of the phone book as the subject or victim – of his powers. He commands her over the phone to come to him, leaving Popeye alone and confused in her apartment. Olive barely avoids traffic as she walks across the streets of the city in a sequence reminiscent of "A Dream Walkin'." In a Superman reference, Popeye eats his spinach and the capital "S" on the label peels off, attaches itself to his chest, he sprouts a cape and he flies up to save Olive. Popeye resists the hypnotist by punching his hypnotic rays just like Superman did in the first Fleischer short "The Mad Scientist." Like in the previous cartoon, when Olive wakes up, she blames Popeye.

"Kickin' the Conga Round" (January 1942) is the second cartoon depicting Popeye in the Navy, this time with Bluto. The ship is in a South American port and they have shore leave to see their girl, a South American version of Olive. Both try to charm Olive. Bluto buts into Popeye's date with Olive and they dance the conga. Popeye sits at his table moping until the waiter brings over a can of spinach. Popeye can effectively dance and fight. The shore patrol breaks it up and brings both of them back to the ship.

It's a new voice for Bluto, supplied by baritone singer Lee Royce in this short, which, effectively foreshadows the format of many cartoons to come.

"Blunder Below" (February 1942) continues the Naval theme. Popeye is in a class to learn how to shoot the ship's artillery. He makes a real mess of things and is assigned to the engine room shoveling coal. When an enemy sub attacks, Popeye whips out the spinach and swims after it. The Japanese on the sub are depicted with glasses and buck teeth making them look sub-human.

"Fleets of Stren'th" (March 1942) opens with Popeye reading a Superman newspaper comic strip when he is ordered to load ammunition on a mosquito boat. His ship is bombed by fighter planes and Popeye attacks it from the mosquito boat. The enemy plane brings in reinforcements but with spinach, he sinks the aircraft carrier. Jack Mercer received his first writing credit.

Animator Seymour Kneitel wrote the story of "Pi-eye, Pup-eye, Poop-eye and Peep-eye" (April 1942) brings back the four imaginary sons of Olive and Popeye from a previous cartoon. Animator Seymour Kneitel wrote the story that re-branded the four sons as four "real" nephews with no explanation. It also brings Popeye back into his Segar-inspired uniform. The nephews don't like spinach despite Popeye's demonstrations that spinach can help you do anything well. Popeye reluctantly spanks them and, of course, once they eat their spinach they seek revenge. The nephews beating up Popeye is just as painful to watch as the dream sequence cartoon that introduced them. There's a great bit of animation with nephews playing the piano together, which is the highlight of a disappointing short. Film Daily called it the cartoon "diverting" and "good for any bill."

One wonders if this short had been in production prior to the start of the war..

With "Olive Oyl and Water Don't Mix," (May 1942) Popeye and Bluto are back in the Navy and declaring they are through with women. Of course, Olive comes walking by on the dock and asks if either of them can show her the ship. Bluto takes the lead and then Popeye steals her back and so on with Olive taking on a bunch of abuse. Olive keeps wanting to "tidy up" in the ship's Powder Room, thinking it's a lavatory. Lighting a match, she blows up the ship and Popeye and Bluto wind up in the brig. The Showman's Trade Review (June 13, 1942) "stated the mishaps are rather funny and make for an entertaining cartoon."

Bluto and Popeye are in the army in "Many Tanks," (June 1942) and Bluto is trying to sneak off-base when he sees Popeye on the other side of the fence on his way to a date with Olive. Bluto ambushes Popeye and steals his Naval uniform. Popeye now must participate in tank training with many mishaps. He manages to get to Olive's house and have the date.

The last cartoon with credits to Max and Dave was "Baby Wants a Bottleship," (July 1942) in which Olive visits Popeye at his ship with Swee'Pea, whom Popeye needs to baby sit. Swee'Pea keeps disappearing putting himself in peril on the ship. This is a re-working of previous cartoons in which Swee'Pea innocently causes havoc but brings no damage to himself.

That would be the second to last theatrical credit for Max.

# Enter Famous

The first Popeye cartoon with simply the Paramount presents credit is "You're a Sap Mr. Jap," directed by Dan Gordon. "Hull of a Mess" is the first short with the Famous Studios credit.

The war made its mark. *Film Daily*, (May 19, 1942) reported the Fleischer Studio would be dropping the idea of producing features for the duration of World War II. *Motion Picture Herald* then reported on May 23, 1942, the studio was "beginning to feel the stringencies of war, according to Sam Buchwald, general manager and Isidore Sparber, studio director at the New York Paramount office on Monday."

Buchwald said materials to make cartoons weren't in demand, and the studio hadn't stocked up on some of them.

"The Fleischer studio [Max was certainly gone by this point] will spend more on the new season cartoons, he added. However, the bulk of this expenditure is caused by increased costs in every category of production. He refused to hazard how much the studio budget would be. "Mr. Buchwald noted that Fleischer financing are done independently from Paramount.

"Although the studio has experimented and has already brought four 'nephews' into the Popeye series it doesn't contemplate introduction of any new characters now, Mr. Buchwald said, remarking the commitments to Paramount were only for the two series named [Popeye and Superman].

"Participation in the war effort is reflected by some short subjects of the Navy theme into the Popeye series, Mr. Buchwald commented. He added that officials of the company had been in Washington recently and that more work directly for the government appeared a prospect."

On July 3, 1942, *Film Daily* noted the name of the Fleischer Studio had been changed to Famous Studios with a staff of about 275 people – a considerable drop of just a few years before.

*Motion Picture Herald* reported on Jan. 9, 1943, that Famous Studios of Miami will "establish a branch at 24 West 45th St., New York City, according to an announcement by Russell

Holman, eastern production manager of Paramount Pictures … The vocal and musical talent shortage because of army personnel in Miami is said to be the reason for the shift, although the Miami studios will operate as before, but on a reduced scale."

In the *Film Daily* column "Along the Rialto" by "Phil M. Daly," (June 10, 1943) the studio is firmly back in New York. "Of decided consequence to Mister Exhibitor, whether he be a circuit solo or the proprietor of only one small cinema emporium, are the current happenings on several floors of 25 and 35 West 45th Street. At those dual addresses, an ace Arsenal of Animation is in high gear, turning out entertainment ammunition of high caliber for the annual box-office battle which we all call the New Season. Said arsenal is Famous Studios, Inc. biz offspring of parental Paramount. Relatively recently, you'll recall, the artistic operations and equipment thereto were moved up here from Miami, with an eye to all-out creation of cartoon shorts – three series of eight, namely 'Little Lulu,' 'Popeye' and 'Noveloons," each and every one in Technicolor."

The column continued about the popular *Saturday Evening Post* cartoons featuring "Little Lulu" was being prepared for animation, and that Popeye would be "freed" from black and white and that the character would benefit from the expertise of Technicolor color consultant, Herbert Kalmus.

It should be noted that Paramount dropped Technicolor for the 1948-49 season and replaced it with Polacolor.


By that time, three series were "Popeye;" "Noveltoons" with Little Audrey (which replaced Little Lulu), Herman the Mouse, Casper the Friendly Ghost and Buzzy the Crow; and Screen Songs, which had been reintroduced in 1946, and became a series in 1947.

Animation fans and scholars can debate how artistically successful the cartoons at Famous were. The emphasis was on funny animal slapstick with the Casper cartoons providing sentimentality. For Popeye, though, the character had become an everyman thrust in all sorts of situations that were too dependent on the Olive/Bluto love triangle and spinach. I don't think Segar would have recognized this incarnation of his creation.

This is not to say the Famous cartoons were technically inferior as the animation, music and voice work were still very good. There seemed to be a lack of innovation and the more sophisticated character-driven humor one saw the in the Warner Bros. shorts, which arguably were the most popular theatrical cartoons of the 1940s and '50s.

A.A.P. acquired the broadcast distribution rights to 234 Popeye cartoons in 1956, an article in *Broadcasting*, (Nov. 11, 1957) noted. The company bought the rights for $2,225,000 from Paramount and King Features and sold the package to "about 88 stations."

For Paramount was probably seen as easy money. For the Popeye character and for the Fleischer legacy, this was a game changer.

For readers who are not Baby Boomers, one needs to understand that in the 1950s and '60s local television stations had many hours to fill and had to produce their own programming.

Children's programming was a staple and most stations had a show aimed at kids. The Popeye cartoons featured on these shows drew big audiences.

How big a success was Popeye for TV stations? A 1962 trade ad from A.A.P. Inc., which distributed the shorts included a testimonial. "We're the independent in a four-station market. Our cost for the Popeye package including prints and AFM is $75,567 plus a participation, We broadcast one half-hour a day, seven days a week and get a 20 percent premium over our card rate for Class B time ($100 per minute for one-time to $75 per minute for 260 times. Except for a few Saturday and Sunday availabilities, we're completely sold out. In the first seven months, we grossed $51,420.39 averaging about $7,347 per month. And at this rate of income, we'll reach the break-even point in a little over three more months. That means we'll show a 17 percent profit on the cost at the end of the first year! With two more years at the same rate of income, Popeye cartoons will net $188,925 on a gross of $264,492! This is money Popeye is making for us – not spinach."

Seeing the success of the Fleischer and Famous cartoons on TV, King Features announced in an ad in *Broadcasting* on Jan. 22, 1962, the Popeye cartoons produced by the syndicate for television that had started the previous fall were a ratings success.

The irony was that a new generation of viewers were being introduced to the Fleischer shorts, the remains of the studio had been downsized in 1956 and redubbed the Paramount Cartoon Studios. That entity stumbled along in several incarnations until 1967.

# Chapter Eleven

## *Legacy*

It's clear the cartoons of the Fleischer Studio have had a lasting impact on popular culture, as well as animation as an art and industry.

In 2024, stories about film restorations or discovery are part of the general coverage about the arts. Companies such as Vinegar Syndrome regularly bring obscure movies back to the public eye in meticulously restored presentations. Today's movie fans seek out restored versions of films.

It is necessary, though, to understand that for most people movies were not necessarily considered art and instead were seen as ephemeral, products of an industry designed to entertain the public. This is why most of the silent films produced no longer exist. The studios saw little reason to save them, especially when the prints had actual value due to the silver in the film stock.

It was not until the advent of commercial television in 1949 that old movies had new value as television stations needed programming and movie packages.

Movie critics of the 1930s and '40s in particular were small-minded when it came to animation. For them, there was simply one studio that produced anything of serious interest, Disney. It didn't seem to matter that the Fleischer cartoons were truly significant in the marketplace of the 1930s and Warners Brother and MGM filled that role in the 1940s.

As I mentioned in the introduction of this book, television screening of cartoons made by almost every studio except Disney were daily content for television stations. These kiddie shows featuring a local host and cartoons set up a new generation of cartoons fans, the Baby Boomers.

The Baby Boom generation has many of the people who then, years later, renewed and restored animation. The efforts of the creators on Nickelodeon, the Cartoon Network and MTV cannot be underestimated in bring back animation from the abyss created by the dreck of Saturday morning.

And the work of the Fleischer Studio can be seen as a major influence in current popular culture. How many times have you seen in TV shows or commercials the use of the bouncing ball? This device is truly part of American culture.

If you want impact and influence, just look at the Rotoscope. The technology endures. Ralph Bakshi used the technique for a series of films. Richard Linklater used it for "A Scanner Darkly" and "Waking Life." Read the credits for many action or fantasy films, and despite all the CGI credits, you're bound to see one for rotoscoping.

I picked up a copy of "The Dark Knight," the graphic novel that changed the venerable character of Batman forever. Author Frank Miller thanked Max and Dave Fleischer in the credits.

The Fleischer Superman shorts were inspiring to the team that created "Batman: The Animated Series."

One of the true legends of animation, Hayao Miyazaki, as stated his admiration for the Fleischer productions, even noting his preference for the Fleischer work over the Disney films.

Another Japanese legend, Dr. Osamu Tezuka, used Betty Boop's large eyes as a model for his character design, which has greatly influenced both manga and anime.

The mere fact that Betty Boop has produced millions of dollars in licensing fees and many, many products in the last 40 years indicates the kind of impact the cartoons made. People who may have never seen a vintage Betty Boop cartoon love the character and its design.

Betty's image has been used in this country and others for decades. Promotional playing cards distributed at a licensing show in the 2000s in New York City by King Features described Betty Boop as "one of the few female licensing properties, Betty Boop is the billion-dollar baby of industry. Every available category has been licensed in the U.S.; she has a huge international following in Asia; great success in the U.K. and a most devoted audience in France."

King Features, which at the time administered the licensing effort with Fleischer Studios, Inc., also tried to launch a secondary licensing effort featuring Betty as a baby. "Baby Boop,

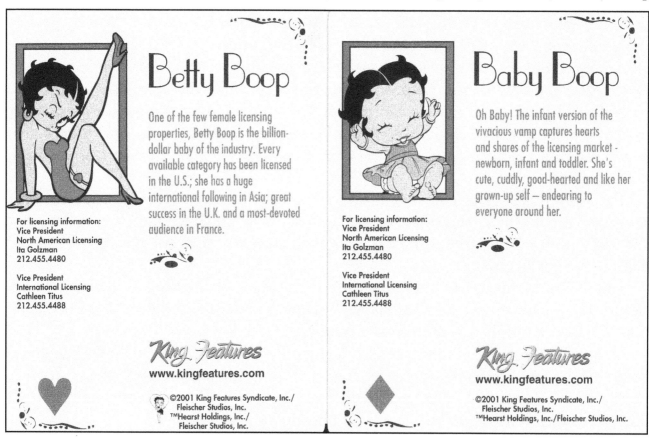

These promotional playing cards, for not just Betty Boop but for "Baby Boop," were distributed at a licensing trade show in 2001.

Oh Baby! The infant version of the vivacious vamp captures hearts and shares of the licensing market – newborn, infant and toddler. She's cute, cuddly, good-hearted and like her grown-up self – endearing to everyone around her."

There were licensed products based on Koko The Clown and Pudgy, Betty's dog, created by Waldman.

The contemporary popularity of Betty Boop spurred the production of two animated specials for TV. As I write this, a musical featuring Betty Boop has started a run in Chicago that is intended to go to Broadway. If this is successful, there will be even more merchandise and attention.

I believe the current Fleischer Studios, Inc., operated by the Max Fleischer descendants, probably has seen more income from licensing that Max and Dave saw at the height of Betty's popularity in the 1930s.

One could argue the popularity of the Fleischer Popeye cartoons kept that character alive after the premature death of creator E.C. Segar. None of Segar's successors were able to gain the type of interest readers had in the Segar strip. The cartoons were incredibly popular when they hit the TV screen in the 1950s.

As previously noted, King Features commissioned Popeye cartoons made for television in order to cash in on the Fleischer and Famous cartoons fan base.

New productions of Popeye over the years have kept, as best as can, the voice used

There was also a licensing promotional deal at the MGM Grand in Las Vegas featuring Betty.

by Jack Mercer. The refinements to the voice made by Mercer are still revered by current voice actors.

The comprehensive release of the Betty Boop cartoons to VHS in the 1990s and the Popeye cartoons to DVD in the 2000s were events that received much attention in the media. As animation fans rejoiced to finally have something more to represent these cartoons than dupey public domain copies.

Thanks to Tommy Jose Stathes' Cartoons on Film company, as well as Steve Stanchfield's Thunderbean Studios, vintage animation, including Fleischer cartoons, is reaching new audiences through beautifully restored shorts featured on Blu-rays.

The animation art boom of the 1990s also saw a resurgence in interest in the Fleischer cartoons. Artists such as Myron Waldman created new images of Popeye and Betty Boop for limited edition cels as did Shamus Culhane. Waldman even did a limited edition cel of the scene he animated for "Gulliver's Travels."

Music videos have used the Fleischer style or elements, such as the 1986 short "Betty's Being Bad" by country rock band Sawyer Brown, which features an actress performing as Betty, but in a blue dress rather than red.

Of course, perhaps the most obvious homage has been "The Cuphead Show," based on the popular video game. The look of the show, the character design and the use of the 3-D sets screams Fleischer.

In my mind, many of the Fleischer cartoons have a contemporary energy to them that have served them well with audiences today. I view them as I view the films of Buster Keaton. They were ahead of their times in many ways. Tommy Jose Stathes regularly stages shows in New York City where he screens 16mm prints from his extensive animation collection, including Fleischer shorts.

I have no idea how Max and Dave would have reacted to how their studio's work has endured into the 21st Century. When the cartoons were made, they were seen as ephemeral – in fact, generally most movies were seen that way. Only a handful of the people who made the cartoons lived into the 1990s to start to see the rise of animation fandom and the appreciation they so richly deserved.

Max and Dave were not the only people who had careers after the studio closed. The following are some of the people interviewed for these two books and what they did after the studio closed.

Animator Myron Waldman served in the US Army during World War II and continued his career in animation with Famous Studios until 1957. During that time, Waldman, who always advised me to work on my own projects, wrote an illustrated a wordless novel, "Eve," to critical acclaim; and was the illustrator for the comic strip "Happy the Humbug." After leaving Famous he worked for Hal Seeger on the Koko television cartoons and did considerable freelance work in animation. With the growing interest in limited edition cels in the 1990s, Waldman did many featuring Popeye and Betty Boop and appeared at animation art galleries. He died at age 97 in 2006, drawing almost up until his death.

Voice actor and writer Jack Mercer performed the voice of Popeye for nearly 50 years, continuing that character and others at Famous Studios. He also wrote cartoons at Famous, as well as working on TV series such as "Deputy Dawg" and "Milton the Monster." He provided all the voices in the TV "Felix the Cat" cartoons. He also did

Myron Waldman is seen at his studio at his Long Island home in the 1980s.

the Popeye voice in commercials and children's records. The only theatrical credit he received for the voice was in the Robin Williams "Popeye" feature film. In 1974 he received some attention when he appeared on the TV game show "To Tell the Truth." He died at age 74 in 1984.

Animator Joe Oriolo worked at Famous Studios, as well as an artist on comic books. He worked on the Felix the Cat strip from 1954 to 1969. He formed a partnership with the brother of Pat Sullivan, Felix's original producer, and was able to produce a TV Felix series starting in 1960. "The Mighty Hercules" series followed along with "Johnny Cypher in Dimension Zero." He died in 1985.

Jack Mercer kept busy up until his death performing as a voice actor, including starring in the Hanna-Barbara version of Popeye.

Animator and producer Hal Seeger produced several films aimed at African American audiences in the late 1940s and returned to animation by producing the Koko the Clown TV shorts. He then produced "Milton the Monster" and "Batfink" for TV. He died in 2005 at the age of 87.

Voice actor Mae Questel resumed the Olive Oyl voice when Famous Studio returned to New ork City. She was busy as an actress on TV and Broadway and gained great fame as "Aunt Bluebell" in commercials for Scott paper towels. She had significant roles in the films such as "National Lampoon's Christmas Vacation"and "New York Stories" and performed the Betty Boop voice in "Who Framed Roger Rabbit." She died in 1998 at the age of 89.

Animator Shamus Culhane worked at Warner Bros. briefly and then had several years at Walter Lantz's studio, where he also directed. After leaving Lantz, he founded his own studio and produced TV commercials. Closing the studio in 1960, Culhane was named the head of Paramount Cartoon Studio until 1967. He wrote two books about animation and passed in 1996 at 87.

Animator John Walworth, who lent me many of the model sheets seen in these two books, worked at Famous Studios but left in the late 1940s. He discovered another career that lasted for decades: designing the toys for Cracker Jacks, as well as giveaway toys for fast food restaurants such as Burger King.

Shamus Culhane (right) spoke about animation at the Ottawa International Animation Festival in the mid-1990s with historian Mark Langer and Myron Waldman.

He died at 78 in 1991.

Writer and animator Alden Getz became a partner in Waterman, Getz, Niedelman Advertising in New York City, a firm specializing in book publicity.

Animator Al Eugster had a very long career in animation. After serving in the US Army in World War II, he returned to Famous Studios until 1957. He then embarked on a career of animating TV commercials. He retired in 1987 and passed the age of 87 in 1997.

Animator Grim Natwick worked at many studios in his very long career, including Disney, Um Iwerks, Fleischer, Water Lantz and UPA. He was one of the veteran animators hired by Richard Williams for his doomed epic "The Cobbler and the Thief," animating the mad witch. He died at age 100 in 1990.

Composer Sammy Timburg contributed many of the songs for the Fleischer Betty Boop and Popeye cartoons, as well as "It's a Hap-Hap-Happy Day" from "Gulliver's Travels," "Boy, Oh Boy" from "Mr. Bug Goes to Town," as well as the scores for the Superman shorts. He had a long career in show business and retired to Scranton, PA, the hometown of his wife. He died in 1992 at the age of 89.

Edith Vernick was in the army in World War II and then had a brief stint at MGM's animation studio, and then worked at Famous Studios. Work in commercials followed as well as time at Hanna-Barbara Studios. Her last job in animation was with producer Larry Harmon – who she gleefully called a "putz" to me in our interview – on the Bozo cartoons for TV. She retired to Atlantic City, NJ, and died in 1992 at age 86.

# Afterword

The Fleischer Studio has been part of my life in one form or another nearly all of my 69 years.

When I was a kid in the late 1950s and early 1960s, my favorite cartoon to watch – and believe me, I watched a lot of animation – was Popeye. I quickly realized that cartoons with the opening and closing ship doors in the introduction were the best.

I also have a vivid memory from my childhood of seeing a Fleischer Superman short on TV. It was "Mechanical Monsters" and I was simply gob smacked. It was incredible, and as a kid who watched George Reeves Superman show, I realized when I was watching this cartoon that it seemed like the "real" Superman. The Superman from the comic books.

Many of us are imprinted by elements of popular culture. The movies or TV shows or music or sports of your childhood frequently leave their mark through your entire life.

As a kid attending high school and college while living in a small town in Massachusetts, I can easily recall how my interest in film exposed me to artists that to this day are still very much a part of my life.

My hope for this book is it either introduces or re-introduces these wonderful cartoons to audiences in the 21st century; perhaps even do to other people what happened to me: have a revelation.

Between what one can find on You Tube and the cartoons that are being lovingly restored and brought out on physical media this is a great time to see and enjoy them.

Not every Fleischer cartoon was a gem, but overall, the output of the studio is truly impressive. The technical advances, the urban style, the wonderful voice artists and animators set a benchmark in animation that few have reached.

What was the secret of the studio's success? I chalk it up to a number of elements that resulted in seeing the animated cartoon in a different way from other studios. The Fleischer cartoons were at their best when they were just true to themselves.

How much of that success was Max, Dave and the rest of the brothers? Frequently in film history, the goal of the historian is to determine who was the auteur, who should get the accolades or the blame. It's always difficult in film, as so many people play a role in the success of a production and animated cartoons are no different.

I really think the Fleischer cartoons that we revere so much came about in an organic process. Part of it came from the New York City background of the studio. Animator Grim Natwick believed Max and Dave were shaped, in part, by the era in which they started – Natwick called it "the jazz age" – and by the fact they were first-generation, Americans.

I think the almost ad lib nature of how they produced the Koko cartoons in the 1920s contributed greatly to a type of filmmaking that for commercial success depended upon planning.

And yet the Koko cartoons were financially successful and popular with audiences.

There was a certain artistic critical mass that occurred at the Fleischer Studio. The right people in the right spot with artistic and humorous senses that were different from their competitors.

The Fleischer cartoons were consistently among the very best in the 1920s and '30s. The studio's work on "Mr. Bug Goes to Town" and "Superman" showed that going into the 1940s the studio was still the only one to rival the reputation of Walt Disney.

The work of the Famous Studio was supervised by three of the people who worked at the Fleischer Studio. Famous still had rights to Popeye and brought back several cartoons with Raggedy Ann, and Hunky and Spunky.

It wasn't the same, though.

There were many talented people at Famous who produced very competently animated cartoons. Something was missing.

Animator Gordon Sheehan told Len Kohl that Seymour Kneitel's – one of the three Fleischer vets who were running Famous – interest in decreasing budgets was well known. "He was great for that! I worked with him enough to know that. I remember him saying – with his Brooklyn accent – 'Let's keep it com-moish-al.' Instead of commercial, he'd say 'commoishal.' And that's typically what somebody manufacturing shoes or garments or whatever. In fact, the 'Hollywood people' that used to come in, they used to 'rib' Seymour because he had this New York accent. He was a typical New Yorker. Business was business – whether it was making cartoons or making buttons for clothing. Seymour always appeared to me to be much more interested in producing animation as inexpensively as possible – rather than aiming for quality and creativity."

That could explain much about Famous.

It's easy to see that Dave's career after he lost the studio never reached the heights it had previously. It wasn't for a lack of trying but Dave's time at Columbia and later at Universal was not distinguished.

Max was the same. He never reached the level of respect in the animation industry or recognition from the public as he once had.

Regardless of that, the cartoons made by the studio are the true legacy of all the Fleischer brothers. Their influence is still far reaching and they are reaching new audiences. Many artists can only dream of those two things happening to them.

## *Many thanks*

These two books could not have been made possible without the help of many, many people. The following list are people I thanked in the first book, but certainly deserve to be mentioned again.

First and foremost is my wife, Mary, who has supported my interest almost since she first met me for more than 45 years ago. Thank you for everything.

My late parents, Sue and Gordon may have been mystified at times by my interests, but they never discouraged me. To accommodate my interest in animation – and to allow me to try it myself – my dad purchased a great Super 8 Bolex camera. Thank you.

The late Rosalie and Myron Waldman became very important friends and mentors to my wife and me.

Although things did not work out as they had hoped, I sincerely thank the late Richard Fleischer and Ruth Kneitel for their initial approval and help. I hope their descendants find some value in my efforts.

The men and the women of the Fleischer Studio who took their time to tell their stories to me were uniformly kind and generous. They included Jack Mercer, Mae Questel, John Walworth, Seymour Reit, Joe Oriolo, James "Shamus" Culhane, Edith Vernick, Al Eugster, Grim Natwick, Sammy Timberg, Alden Getz, Hal Seeger and Hi Neigher.

Other people who provided invaluable opinion and information were JJ Sedelmaier, Len Kohl, Stephen Worth, Ray Pointer, Karl Cohen, Mark Langer, Patricia Timberg, Jackson Beck, Bill Melendez, George Evelyn, Ron Magliozzi and Dan Dalton.

Donald Crafton's essential book "Before Mickey" was an inspiration, as was Leonard Maltin's "Of Mice and Magic." Thank you to both authors. You should add them to your library.

I have great admiration for the restoration work of Tommy Jose Stathes and his Cartoons on Film (http://www.cartoonsonfilm.info) and Steve Stanchfield and his Thunderbean Animation (https://thunderbeanshop.com).

Others that deserve a deep tip of Koko's hat include the late Richard Gordon, Stephen R. Bissette, Joseph Citro, Patrick Dobbs, as well as Kyle Macabee, the late David Mruz, Jerry Beck and the late Michael Sporn for their good will and help.

My good friend, the talented artist Mark Masztal, designed this book and I deeply appreciate his help. Check out his work at https://markmasztalbooks.bigcartel.com

And thank you for reading. I can be reached at gmdobbs@comcast.net.

G. Michael Dobbs
*Springfield, MA*
*2024.*

With the influx of new artists, the following Production Guide was written to provide everyone with the same information about the process of producing cartoons at the studio. This provides a valuable insight into the details of the how the studio worked.

The material for this book has been compiled by Izzy Sparber and Seymour Kneitel.

If clarification of any section of its contents is necessary, the above should be consulted for a verbal explanation.

FOREWORD

The purpose of this book is to familiarize Animators and their Assistants with the technical requirements necessary to the production
of Animated Cartoons.

To produce cartoons efficiently, it is
important to know how to obtain the best results
with the least amount of work.

Established short cuts, if used to advantage, make for high efficiency and enhance
the artists value to himself and to the company.
Animation on TWOS--clever use of repeats--
elimination of unnecessary tracebacks by use
of the three cel levels--handling crowds by
impression  rather than drawing each character--
the use of an overlay blocking off a large part
of the crowd--these are but a few of the practices
which make for efficiency.

It is important that artists thoroughly
acquaint themselves with these methods and plan
their scenes with the standards established herein.
Read the book carefully and keep it on your desk
at all times for a handy reference.   For your
convenience, it is indexed so that solutions for
everyday problems may be found with a minimum of
delay.

TABLE OF CONTENTS

## TABLE OF CONTENTS

### (Cont'd.)

-1-

### GENERAL NOTES

Before starting a scene, be sure you understand the necessary "business" called for. If in doubt about anything, please check with your Head Animator.

Originality is desirable but it must be in keeping with what your particular scene is designed to "put over". The Head Animator must be consulted about any new business that you wish to insert into a scene. The production as a whole must appear unified. The characters must be uniform in appearance and have the same touches of personality. Where model charts have been established, check with them frequently.

Don't put unnecessary details on props which are introduced by you into a scene for which no models have been made. Keep shading and highlighting down to greatest possible simplicity and if in doubt, check with the Head Animator. Don't use highlights on eyelids, except in very unusual cases or in extreme close-ups. It is imperative that all layouts and action be carried at least half inch outside the cutting field on all sides.

Make it a point to notify the Head Animator at least a day before you expect to finish your scene.

Don't spend time cleaning up or breaking down drawings which your Assistant is capable of doing.

Before a scene is turned over to your Assistant to be broken down, it must be checked with the Head Animator to determine whether the basic idea has been carried out. His initialed O.K. must appear in the upper left hand corner of the first exposure sheet.

After a scene is broken down and ready for Inbetweening, it must be checked by the Animator and his initialed O.K. must appear under the Head Animator's on the first exposure sheet.

The footage of a scene is reported on the Time Card by the Animator when it is completely cleaned up by his Assistant and ready for Inbetweens. In the case of an Animator doing his own Breakdowns, footage is to be reported when he has completed the Breakdowns.

DON'T REMOVE DRAWINGS, EXPOSURE SHEETS, LAYOUTS, ETC., FROM ANY SCENE WHICH IS NOT ON YOUR OWN DESK, without leaving a memo with the scene clearly stating where the removed drawings, layouts, sheets, etc., were taken.

<u>ABBREVIATIONS</u>

The following abbreviations have been standardized in
order to simplify the writing of notes and instructions.
Familiarize yourself with them and if a term is to be
abbreviated, be sure to use the correct one.  <u>DO NOT
USE</u>  any other abbreviations for these terms as it will
confuse all departments required to handle the scene.
After determining which abbreviation you desire to use,
<u>PRINT IT CLEARLY</u>.

| | |
|---|---|
| A  (With circle around it) | Action.  (This abbreviation used <u>only</u> for indicating in which fields action is to be inked on sliding cels.) |
| Act. | Action |
| Anim. | Animation |
| Anim'r. | Animator |
| Anim-Str-Ahd. | Animate straight ahead |
| App. | Approach |
| Ass't. | Assistant |
| | |
| B  (With circle around it) | Blank Field. (This abbreviation used <u>only</u> for indicating which fields are to be blank on sliding cels.) |
| Bkg. | Background |
| Blk-Mask-F. | Black Mask Field |
| Bot. | Bottom |
| BP. | Bottom Pegs |
| BCP | Bottom Center Peg |
| BLP. | Bottom Left Peg |
| BRP. | Bottom Right Peg |
| Brk-Dwn. | Break Down |
| Bt.  ($\frac{1}{2}$-BT, $\frac{1}{4}$-BT.) | Beat  ($\frac{1}{2}$ Beat, $\frac{1}{4}$ Beat) |
| Cam. | Camera |
| CD. | Complete Drawing |
| Cel. | Celluloid |
| Col. | Color----Coloring |
| C.O. | Cut Out |
| CP. | Center Peg |
| C.U. | Close-Up |
| Cut. | End of a Scene |
| X-diss. | Cross Dissolve |

| | |
|---|---|
| Dwg. | Drawing |
| Dept. | Department |
| Diag. | Diagonal |
| Dial. | Dialogue |
| | |
| X's. | Exposures |
| Exp. | Expose---Exposures |
| Ext. | Extreme |
| | |
| F. (F-A, F-B, etc.) | Field (Field A, Field B, etc. |
| Fol. . | Follow---Follows |
| Fin. | Final |
| Forgnd. | Foreground |
| Fr. | Frame |
| Ft. | Foot----Feet |
| Ftg. | Footage |
| FTO. | For Tracing Only |
| | |
| H (With circle around it) | Hold (Only used for indicating pan move holds on Exp. Sh.) |
| Hor. | Horizontal |
| H.U. | Hook-up |
| | |
| In. or (") | Inch------Inches |
| Inb. | Inbetween |
| Inb'r. | Inbetweener |
| | |
| L. | Left (Only used when referring to direction of pan or cel moves.) |
| LF. | Large Field |
| LFSB | Large Field Set-back |
| LFSP | Large Field Sliding-Pegs |
| LP | Left Peg |
| L.S. | Long Shot |
| Lev. | Level |
| | |
| M-to-18 | Match to Drawing 18 |
| Mod. | Model |
| Med. | Medium |
| Mid. | Middle |
| Mus. | Music |
| | |
| O-lay | Overlay |
| ONES | One exposure for each move |
| O.R. | Off Register |

- 4 -

| | |
|---|---|
| P # | Punch number |
| Pan | Panorama |
| Pos. | Position |
| Ppr. | Paper |
| Pre-sync. | Pre-synchronized. (Recorded before cartoon is made) |
| Post-sync. | Post-synchronized (Recorded after cartoon is made) |
| Prod. | Production |
| PT. | Pencil Test |
| R. | Right |
| Reg. | Register or Registry |
| Rpt. | Repeat |
| Rev. | Reverse |
| RP. | Right Peg |
| S-1, S-2, S-3, etc. | Sync 1, Sync 2, Sync 3, etc. |
| SB | Set-back |
| Sc. | Scene |
| Sc-# | Scene Number |
| Sh. | Sheet |
| SE. | Sound Effect |
| Sldg. | Sliding |
| SF. | Standard Field |
| Sm. | Small |
| Sync. | Synchronize |
| T-# | Take Number |
| T-18 | Trace Drawing 18 |
| TP. | Top Peg |
| TB. | Trace Back |
| TCP. | Top Center Peg |
| TRP. | Top Right Peg |
| TLP. | Top Left Peg |
| TWOS | Two Exposures for each move |
| THREES | Three exposures for each move |
| U-lay | Underlay |
| Vert. | Vertical |
| X-diss. | Cross Dissolve |
| X's. | Exposures |

INSTRUCTIONS TO THE ANIMATION DEPARTMENT

In order that scenes go thru the various production
departments with the least amount of inter-departmental
discussion (due to errors, confusing notes and bad
planning by the Animator or the Assistant Animator)
the following instructions MUST BE OBSERVED.

"Circle In" or
"Circle Out"    There are 32 standard circles planned to
                work to or from the center of the Stand-
                ard or Large Field.  If it is necessary
                to "Circle In" or "Circle Out" on either
                of these fields, just call for the Stand-
                ard Circles.

                If it is necessary to "Circle In" or
                "Circle Out" off center, a chart for a new
                set of circles will have to accompany
                the scene.

                Except for special effects, the standard
                length for a "Circle In" is one foot and
                two feet for a "Circle Out".

                When circles are used, the following notes
                must appear on the Exposure Sheet and in
                the Camera Department section of the
                Large Pink Card:

                    Length of "Circle In" or "Circle Out".

                    Whether Standard or new set of circles
                    is to be used.

Cross-          Cross-dissolves between scenes are limited
Dissolves       to exactly 2, 3, or 4 feet, except for
                special effects.

                Dissolves within a scene are not limited
                in length.

                When scenes dissolve to other scenes, it is
                necessary for them to reach the Camera
                Department simultaneously. If there is a
                long stretch of dissolves without a cut,
                it will not be possible to photograph any
                of the scenes involved until all have
                been colored, planned, etc. If a retake is
                necessary in any of these scenes, all other
                scenes that it dissolves to or from, will
                also have to be rephotographed.

                Therefore, do not call for a dissolve unless
                you feel that it is absolutely necessary.
                If too many scenes are combined by dis-
                solves, plan for a cut somewhere in this
                section to break it up.

- 6 -

Registry marks
for Pans

All horizontal pan registry marks should register to the line on the center peg, except when the Pan changes to a vertical or diagonal Pan moving down. In this case, use a registry mark at the bottom of the field corresponding to line on top center peg.

For vertical and diagonal pans, a registry mark must be made on a separate sheet of paper to accompany the scene. This mark should be about one inch below the pegs on the right or left hand side of the field, depending on which side will keep the Pan Move Scale outside of the action part of the background.

If a pan changes from a horizontal to a vertical or diagonal pan, be sure you have the background on the pegs in register to its last horizontal pan position before creating a new registry mark. (Use the same procedure in going from a vertical or diagonal pan to a horizontal, or from a vertical to a diagonal pan.)

How to in-
dicate START
and STOP re-
gistry posi-
tions on pans

ALL START and STOP positions on a pan (with the exception of HORIZONTAL SLIDING-PEG PANS) must be marked with a letter underneath the number of the pan move. Thus, the START of a pan would be marked "1-A". If the background starts to pan and is stopped at PAN POSITION 43, it would be marked "43-B". If the background starts panning again, stopping at PAN POSITION 84, it would be marked "84-C"-etc.

If you cut away from a scene and pick it up again in a new position, it must be marked with a new letter picking up alphabetically from where the last pan position left off.

| | |
|---|---|
| Exposing of pans | All pan moves and the letters with them indicating the START and STOP positions must be exposed on the exposure sheets thru-out the scene. (See SAMPLE EXPOSURE SHEET) |
| Timing of pans | All pans must be exposed on ONES. All action in direct contact with a pan must also be exposed on ONES. But, if it is a bird flying, a waist-up shot, or any other similar action where there is no direct contact with the background, the action can be exposed on TWOS, while the pan background is exposed on ONES. |
| Starting and Stopping of pans | Graduate the speed of a pan to ease out of the starting and also into the stopping position. The only exception to this rule should be where an effect of a sudden start or stop is necessary. |
| Pan Marking Strips | These strips have been printed to save the time of marking off pan moves on the back-ground and trace-up guides on the SHIFT CHART.

They are printed in 16-inch lengths with a gummed surface on the reverse side. They are to be cut down to the necessary length and pasted in position on the background where the pan moves would ordinarily be marked. Where a pan length totals more than 16 inches and additional strips are necessary, these strips are to be matched up at the inch lines.

For accuracy, it is advisable to wet only about three inches at a time when pasting the strips down.

The markings on these strips are spaced down to a 32nd of an inch. A dot, made with a black pencil, should be on every marking intended for use in panning. By this method, speeding and slowing up of a pan can easily be taken care of. To move a pan at a 64th of an inch, call for the pan to be registered on and inbetween the 32nd inch markings.

These strips may also be employed as guides for animating in one spot an action used with a pan background, by marking off the speed of the pan with dots and animating the action sliding back to match these dots. |

- 8 -

Animation on
TWOS

Instead of planning animation to be
exposed on ONES, leaving TWOS the exception to the rule, ALL ANIMATION
SHOULD BE PLANNED TO BE EXPOSED ON TWOS,
AND ONES SHOULD BE THE EXCEPTION.
Actually, about 80% of all action can
be shot on TWOS without harmful effect
to the picture.

In fast actions, it is necessary that
exposures be retained on ONES, where it
is impossible to have the action follow
in arcs on TWOS, and where the spacing
between drawings lacks overlapping of
the action.  Also pans, which must be
exposed on ONES are those having characters or objects in contact with the
pan.  But if it is an action that has no
direct contact with the pan, it should be
exposed on TWOS, while the PAN is on
ONES, providing the action itself permits
it.  Even so-called "LIVELY ACTION"
can be successfully shot on TWOS.

Where mouth actions occur with a character that can be exposed on TWOS, don't
figure it for ONES because of this.
Actually mouth actions can work just
as well on TWOS as they do on ONES,
except in very fast mouth actions.
In this case call for the heads to be
inked on separate cels from the body,
exposing them on ONES and expose the
main body action on TWOS.  In this
case the jump in the cel-level will be
taken care of by using the necessary top,
middle and bottom opaques.

Don't plan action on ONES, where it can
be on TWOS because of a camera approach
or recede.  The Timing Department will
check the scene for this before it
goes to the Inbetween  Department and
if necessary they will call for the
extra inbetweens and expose them on the
exposure sheets.

Animation
on THREES

It is possible to animate an action on
THREES only if there is no more than the
thickness of a pencil line between each
of the drawings when all the inbetweens
have been completed.  The close spacing
must be drawn carefully and inbetweened
just as carefully.

Do not animate an action on THREES
during an APPROACH, RECEDE, or a CAMERA
PAN.

- 9 -

| | |
|---|---|
| Spacing of Inbetweens | If there is a particular spacing required for the inbetweens, a guide should be drawn on the extreme into which the inbetweener is supposed to work. |

EXAMPLE:

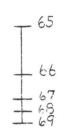

| | |
|---|---|
| Trace-Backs | Do not call for Trace-Backs unless you are already working on a three cel level. It is not necessary to keep a scene on a one or two cel level if it necessitates unnecessary trace-backs. |
| Sliding-Cels | Sliding-Cels are not to be generally used, except under the SLIDING-PEG CAMERA. |

For this type of action on any of the other cameras, a SHIFT CHART must be made to carry the action in, out, or to any section of the scene.

You are permitted the use of one sliding cel on any of the cameras if a drawing that cannot be a cut-out must pan in or out of the scene.

Where a drawing can be used as a cut-out instead of a sliding-cel, it is better to use it as a cut-out (in a pan only), regardless of the cel-levels.

If the use of sliding-cels on any of the other cameras will avoid considerable trace-ups, obtain an initialed O.K. on the pink card from the head of the Timing Department.

| | |
|---|---|
| Registry for Sliding Cels | Sliding-Cels must be planned to register to the line on the center peg. |

JOB NO._____ SCENE NO._____ FOR MAKING CELS_____ TO_____ TRACED FROM DRAWINGS_____ TO_____

DRAWINGS_____ TO_____ ARE ALSO USED IN THEIR REGULAR POSITION ON THE PEGS.

# SHIFT CHART

THIS SHIFT CHART PAPER CAN BE OBTAINED FROM THE SUPPLY DEPARTMENT IN BOTH SMALL AND LARGE FIELD PAPER.

We are limited to using SLIDING CELS in HORIZONTAL PANS, only on the STANDARD & LARGE FIELD SLIDING PEG CAMERA. A SHIFT CHART must be laid out for this type of action to be used on any of the other cameras and in all DIAGONAL & VERTICAL PANS.

## METHOD OF LAYING OUT SHIFT CHART:

A line running parallel with the direction in which the PAN or ACTION is moving is drawn on the SHIFT CHART. A guide mark, indicating the peg registry to the action, is made as a cross on this line. Guide moves are then similarly drawn from the Peg registry mark in the direction toward which the action is moving, until it is in its new position or out of the scene. With regard to slowing in and out of holds, these moves must be calculated the same as pan moves. Each guide move must be numbered to indicate which drawing must be traced in that position. If it is a repeat, or drawings previously used on the pegs that are to be traced this way, new numbers must be used to take care of the additional cels. The repeated drawing must be numbered below each guide move and the new number above each corresponding guide move. The new numbers must be exposed on the exposure sheets. (Pan mark- ing strips may be used for laying out guide moves.) Be sure to fill out the heading on the shift chart sheet.

- 11 -

**Animation to Background Layout**

Always use your Background Layout on the animation board while you are animating so that your characters will always be in the correct perspective and proportion to it. The animator is not permitted to change any lines on the Background Layout. If this is necessary, the layout man must be consulted to make these changes. Notate all intricate matching lines on the background.

**Scene Numbers on Backgrounds**

All backgrounds must be stamped with the JOB STAMP in the upper left hand corner and the JOB NUMBER, SCENE NUMBER and FOOTAGE of all scenes used with the background must be written in.

**Numbering the Drawings**

Don't mix up the numbers of the drawings in your scene any more than is necessary. Keep the drawings in straight numerical order as much as possible. A mixed combination of numerals will result in needless waste by confusing every department and may eventually ruin the scene.

Do not put numbers in odd places on your drawings. Always place final numbers in the upper right hand corner.

**Exposure Sheets**

There are two types of Exposure Sheets:

1. GREEN EXPOSURE SHEETS...To be used with any action <u>planned to definite music.</u>

2. WHITE EXPOSURE SHEETS...To be used for action that is not planned to definite music. This means Ad-lib action or action planned to Beats, Phrases, or a pattern of music.

<u>ALL POST-SYNC DIALOGUE MUST BE PREPARED BY THE MUSIC DEPARTMENT.</u>

| HEAD ANIMATOR'S O.K. | | FLEISCHER STUDIOS INC. | | SHEET No. |
|---|---|---|---|---|
| ANIMATORS O.K. | | EVERYTHING CHECKED ON THE HEADING OF THIS SHEET MUST BE | | Scene No. |
| Job No. | | FILLED IN ON EVERY EXPOSURE SHEET IN THE SCENE. | | |
| Animation by | | Inbetween by | | Inking by |

| MUSIC | | | ANIMATION | | | CAMERA |
|---|---|---|---|---|---|---|

List each action & CUT-OUT by name in these boxes on every sheet thru-out the scene.

Be sure that DIAL NUMBERS run in consecutive order thru-out the scene.

This column is for the animator to use if necessary for planning his action.

This EXPOSURE SHEET must be a numerical picture of your scene.

Clearly indicate all the background during scene STARTS & CUTS.

Any DWGS. that are used from another scene must be exposed with a red pencil and the scene from which they are used indicated.

All other DWGS. must be exposed using black pencil.

CUT-OUTS are to be exposed, in this column only, thru-out the scene on every sheet.

If a CUT-OUT goes on a PAN--indicate to what PAN POSITION the CUT-OUT must REGISTER.

THE ANIMATOR IS REQUIRED TO PLAN HIS SCENE FOR INKING AND PHOTOGRAPHY AS HE ANIMATES AND POSES.

(There A & B Exposure sheets, both completing a section of 100 exposures.)

After DIAL 100 add a one to the Dial No. at the beginning of the subsequent sheets until DIAL 200. Add twos to the Dial Nos. thereafter etc. to the end of the scene.

When an ACTION is on TWOS and there is another action exposed with it on TWOS, expose the drawings so that they work together.

Do not use more than a THREE CEL LEVEL.

List all post-sync sound effects ON THAT FRAME to which animation synchronizes.

Use CUT-OUTS only where they permit you to avoid a FOUR CEL LEVEL, except in PANS where a cut-out would eliminate the use of a sliding cel.

If you cannot possibly work your action on a total of three cels, it will be necessary to combine some of these actions on a TRACING GUIDE. (Look up, "HOW TO USE TRACING GUIDE")

Should you find that in keeping the scene down to a THREE CEL LEVEL it requires an abnormal amount of TRACE BACKS see IZZY SPARBER or SEYMOUR KNEITEL about the possibility of making the scene a FOUR CEL LEVEL and get his initialed O.K. on the PINK CARD.

Exposure Rolls are clipped to the Exposure Sheets in this section.

Drawings must be exposed in their respective CEL LEVELS thru-out the scene. If necessary you are permitted to jump an action ONE CEL LEVEL once only if these jumps are not less than 15 feet apart. All main actions should be exposed on the MIDDLE LEVEL giving you the chance to jump it one level up or down if necessary. You cannot jump cel levels during a repeat or jump an action TWO CEL LEVELS at one time in any case.

When two or more Sound Tracks are being used together they must be clipped to the Exposure Sheets, one over the other. The top ones must be clipped along the side only, to permit those underneath to be read.

1-A   8

9

2

3

Draw a RED CIRCLE around all HOOK-UP drawings.

Line drawn at bottom of last frame of a hold indicates where cel is to be removed.

During a CROSS-DISSOLVE EXPOSE SCENE dissolving out here

Use this column for exposing CUT-OUTS of scene dissolving out.

Scene that is being dissolved in must be exposed here.

Except when using pegs (See sample exposure sheet for sliding peg action.) Do not write in these three columns. They are used by the Camera Dept.

Expose all pan moves with their start & stop letters thru-out the scene. The PAN move must be with the change of BKG. POS. directions to which for PANS in the DWGS. used in at the exposure on that frame which it register. occurs.

Be sure you call for the proper camera to be used in the "instruction" column. If an OVERLAY is to be used indicate it in this column.

All notes for APPROACHES or RECEDES must appear here and fields be indicated in the "fields" column. FIELDS must be exposed thru-out the scene.

Indicate length of all camera PANS, APPROACHES or RECEDES.

EXAMPLE Start 3 ft. APPROACH TO FIELD 3. Indicate length of X-Dis. FADE IN, FADE OUT that the CIRCLE IN OR PAN is OUT. held in the (A) EXAMPLE POS. on START 3 ft. X-the BKG. DIS. TO 3C. for the Be sure APP-dwgs. ROACHES RECEDES with X-DIS. CIRCLES frame pos. and FADES are 22 To 26. exposed for The dwgs. lengths indiwith cated. frame 27, 28 are used with Pan Pos. 2 Frame 29 used with Pan Pos. 3 etc. This removes any doubt as to which DWG. goes with WHICH PAN MOVE.

A line running thru the exposures from the hold Pos. of the pan is sufficient to the next PAN MOVE.

| | | | | |
|---|---|---|---|---|

FILL OUT THE HEADING OF <u>EVERY TRACING GUIDE</u> USED WITH THE SCENE.

# TRACING GUIDE

Indicate what No. guide this is ?                                        No _____ -13-

Job No._____                        Scene No._____

Drawings ___ to ___ also inked separately.

| CEL NO. | TRACE DRAWINGS AS FOLLOWS: |
|---------|----------------------------|

The TRACING GUIDE is used to combine some of the actions in the scene in order to retain a three cel level.

It is very important in combining repeats, that you make every effort to keep them in MULTIPLES OF THE SAME NUMBER OF DRAWINGS, so as to avoid unnecessary trace-ups to get into a hook-up.

List the drawings to be combined in the order in which they are to be traced, reading from left to right. A drawing, that overlays another with which it is to be combined, should be inked first. Hook-up drawings must be circled in the same manner as those appearing on exposure sheets.

Give the combined drawings a new set of numbers. Unless any of the separate drawings making up a combination are to be used alone, let these new numbers be the only ones to appear on the exposure sheets.

THIS CARD SHOULD BE A CONDENSED VERSION OF THE TECHNICALITIES OF THE SCENE.

## FLEISCHER STUDIOS

Job No._____    Title_____    Scene No._____

| MODEL | DWG. No. | Description _____ FILL OUT HERE A BRIEF DESCRIPTION |
| --- | --- | --- |

IN THIS BOX LIST AT
LEAST ONE DRAWING OF
EVERY CHARACTER AND
PROP IN THE SCENE,
PREFERABLY THE DRAWING
WHICH REVEALS IT MOST
CLEARLY AND COMPLETELY.

Description _____ FILL OUT HERE A BRIEF DESCRIPTION
OF THE MAIN ACTION IN THE SCENE.

((This card must accompany the scene thru
all the production departments. All the
details for the technical handling of
the scene must be properly filled in.)

Animated by_____    Footage_____

## DEPARTMENTAL INSTRUCTIONS

BACKGROUND DEPT.  Type Bkg. Used_____    Bkg. Used with Sc._____
Bkg.—Overlays  FILL IN ALL NOTES CONCERNING ANY SPECIAL HANDLING OF BKG.
Bkg.—Underlays  LIST ALL CELS TO BE RETOUCHED BY BKG. DEP'T.  LIST ALL
List C. O.'s to be rendered by Bkg. Dept  OVER-LAYS AND UNDER-LAYS.  NOTE WHETHER BKG.
IS A STILL OR A PAN AND IF USED FROM, OR WITH, ANOTHER SCENE.  OK'ed by_____

TIMING DEPT.  Exp. Sheets #_____To #_____
(LIST ANYTHING OUT OF THE
ORDINARY THAT WILL HAVE TO
BE WATCHED IN CHECKING.)
OK'ed by_____

MUSIC DEPT.
(LIST PRE-SYNC AND POST-SYNC
TALKS AND EFFECTS IN SCENES.
OK'ed by_____

INBETWEEN DEPT._____  ALL SPECIAL NOTES TO THE INBETWEENER MUST APPEAR HERE.
IF THE INBETWEENER IS TO SEE THE ANIMATOR BEFORE INBETWEENING THE
SCENE, THE NOTE MUST APPEAR HERE.
OK'ed by_____

INKING DEPT._____  ALL SPECIAL NOTES TO THE INKER MUST APPEAR HERE.
Cels Used From Other Sc's_____
Tracing Charts_____
Tracing Guides_____
Sliding Cels_____    OK'ed by_____

PLANNING DEPT._____

COLORING DEPT.  Sample Cels_____
ALL SPECIAL NOTES PERTAINING TO THE COLORING
OF THE SCENE MUST APPEAR HERE.

Planned by_____    Matched by_____    OK'ed by_____

CAMERA DEPT.  Type Camera Used_____    Fields Used_____

| Cut From Sc. | Cut To Sc. | (ALSO NOTE HERE IF BKG. |
| --- | --- | --- |
| ☐ Ft. Diss. From Sc. | ☐ Ft. Diss. To Sc. | OR DWGS. ARE USED FROM |
| ☒ Ft. Fade In | ☐ Ft. Fade Out | ANOTHER SCENE — IF BKG. IS |
| ☐ Ft. Circle In | ☐ Ft. Circle Out | STILL OR PAN, AND ANGLE OF PAN.) |

Photo by_____    OK'ed by_____

...cel scene O.K'd by
...verse side of this card properly filled out

**DRAWINGS**

Ass't. — Timing Dept.

1. Details on drawings check through
2. Hook-ups clearly noted on drawings
3. Cut-outs clearly marked on drawings
4. Matching indicated where necessary
5. Trace-backs clearly noted on drawings
6. Check movement of acr: with Pan Bkg.
7. Acr: completed ½" beyond cutting field
8. Top and Bottom Pegs clearly indicated
9. Tracing Guides properly laid out
10. Shift Charts properly planned out
11. Registry of cut-outs or sliding cels in relation to pan noted
    on drawings and sheets

**BACKGROUNDS**

1. Job No., Scene No. and Footages indicated
2. Start and Stop positions indicated on Pan Bkg.
3. Handling of O-Lays and U-Lays indicated
4. Special handling indicated on drawings and Pink Card

**EXPOSURE SHEETS**

1. Characters listed in column headings
2. Drawings or Bkgs. from other scene listed
3. Necessary Field notes exp. thru-out Scene
4. Fades, start and cut indicated
5. Proper camera called for
6. Approach's and Recedes clearly exposed
7. Cross dissolves (to or from) exposed
8. Cel levels taken care of
9. Cut-outs exposed thru-out scene
10. Drawings on TWO'S working together
11. Hook-ups indicated with red circle
12. Pan moves exposed thru-out scene
13. Exp. sheet headings filled out
14. Dial Nos. in consecutive order (Numbered)

Assistant's Name                    Timer's Name

- 15 -

| | |
|---|---|
| Characters and Props | Keep characters uniform by checking with the original models.  Be sure that all color separations are drawn in with a definite line closing in these areas. Check props handled in your scene with other scenes using these props, for uniformity in handling. |
| Handling of Shadows | Don't make large shadows under characters except for special effects.  Keep them small and narrow, bearing in mind that usually their purpose is simply to indicate how far off the ground the character is.  Make them disappear entirely  when the character stops in one place, unless, of course, it is a special effect. |
| Presentation of two or more characters in a scene | Don't forget to check on the coordination of the action when two or more characters are working in a scene at the same time.  Not only should they look as if they react properly to each other, but they should be planned to give each other working space. This requisite may often be overlooked if each character is animated by itself, instead of using the others at the same time, as a check. |

- 16 -

| Animation of Effects | Do not pass lightly over Animation Effects such as splashes, dust, smoke, fire, water and blur or speed effects, believing them to be of no importance. They help the presentation of your scene and the proper number of drawings should be used for the right effect. It is also important to indicate with colored pencils, the various tones necessary, so that the inbetweeners can follow the action and the opaquers apply color with the least amount of color flashes. See that all differently toned areas are closed in with definite lines. |

| Effects Card | Wherever possible, all effects will be planned to be carried out with "straight opaqueing." |

SPECIAL EFFECTS
FLEISCHER STUDIOS

JOB NO._____ SCENE NO._____

NAME EFFECT_____

AUTHORIZED BY_____

FIND INSTRUCTIONS_____

RETOUCH CELS FROM_____ TO_____
- - - - - - - - - - - - - - - - - - - -
TRANSPARENCIES ☐   DRY BRUSH ☐
AIR-BRUSHING ☐   MISC. RETOUCHING ☐

USE SAMPLE_____ O.K'd BY_____

SCENE TO BE SENT TO_____
(BEFORE)-(AFTER)OPAQUING(Cross out)

NO. OF CELS TO BE RETOUCHED_____

CELS POLISHED FOR RETOUCHING BY____

CELS RETOUCHED BY_____

RETOUCHING CHECKED BY_____

CELS POLISHED FOR CAMERA BY_____

O.K. FOR CAMERA_____

If it is necessary to use transparent colors, dry brush, air brush or any retouching on a cel or a series of cels, an effects card, properly filled out, must accompany the scene. The animator need only fill in the information up to the dotted line. This card must go behind the regular window card on the folder.

If the effect involves more than one scene or has to be carried thru-out a picture, it must be O.K'd by Izzy Sparber or Seymour Kneitel.

- 17 -

Window Cards
for folder

Two differently colored cards are used
each for a separate purpose. The
proper one for each scene, must be
used.

FLEISCHER STUDIOS

Job No................................ Sc No..........................

ANIMATOR................................ Ft...........................

Scene used with Sc No..........................

Scene used with Sc No..........................

Colors marked................ Timed.................

Dwgs Stamped              Stamped
for Inb'tnrs................    for Inkers................

Foreign & Production Script OK................

Inbetweened.............. No. Dwgs..............

Inb'twns Ck'd............. OK to Ink.............

Inked............. Planned .............

Colored............. Matched.............

PINK WINDOW CARDS . . .
This card is to be used
when:

a) The scene dissolves to
   or from another scene.

b) You use drawings from
   another scene or draw-
   ings from your scene are
   used in another.

c) Background from one scene
   is used in another.

FLEISCHER STUDIOS

Job No........................ Sc No..........................

ANIMATOR................................ Ft...........................

Colors marked................ Timed.................

Dwgs Stamped              Stamped
for Inb'tnrs................    for Inkers................

Foreign & Production Script OK................

Inbetweened.............. No. Dwgs..............

Inb'twns Ck'd............. OK to Ink.............

Inked............. Planned .............

WHITE WINDOW CARD . . .
This card is to be used
when the background or
drawings in your scene
are NOT used in any
other.

INSTRUCTIONS FOR PENCIL TESTS

PENCIL TEST WINDOW CARDS.

This card, properly filled
out, must appear in the
folder of the scene or
action to be Pencil Tested.

```
PENCIL TEST

Job No. _____   Sc. No. _____

Inbetweened _____   No. Dwgs ____

OK for Camera _____

Pencil Test Photo'd _____

Pencil Test Ok'd _____
```

Job Sheet

A Job Sheet, properly filled out,
must accompany each scene.  This
Job Sheet will be photographed
at the beginning of each pencil
test.

```
JOB _____ SEQ. _____ SCENE _____
TEST# _____ TYPE _____
DIRECTOR _____
ANIMATOR _____
FOOTAGE _____
REMARKS:


                           DATE _____
```

- 19 -

Pencil Test
Exposure
Sheets

Each scene must be exposed on Pencil
Test Exposure Sheets.

Dialogue...music...sound effects...and
sound analysis, must be duplicated on
the Pencil Test Exposure Sheets, using
the same dial numbers as on the production exposure sheets.  If the scene
is being animated to beats, these must
also be on the Pencil Test Sheets in
their proper dial positions.

All camera instructions pertaining to
the Pencil Test must be indicated on
these sheets.

If the background is to be used with the
pencil test, it must be called for on
the Pencil Test Exposure Sheet, otherwise the scene will be photographed
without a background.

Camera fields must be indicated.

Pencil Test Exposure Sheets for an
O.K.'d pencil test must remain in the
folder with the scene when it goes
through for production.

If the timing of any part of an O.K.'d
pencil test is changed, mark a cross
thru that section on the Pencil Test
Sheets.

Animation
for Pencil
Tests

If the action to be pencil tested is
rather lively, it should be drawn in
the rough only.  This action should be
handled as simply as possible, minus
details, but still keeping its propor-
tions and perspective relative to the
background.  Mouth actions are not
necessary on these roughs.

If the action is rather closely spaced,
it is advisable to animate for the
pencil test in the clean up.

All mob and crowd scenes should also
be animated in the clean up for the
pencil test.

Rough animation will not go to the
Inbetween Department.  In this case the
necessary inbetweens for the pencil
test must be filled in by the Assistant.

A scene, animated in the clean up for a pencil test, should be sent to the Timing Department complete with all necessary information for the test. The Timing Department will check it; send it to the inbetween Department for any necessary inbetweens, and return it to the animator before the test for checking. The scene should then be returned to the Timing Department O.K.'d for the pencil test.

A single scene may be animated for a pencil test, part in the rough and part in clean up, depending on the action involved. If this is done, the Assistant will complete the roughs. The completed scene will than be sent to the Timing Department with a sheet of written instructions folded over the drawings requiring clean up inbetweens.

A scene animated for pencil test, whether in rough or clean up, should be handled just as you expect to have the action appear in final production.

After cleaning up a scene that has been animated in the rough for a pencil test, the inbetweened roughs should be kept separately with a note to the inbetweener indicating whether or not roughs are to be used for inbetweening and if so, to what extent; i.e. whether to clean up the roughs or just use them for the general swing of the action, cleaning them up on new sheets.

**Limit of Paper Levels**

No more than three (3) sheets can be photographed for a pencil test at one time. It must be remembered that each sheet photographs transparently, and that all lines on the underlay drawings and on the background, will appear on the film.

The background must be counted as one sheet unless the background IS put on a cel for that purpose.

**Type of Background**

A shaded or colored Background cannot be used for pencil tests. When a background is required, it should be drawn in outline, minus unnecessary details. For a pencil test, try to keep the action area in the background clear.

- 21 -

Color of
Pencil Lines

Drawings for pencil tests must be drawn
with black, red or sepia pencil lines.

Green, blue and violet do not photograph
and cannot be used for pencil tests.

Approaches

An approach from one field to another must
be arranged as follows:

Make a cel of the Cutting Fields, you
are approaching or receding from,
with a line drawn from each of the four
corners of one field, to each of the four
corners of the other.

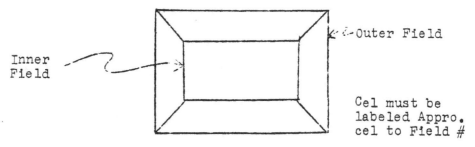

Inner
Field

Outer Field

Cel must be
labeled Appro.
cel to Field #

This Approach Cel must be indicated on
the Pencil Test Exposure Sheet and is to
be held for the length of the camera
approach.

Approach
Field Mask

When Approach Field is reached, a mask
labeled "FIELD #_____" must be called for
on the exposure sheet, and is to be held
as long as the Approach Field is used.

Recede

If a Recede IS desired, reverse the above
process.

Cross
Dissolves

When one scene cross-dissolves to another,
it should be handled as follows:

A cross is to be drawn over the field of
a cel with instructions on the Exposure
Sheets for the Camera Department to
hold this cel for $\frac{1}{2}$ the length of the
dissolve at the end of the scene fading
out, and for $\frac{1}{2}$ the length of the dissolve at the beginning of the scene
fading in.

| | |
|---|---|
| **Fade Out and Fade In** | If a scene is to Fade Out or Fade In, call for a cross-cel to be held over the field for the full length of the fade. "FADE OUT" or "FADE IN" should be lettered across the bottom of the cel in this case. |
| | If an action is to Fade In or Fade Out, a cel lettered "FADE IN" or "FADE OUT" should be called for to flash on at the beginning of the fade and off at the end. This lettering should be clear of the action. The action should also flash on at the beginning of the fade, and flash off at the end of it. |
| **Sliding Pegs** | There are no Bottom Sliding Pegs on the Pencil Test Camera, only Top Sliding Pegs. |
| | If your scene calls for Top and Bottom Sliding Pegs, the test will have to be shot in two sections. |
| | Action that must be traced on a Shift Chart for final production, may be used for a pencil test on the sliding pegs under the Pencil Test Camera. |
| **Pans** | Horizontal Pans are the only ones that can be used with action drawings on the Pencil Test Camera. |
| | Fast diagonal or vertical pans, however, can not be used with action drawings and may be shot as follows: |
| | Make a paper layout of the pan with pan moves indicated and the background roughly traced. At the beginning of this pan layout, trace the drawing used when pan starts moving, and at the end of the layout, trace drawing used when the pan stops. |
| **Loop Shots** | Loop Shots must be exposed for not less than four feet. |
| | **All instructions must be in writing and must accompany the scene.** Verbal instructions will be considered as NO INSTRUCTIONS. |
| | If it is necessary that the Inbetweener see the Animator before inbetweening the clean-ups for a Pencil Test scene, a note to that effect must be clipped to the folder. |

THE HEADING OF EACH PENCIL TEST EXPOSURE SHEET IN A SCENE MUST BE
PROPERLY FILLED OUT AT CHECKS.

---

**FLEISCHER STUDIOS INC.** **PENCIL TEST** **SHEET NO.** ✓

**JOB NO#** ✓  **TITLE** ✓  **SEQ#** **SC#** **TEST#** ✓

**DIRECTOR** ✓  **ANIMATED BY** ✓  **INBETWEENED BY** ✓

| MUSIC | | | | DIAL | DRAWINGS | | | CAMERA | | | MUSIC | | | | DIAL | DRAWINGS | | | CAMERA | | |
|---|---|---|---|---|---|---|---|---|---|---|---|---|---|---|---|---|---|---|---|---|---|
| | M | A | B | NO | T | M | B | PAN | FIELD | INSTRUCTIONS | | M | A | B | NO | T | M | B | PAN | FIELD | INSTRUCTION |
| COPY ALL | | | | 01 | | | | ALL CAMERA | | | | | | | 51 | | | | | | |
| DIALOGUE, | | | | 02 | | | | | | | | | | | 52 | | | | | | |
| MUSIC, | | | | 03 | | | | NOTES MUST | | | | | | | 53 | | | | | | |
| SOUND | | | | 04 | | | | BE INDICATED | | | | | | | 54 | | | | | | |
| EFFECTS & | | | | 05 | | | | IN THESE | | | | | | | 55 | | | | | | |
| SOUND | | | | | | | | COLUMNS. | | | | | | | | | | | | | |
| ANALYSIS | | | | 06 | | | | (FIELDS-- | | | | | | | 56 | | | | | | |
| FROM | | | | 07 | | | | DISSOLVES | | | | | | | 57 | | | | | | |
| PRODUCTION | | | | | | | | FADES FIELD | | | | | | | | | | | | | |
| SHEETS | | | | 08 | | | | MASKS ETC.) | | | | | | | 58 | | | | | | |
| AND | | | | 09 | | | | | | | | | | | 59 | | | | | | |
| COPY | | | | | | | | | | | | | | | | | | | | | |
| ALL BEATS | | | | 10 | | | | BE SURE TO | | | | | | | 60 | | | | | | |
| AT PROPER | | | | 11 | | | | NOTE IF | | | | | | | 61 | | | | | | |
| DIAL NOS. | | | | 12 | | | | BACKGROUND | | | | | | | 62 | | | | | | |
| | | | | 13 | | | | IS TO BE | | | | | | | 63 | | | | | | |
| | | | | 14 | | | | USED. | | | | | | | 64 | | | | | | |
| | | | | 15 | | | | | | | | | | | 65 | | | | | | |
| | | | | 16 | | | | | | | | | | | 66 | | | | | | |
| | | | | 17 | | | | | | | | | | | 67 | | | | | | |
| | | | | 18 | | | | | | | | | | | 68 | | | | | | |
| | | | | 19 | | | | | | | | | | | 69 | | | | | | |
| | | | | 20 | | | | | | | | | | | 70 | | | | | | |
| | | | | 21 | | | | | | | | | | | 71 | | | | | | |
| | | | | 22 | | | | | | | | | | | 72 | | | | | | |
| | | | | 23 | | | | | | | | | | | 73 | | | | | | |
| | | | | 24 | | | | | | | | | | | 74 | | | | | | |
| | | | | 25 | | | | | | | | | | | 75 | | | | | | |
| | | | | 26 | | | | | | | | | | | 76 | | | | | | |
| | | | | 27 | | | | | | | | | | | 77 | | | | | | |
| | | | | 28 | | | | | | | | | | | 78 | | | | | | |
| | | | | 29 | | | | | | | | | | | 79 | | | | | | |
| | | | | 30 | | | | | | | | | | | 80 | | | | | | |
| | | | | 31 | | | | | | | | | | | 81 | | | | | | |
| | | | | 32 | | | | | | | | | | | 82 | | | | | | |
| | | | | 33 | | | | | | | | | | | 83 | | | | | | |
| | | | | 34 | | | | | | | | | | | 84 | | | | | | |
| | | | | 35 | | | | | | | | | | | 85 | | | | | | |

- 24 -

STANDARD FIELD CAMERA
(Black & White or Color)

Field Range    The abbreviated term for this camera
               is "SF-CAM." This camera is a set
               field camera and cannot be moved in
               any direction. It is the smaller
               of our two set fields.

Background     On this camera you can pan vertically,
Panning        horizontally, or diagonally at any
Range          angle.

Limitations    You cannot shoot an Approach or a
               Recede or use any of the Approach
               Fields on the Standard Field Camera.
               You cannot shoot a scene using Slid-
               ing Pegs on it. (A shift chart
               must be used instead.) However you
               can make use of the Standard Field
               Sliding Peg Camera on the Standard
               Field.

When to        If your scene does not call for an
Use the        Approach, Recede or Sliding Pegs, either
Standard       the Standard Field or Large Field
Field          Camera must be used.
Camera
               The only exceptions to this, would be
               in the animation of a close-up where
               it would save the making of
               unnecessarily large drawings by
               shooting it on a smaller field on
               the Approach Camera, or a cut to an
               action or background already used, that
               would necessitate a different size
               field. In other words, use this
               camera as much as possible.

- 25 -

## <u>LARGE FIELD CAMERA</u>
(Black & White or Color)

| | |
|---|---|
| Fields Range allowed | The abbreviated term for this camera is "LF-CAM." |
| | This camera is a set field camera and can not be moved in any direction. It is the larger of the two set fields. (#1 field on the pegs.) |
| Background Panning Range | You can pan vertically, horizontally, or diagonally at any angle with this camera. |
| Limitations | You cannot shoot an Approach or a Recede or use any of the Approach Fields on the Large Field Camera. You cannot shoot a scene using Sliding Pegs on it. (A Shift Chart must be used instead) However, you can make use of the Large Field Sliding Peg Camera on the Large Field. |
| When to Use the Large Field Camera | This camera should only be used for animating long shots that would be more difficult to handle on the smaller field. |

<u>APPROACH CAMERA</u>
(Black & White)

The abbreviated term for this camera is
"APP-CAM."

It is important that you do not use
any of the Approach Cameras unless the
action in the scene necessitates it.
Don't make a layout and then lay the
various fields over it to see which
one will fit best.  If the Approach
Camera is not necessary, compose your
layout in either the Standard or
Large Field.  Don't plan your scene
<u>with slight shifts of the field.</u>

Extent of          This camera can be used for Approach-
Approach or        ing or Receding between field #1 and
Recede             the smallest field, #16, used in any
                   section within the cutting field of
                   the #1 field.

Limitations        There are no limitations in the scene
for Handling .     if you are <u>panning horizontally only.</u>
Pans
                   Vertical pans can be used if they
                   do not exceed the width of the large
                   field paper.

                   If a horizontal pan is on either end
                   of a vertical pan, you must plan your
                   background with a splitting section,
                   so that the horizontal section of the
                   pan can be disconnected during the
                   vertical panning.

                   In a horizontal pan, you cannot pan
                   a vertical pan in or out if it is
                   above the pegs, without a splitting
                   section planned to be disconnected
                   during the horizontal panning.

Diagonal           There are extreme limitations on the
Pans               angle for a diagonal pan on the
                   Approach Camera.  Check with steel-
                   plate "Diagonal Pan Guide for the
                   Approach Camera", showing the extreme
                   angles and limitations of cutting field.
                   If the diagonal pan is necessary, lay
                   out the angle you intend to pan, and
                   the size cutting field you intend to
                   use, and check them with the Camera
                   Department.  A Camera Department
                   O.K. must be initialed on the back-
                   ground layout.

- 27 -

| | |
|---|---|
| Use of Cutting Fields | Black Mask Fields (number 1 to 16) are all projection cutting fields. These are the only fields you are permitted to use at any stopping point in an approach or a recede. Do not call for intermediate fields. |
| How to Indicate Camera Arc in Curved Camera Pans | Find the exact centers of your fields by drawing a cross from the corners of the cutting field, then indicate the desired arc for the camera pan by drawing this curve from the center of one field to the other. |
| | Dotted lines on cels attached to fields are the Safety Fields. All important action and lettering must be inside of this Safety Field. The Safety Field is to be used only as a guide to make certain that important action is within its limits. Never put the safety field on any of the drawings. It may become confused with the Cutting Field. In other words, the only fields that will go thru production with a scene are the Cutting Fields. Each Scene, designated for the approach camera, must be accompanied by a tracing of the cutting field used in that particular scene. |
| Composition of Scene | All scenes will be laid out in composition with the Cutting Fields. |
| How to Call for Cutting Fields | Never refer to the Cutting Fields by the numbers indicated on them. Instead call them, Field A--B--C--etc. Be sure a tracing of the field or fields used accompanies the scene thru production. When the same field is used in two or more scenes, a tracing of the field or fields must accompany each scene. |
| | Fields must be exposed on the Exposure Sheets thru-out the scene in the Field Column and also noted in the camera section of the Large Pink Card. |
| Distance that Action Must be Carried Out-side of Cutting Fields | IT IS IMPERATIVE THAT ALL LAYOUTS AND ACTION BE CARRIED AT LEAST HALF AN INCH OUTSIDE OF THE CUTTING FIELD ON ALL SIDES. Be sure that the size of paper on which you are animating permits the action to be carried this distance beyond the cutting field. |
| Effects that can Be Handled with the Approach Camera | You can completely revolve a scene, including the cel action, on a still background only if it is within the size of our #9 field centered on the pegs. The background, in this case, must be rendered to our #1 Cutting Field. |
| | You can also obtain swinging and rocking effects, but do not plan these scenes without first consulting the Camera Department. |

27-A

L.F. <u>Sliding Peg Approach Camera</u>

The abbreviated term for this camera is
"S.P. App. Cam.

The camera is equipped with sliding pegs top
and bottom.

You can approach or recede between fields #1
and #16 both in color and Black and White.

Fields and pegs can revolve in a complete circle.
Size of field must be considered - due to the
corners being cut off as the field is turned.

Sliding pegs can be used with the platten in still
position or revolving or at any angle.

The platten must be turned sideways for vertical
pans, because they do not fit under a peg bar.
This reduces the size of the field and requires
animation to be drawn in relation to the camera
rather than to the relation of the pegs.

The diagonal pan problem is the same as the
vertical pan problem.

Before an animator lays out a scene for this
camera it will be well to have him check with
Charles Schettler.

- 28 -

APPROACH CAMERA
(color)

The abbreviated term for this Camera is also "APP-CAM."

The instructions for the use of this camera are the same as for the Black and White Approach Camera with the exception of the size field you can approach.

The smallest field you can approach in the center of your #1 field is field #13.

The smallest field you can approach in any corner of the #1 field is field #12.

- 29 -

STANDARD FIELD SET-BACK CAMERA
(Black & White or Color)

The abbreviated term for this camera is "SFSB-CAM".

The purpose of this camera is to give a third dimensional
effect to the background. The glass on which the cels are
shot is mounted vertically in front of a large turntable
where an actual miniature set is constructed. This set
is built in perspective and turns on a pivot point so
that the farther an object is from the lens, the slower
it moves, thus creating an illusion of depth in the background.

This camera should only be used in PANS and for scenes that
will show up this effect to best advantage.

| | |
|---|---|
| Fields Allowed | This camera is a set field camera and can not be moved in any direction. It is the smaller of the two Set-Back Fields. (Check with steel-plate standard field for exact size of field.) |
| Background Panning Allowed | You can use horizontal, vertical or diagonal pans on the Set-Back Camera. You can go from a horizontal to a vertical to a diagonal or any combination of the three. |
| Limitations | You cannot shoot an approach, a recede, or any approach field, or call for sliding pegs on this camera. |
| Background Layout | A layout to be used for this camera is drawn up the same as it would be for the ordinary pan, but efforts should be made to have an arrangement to allow for objects in the background to cross each other in panning. |
| Pan Moves | Plan your pan moves the same as you would for the ordinary pan. |
| Animation | Action must be planned so that there is no direct matching to anything in the Set-back Set. |

- 30 -

| | |
|---|---|
| Overlays | If an overlay is arranged to extend below the bottom Cutting Field, it can be a Cut-out, thereby saving a cel. |
| | If the overlay is within the Cutting-Field, it must go on a sliding cel. |
| Cel Levels | Three cel levels are allowed. The general rule for jumping cel levels applies here too. Cut-outs or repeats on sliding cels cannot be used, but one sliding cel may be used to pan a cut-out in, out, or thru a scene. |
| | It is a good principle in animating for the set-back camera to keep the cel levels down as low as possible, that is, if it does not necessitate unnecessary trace-backs. Best results are obtained with single cel action. |
| How to Arrange for a Set-Back | Before you definitely plan your scene for a Set-Back shot you must consult Johnny Burks. |

LARGE FIELD SET-BACK CAMERA
(Black & White & Color)

The abbreviated term for this camera is "LFSB-CAM".

Field Allowed      This camera is a set field camera and
cannot be moved in any direction.  It
is the larger of the two set-back
fields.  (Check with steel-plate Large
Field for exact size of field.)

Background        Only horizontal pans can be shot on
Panning Allowed   this camera.

The same instructions that hold for
the Standard Field Set-Back Camera
hold for the Large Field Set-Back Camera
with the above exceptions.

Be sure to see Johnny Burks before definitely planning
to lay out a Large Field Set-Back shot.

- 32 -

STANDARD FIELD SLIDING PEG CAMERA

LARGE FIELD SLIDING PEG CAMERA
(Black & White or Color)

The abbreviated term for the Standard Field Sliding Peg
Camera is "SFSP-CAM".

The abbreviated term for the Large Field Sliding Peg
Camera is "LFSP-CAM."

The purpose of these cameras is to save unnecessary
work and trace-ups. They should only be used where
such savings can be accomplished.

The sliding-pegs can only be used in horizontal
actions and pans.

Both cameras have practically the same limitations,
the only exception being that no more than four field
sliding-cels may be used on the large field camera.

Types of Action          A repeat action, used in various sec-
Adaptable to             tions of the scene, is adaptable. If
Sliding-Pegs             otherwise, it is advisable to call for
                         a Shift-Chart instead of using sliding-
                         cels.

  a.    For bringing a repeat action
        through, in or out of a still
        scene;

  b.    For bringing a repeat action
        through, in or out of a pan;

  c.    For panning an action, (not in
        a panning action itself) in, or
        out of a scene. The advantage
        in this case, is that on the
        sliding-pegs, this action may
        be exposed on twos, whereas, in
        the regular pan it must be on
        ONES.

- 34 -

| | |
|---|---|
| Registry<br>Marks<br>Cont'd. | <u>Before making this new Registry Mark, be<br>sure the background is on the pegs in<br>its last Horizontal Pan Registry.</u> |
| Operation<br>of Sliding-<br>Peg Camera | These cameras have top and bottom sliding-<br>pegs and a movable background board that<br>can be used only in horizontal pans.<br><br>Top or bottom sliding-pegs, or the<br>background board can be moved together<br>or separately, in the same or oppos-<br>ing directions.  Also, anyone of the<br>three may be held while the other two<br>are panning.<br><br>If only one set of sliding pegs are<br>necessary, give the top pegs the pre-<br>ference. |
| Overlay<br>Flaps | An Overlay Flap attached to the back-<br>ground can be used if the bottom<br>sliding-pegs are not used at the same<br>time.<br><br>An Overlay Flap can be used with the<br>top and bottom pegs in operation if the<br>Overlay Flap is punched and used on<br>either the top or bottom pegs, and<br>the pegs with which it is used are<br>moving at the same speed as the back-<br>ground. |
| Pan Moves | All Pan Moves for the Top and Bottom<br>pegs or the background must be figured<br>in multiples of <u>128th of an inch</u>  which<br>is the slowest movement possible.<br>(It will not be possible to use the<br>sliding pegs for your scene if it is<br>not figured in multiples of this speed). |
| Exposing<br>of Pan Moves | A separate column of Pan Moves will have<br>to be exposed for each of the three<br>movable sections.  <u>Do NOT call for the<br>Pan Moves by numbers as in an ordi-<br>nary pan.</u>  Instead, call for the<br>exact speed in inches or fractions<br>thereof, in which each particular<br>section is moving, and precede each<br>marking with the abbreviation for the<br>direction in which it is panning.  The<br>abbreviated terms used for simplicity<br>in marking are: |

- 35 -

```
"TP"----------Top Pegs
"BP"----------Bottom Pegs
"BKG"---------Background
"L"-----------Left
"R"-----------Right
"H"-----------Hold
```

The "right" (R) and "left" (L) must
be the directions the pegs are to be
moved and not the directions of the
section in the scene.

Enumerate carefully each increase or
decrease in speed for every frame.
When the pan is moving at a steady speed,
a line carried down through every exposure required to move at this speed,
is all that is necessary.  To avoid
confusing the symbol for a two exposure hold, with that used for pan
speeds, do not use ditto marks when
the same speed is required for only two
exposures, WRITE EACH MOVE OUT. (Whether
an action is held or in a pan, the Pan
Moves must be exposed on every exposure
sheet of the scene.)

As in an ordinary pan, you must slow in
and out of holds.

 Also, above each action exposed, indicat
on which pegs they are to be used, i.e.
"TP" or "BP".

(See sample Exposure Sheet showing
columns used for sliding-peg moves.)

Animation         Normally, for action animated on the
Paper for         standard peg position (to be inked on
Sliding-Peg       sliding-cels), single field sheets of
Action            Animation Paper may be used.

The sheet, on which the last possible
action can be drawn, is shifted one peg
positon, centering it in the field.
The next sheet is placed on the pegs in
normal position to animate subsequent
action.  Extreme care must be taken to
number properly the center peg position
on every drawing.

The pegs are exactly four inches apart.
You cannot punch new peg holes  between
the pegs, altering this distance.  If
 you do, your scene cannot be photographed on the sliding-peg camera.

If, at the end of a sliding-peg pan your

**Animation Paper for Sliding-Peg Action (cont'd.)**

action happens to be off-center in the field, you must continue animating in this position until the end of the scene, depending on the sliding-peg registry to keep it centered in the field. This pertains to the top and Bottom sliding-pegs and to the background.

**Two-Field Animation Paper**

There are also Two-Field papers punched for use when necessary. They are to be used for repeats occurring in a setting having actions that stretch two fields long.

For repeats longer than two fields, double and single sheets may be pasted together to get the necessary length. When this is done, make sure the distance between each peg position is four inches, no matter how long the sheet. (When the longer sheets are necessary, call the supply department for them.

**Sliding-Cel Sizes**

There are 2, 3, 4, 5, and 6 field Sliding-Cels available for use with the standard field.

Four Field Sliding-Cels are the limit on the large field.

**Method of Handling an Action Animated in a repeat in One Place**

In planning for inking a sliding-pegs, the general idea is to have a blank field precede the action when it comes into the scene, and a blank field follow when it goes out of the scene. This limits your longest action in a scene, to four fields on the standard field, and two on the large field.

If an action is in the field at the start of the scene or remains in the field at the end, the repeat may stretch five fields on the standard field and three on the large field.

- 37 -

Method of
Handling an
Action Anim-
ated in a
Repeat in
One Place
(Cont'd.)

If an action is in the field at the
start of a scene and also at the end,
the repeat may be as long as the full
six fields on the standard field, and
four fields, long on the large field.

The animator must plan his scene with
notes to the inker as to which cel
lengths are to be used, side of cel on
which the action is to be inked, (Right,
Left or Center) and which pegs are to
be used (top or bottom).  When these
notes are missing, the drawings may
erroneously be inked on single field
cels.

On the first drawing of every new set
of action, planned for Sliding Pegs,
a diagram must appear in the upper
right hand corner under the number.

Following is the standard diagram to
be used.

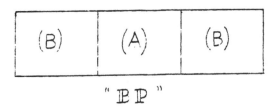

DWGS. 1 to 32

| (B) | (A) | (B) |
|-----|-----|-----|

" B P "

("B" stands for "BLANK" --- "A" stands
for "ACTION".)

The inker in this case will know that
drawings 1 to 32 are to be inked in
the center field of a Three Field
Sliding Cel on the bottom pegs.

DWGS. 64 to 130
" T P "

| (B) | (A) | (A) | (A) | (A) | (B) |
|-----|-----|-----|-----|-----|-----|

In this case drawings 64 to 130 are to
be inked on the four center fields
of a Six Field Sliding Cel on the top
pegs.

| | |
|---|---|
| Method of Handling An ACTION Animated in a Repeat in one Place | The Animator must call for the correct sliding cel lengths in order to avoid handling longer cels than is necessary. |

| | |
|---|---|
| Registry Marks for Repeats on Sliding Cels | With this type of action, a Registry Mark must be drawn on the first drawing of the repeat. This Registry Mark is determined by planning the drawing on the board as it will appear in relation to the field at the start of the scene; then marking the center peg line on the drawing. |

| | |
|---|---|
| Pan Lengths must be accurate | Keep track of the over-all lengths of your pan in order to know just where the action is in the field, in relation to other actions being used with it. This must be done accurately since the panning under the camera is mechanical and should you miscalculate, your scene will not turn out as you had planned. |

| | |
|---|---|
| When Straight Ahead Action is Animated for a Repeat: | When animating straight ahead action to be used as a repeat on sliding-cels, a Shift Chart must be planned so that the drawings can be inked in one registry on the sliding-cels. |

| | |
|---|---|
| Exposing Repeats on TWOS | The standard rule for TWOS in a pan, also applies to sliding peg action. (Where an action is in contact with the background, as in walks, etc., it, too, must be exposed on ONES.)<br><br>Sliding-Cel action, not in a panning action itself, may be exposed on TWOS during a pan. |

- 39 -

**Method of Handling Action Animated Straight Ahead on the Pegs**

Only Two field Cels need be called for when animating straight ahead on the pegs.

The center line on the center peg, is the key registry position. All the drawings in the scene must have a Registry mark registering to this line. The peg position used for the progression of the action is referred to by a number preceeded by the letter "R" (right) or "L" (left) indicating the direction in which the action is moving.

**Method of Marking Peg Registry Positions on the Drawings.**

The first registry Position at the start of the scene would be "CP-1" (Center Peg 1). If the action moved to the left, the next Registry Position would be "RP-2" (Right-peg 2). Then "RP-3"-----"RP-4"---etc.

For example, if the action should stop on "RP-6" and then start animating the other way, the new Registry Positions would be "LP-5"--"LP-4"---etc.

This method keeps the numbers of the sliding-peg positions in register with the peg positions on the background, for checking purposes.

The peg positions on the background must also be numbers 1---2---3--etc., and these must be the positions corresponding to the animation.

**Method of transferring Papers on Board to Animate Straight Ahead**

Single field paper is all that is necessary to animate this type of action.

Animate straight ahead, and as the action reaches the edge of the paper, bring it back on the pegs (calling for the next peg position on ensuing drawings) and continue animating.

**Cel Levels**

The general rule applying to Cel Levels also applies to sliding-cels.

# G. MICHAEL DOBBS

| HEAD ANIMATOR'S O.K. | | | | FLEISCHER STUDIOS INC. | | | | SHEET No. |
| --- | --- | --- | --- | --- | --- | --- | --- | --- |

EXPOSURE SHEETS FOR SCENES ON THE SLIDING PEG CAMERAS MUST BE
Title LAID OUT AS FOLLOWS:

ANIMATOR'S O.K.

Job No._____    Scene No._____

Animation by._____    (THIS IS IN ADDITION TO THE GENERAL INFORMATION ON THE SHEETS.___   Inking by___

Inbetween by___

SEE SAMPLE EXPOSURE SHEETS)

| MUSIC | | | | | | ANIMATION | | | | | | | | CAMERA | | | | |
| --- | --- | --- | --- | --- | --- | --- | --- | --- | --- | --- | --- | --- | --- | --- | --- | --- | --- | --- |
| Music Instructions | Mouth Actions | Beats | Dial No. | ACTION | | ACTION DWGS. | | | | CUT-OUTS | | Dial No. | Pan Moves | Fields | Instructions | | TP | BP |
| | | | | | Top | | | Bottom | | | | | BKG | | | | | |
| | | | | | OLIVE | POPEYE | DOG | | | | | | | | | | | |
| | | | | | TP | BP | BP | | | | | | | | | | | |
| | | | 01 | | 31 | 47A | 63 | | Expose all PAN and | | | 01 | R-¾ | | | | R-¼ | L-⅝ |
| | | | 02 | | ⌐ | 48 | 64 | | SLIDING PEG moves | | | 02 | ⅛ | | | | ⅛ | |
| | | | 03 | | 32 | 49 | 65 | | throughout the scene. | | | 03 | ¼ | | | | ¼ | |
| | | | 04 | | ⌐ | 50 | 66 | | All moves must be | | | 04 | | | | | | |
| | | | 05 | | 33 | 51 | 67 | | figured in multiples | | | 05 | | | | | | |
| | | | 06 | | ⌐ | 52 | 68 | | of 128th of an inch | | | 06 | | | | | | |
| | | | 07 | | 34 | 53 | 69 | | which is the slowest | | | 07 | | | | | | |
| | | | 08 | | ⌐ | 54 | 70 | | movement possible. | | | 08 | ⌐ | | | | | |
| | | | 09 | | 35 | 55 | 71 | | Moves must be called | | | 09 | ⅛ | | | | ⅛ | |
| | | | 10 | | ⌐ | 56 | 62 | | for in inches or frac- | | | 10 | ¼ | | | | ¼ | |
| | | | 11 | | 26 | 57 | 63 | | tions thereof. | | | 11 | ⌐ 3/32 | | | | ⌐ 3/32 | |
| | | | 12 | | ⌐ | 48 | 64 | | To avoid confusing the | | | 12 | Ⓗ | | | | Ⓗ | |
| | | | 13 | | 27 | 49 | 65 | | symbol for an ex- | | | 13 | | | | | | |
| | | | 14 | | ⌐ | 50 | 66 | | posure holds with that | | | 14 | | | | | | |
| | | | 15 | | 38 | 51 | 67 | | used for pan speeds, | | | 15 | | | | | | |
| | | | 16 | | ⌐ | | 68 | | do not use ditto marks | | | 16 | | | | | | |
| | | | 17 | | 39 | | 69 | | when the same speed is | | | 17 | | | | | | |
| | | | 18 | | ⌐ | | 70 | | required for only two | | | 18 | | | | | | |
| | | | 19 | | 40 | | 71 | | exposures. WRITE OUT | | | 19 | | | | | | |
| | | | 20 | | ⌐ | | 72 | | each move. | | | 20 | | | | | | |
| | | | 21 | | 31 | | 73 | | Direction (R or L) must | | | 21 | | | | | | |
| | | | 22 | | ⌐ | | 74 | | precede every move. | | | 22 | | | | | | |
| | | | 23 | | 32 | 52 | 75 | | Hold is indicated with | | | 23 | | | | | | |
| | | | 24 | | ⌐ | | 76 | | an (H) on frame which | | | 24 | | | | | | |
| | | | 25 | | 33 | 53 | 77 | | PAN stops. | | | 25 | | | | | | |
| | | | 26 | | ⌐ | | 78 | | Above each section indi- | | | 26 | | | | | | |
| | | | 27 | | 34 | 54 | 79 | | cate the pegs on which | | | 27 | | | | | | |
| | | | 28 | | ⌐ | | 80 | | they are to be used... | | | 28 | | | | | | |
| | | | 29 | | 35 | 55 | 81 | | TP or BP. | | | 29 | | | | | | |
| | | | 30 | | ⌐ | | 82 | | It is important that | | | 30 | | | | | | |
| | | | 31 | | 36 | 56 | 83 | | you keep your exposure | | | 31 | | | | | | Ⓗ |
| | | | 32 | | ⌐ | | 84 | | sheets clean and neat. | | | 32 | | | | | | |
| | | | 33 | | 37 | 57 | 85 | | All cut-outs must be | | | 33 | | | | | | |
| | | | 34 | | ⌐ | | 86 | | placed on the back- | | | 34 | | | | | | |
| | | | 35 | | 38 | | 87 | | ground registered to | | | 35 | | | | | | |
| | | | 36 | | ⌐ | | 88 | | the center peg. | | | 36 | | | | | | |
| | | | 37 | | 39 | | 89 | | Be sure to indicate | | | 37 | | | | | | |
| | | | 38 | | ⌐ | | 90 | | on the EXPOSURE SHEET | | | 38 | | | | | | |
| | | | 39 | | 40 | 58 | 91 | | whether an OVERLAY is | | | 39 | | | | | | |
| | | | 40 | | ⌐ | | 92 | | to be used and whether | | | 40 | | | | | | |
| | | | 41 | | 31 | 59 | 93 | | it is to be a flap | | | 41 | | | | | | |
| | | | 42 | | ⌐ | | 94 | | attached to the Bkg. | | | 42 | | | | | | |
| | | | 43 | | 32 | 60 | 95 | | or on TP. or BP. | | | 43 | | | | | | |
| | | | 44 | | ⌐ | | 96 | | | CHAIR | | 44 | | | | | | |
| | | | 45 | | 33 | 61 | 97 | | | 10-B | | 45 | | | | | | |
| | | | 46 | | ⌐ | | 98 | | | | | 46 | | | | | | |
| | | | 47 | | 34 | 62 | 99 | | | | | 47 | | | | | | |
| | | | 48 | | ⌐ | | 100 | | | | | 48 | L-1/32 | | | | L-1/32 | R-1/32 |
| | | | 49 | | 35 | 63 | 101 | | | | | 49 | 1/16 | | | | 1/16 | |
| | | | 50 | | ⌐ | | 102 | | | | | 50 | ⌐ ⅛ | | | | ⌐ ⅛ | |

- 41 -

ANALYSIS OF SOUND TRACKS

| | |
|---|---|
| Recording | Sound is recorded with the following identifications: |
| Job Number | Job Number-Spoken into the sound track. (Example)  P 9-4, C 9-7, etc. |
| Punch Number | Punch Number - The sound is usually recorded in sections.  Each time the camera is set in motion, a Punch Number is spoken into the sound track. (Example)  Punch 864, etc. |

Each Punch may also be divided into sections.  For identification purposes, prior to the recording of each section, the Punch Number is repeated, followed by the letter A--B--C--etc.
　　(Example)　Punch 864-A

Should a retake be made during a recording session or at a later date, a new Punch Number must be spoken into the sound track followed by the original punch number.
　　(Example)　　Punch 963--Retake of
　　　　　　　Punch 864.

| | |
|---|---|
| Take Number | Each section of a Punch is usually recorded more than once.  These repeated recordings are referred to as Takes.  The second and ensuing Takes of a section are identified by a corresponding number of "claps" recorded into the sound track preceding each Take. |
| Identification of Selected Sound Tracks | On the first frame preceding the sound of each Take, a Sync Mark is punched into the film. (example)  S-1. |

The Job, Punch, and Take Numbers are written in ink below the Sync Mark as close to it as possible.  (Example)
　　　S-1　　　　　(Sync Mark)
　　　J-P-9-4　　　(Job No.)
　　　P-864　　　　(Punch No.)
　　　T-2　　　　　(Take No.)

| | |
|---|---|
| Reprints | Should the Animator want all or part of a sound track to be used more than once, they should notify the Music Dept. to order a Reprint of the Sound and give him an additional Exposure Roll identified in the following manner. (Example) 2nd Print (3rd-4th-etc.) S-1, J-P-9-4, P-864, T-2. |

Accents    After the Takes have been selected, the
Music Department assembles them in the
approximate order of their appearance in
the picture, and prepares an O.K. Takes
Acetate and a typewritten copy of the
Takes recorded on it.

The Head Animator will then underline those
syllables which he judges the most suited
for accents in animation.

The most emphatic accents will be underlined
with red pencil and the secondary accents
will be underlined with a brown pencil.
These will be the accents indicated on the
Exposure Sheets and Exposure Rolls.

Exposure    For Pre-sync Dialogue and Sound Effects,
Rolls.      the analysis of the sound track is trans-
Pre-sync    ferred to Green Exposure Rolls, which are
Sound.      clipped on the Exposure Sheets where the
(Green Ex-  tracks are to be used.
posure Rolls)

The Sync Mark (S-1) must be printed on the
Green Exposure Roll by the Music Department,
on the same frame as punched in the Sound
Track; and the Job Number, Punch Number and
Take Number must be printed above each Sync.
Mark.

Post-sync Sound.
(White Exposure
Rolls.)      Post-sync Dialogue will be given to the
Animator on White Exposure Rolls, to be
clipped on Exposure Sheets where the dialo-
gue is to be used.

Exposure    There are two types of Exposure Sheets:
Sheets.
1.  GREEN EXPOSURE SHEETS...used with any
action planned to definite music. (Pre-
sync or post-sync). These sheets are
laid out only by the Music Department
and no sheets or Exposures are to be
added or eliminated without this
department's O.K.

2.  WHITE EXPOSURE SHEETS....used for action
that is not planned to definite music.
This means Ad-lib action or action
planned to Beats, Phrases or a pattern
of music.

MADE OF PEN & INK: FLEISCHER STUDIOS - THE FLORIDA YEARS

- 43 -

Green Exposure
Sheets

If the Recording is a song, (vocal or instrumental) the analysis of the sound track will be given to the Animator on Green Exposure Sheets with the Sync. Mark, Job Number, Punch Number and Take Number properly written in.

When the Animator has finally planned his Scene Cuts on the Green Exposure Sheets, they must be returned to the Music Department to have a new Sync Mark written on the sheets for each cut (S-1, S-2, S-3 etc) These new Sync Marks must all be initialed and dated by the Music Department and immediately punched into the Sound Track in its corresponding position.

Where the Sound "carries over" from one scene to the next, it will not be possible to punch S-2, S-3, etc. on the first frame preceding the sound.  In this case, S-2, S-3,etc, must be punched about 2 feet from the beginning of the Scene.

Two or More
Sound Tracks
used Together

When two or more Sound Tracks are being used together they must be clipped to the Exposure Sheets, one over the other.  The top ones must be clipped, along the side only, to allow them to be turned for reading those underneath.

In the above case, each Sound Track must have its own Sync Mark.

In the event of Double Tracks, the Timing Department will send these Exposure Sheets to the Music Department for a combination recording.

After the Timing Department has checked the picture in preparation for the Inbetween Department, all Exposure Sheets containing Double Tracks, will be sent to the Music Department for combination into a single track.  After these tracks have been combined, the first Exposure Sheet must carry the following note at the top of the Music Column:

TRACKS COMBINED
(Initialed---dated)

- 44 -

| | |
|---|---|
| Splitting a Take into Sections | If the length of a Take must be altered in any way, (i.e. part cut out---leader added in the middle---sections of the Take switched) the Exposure Roll must be returned to the Music Department for necessary adjustments. |

Should the Exposure Roll be split into two sections, the new section will be called Sync #2 with the same job, Punch, and Take Numbers.  If in three sections, the third will be called Sync #3, etc.

When a sound "carries over" from one scene to another, an additional Sync Mark must be made for the new scene.  In this case it must be within 2 Ft. in the second scene.  (This is because a Sync Mark on the first frame before the sound, would be out of the length of the scene.)

Should the change in the Exposure Roll consist of adding or cutting but a few frames, a new Sync Mark will not be necessary. Instead the Music Department will adjust the Exposure Roll and the corresponding sound track.

When the above changes become necessary, the Exposure Rolls must be returned to the Music Department where immediate adjustments will be made on both the Exposure Rolls and the corresponding sound tracks. All changes are initialed and dated by the Music Department.

Sounds cut from a Selected TAKE, must not be discarded.  They must be filed away with their Job, Punch and Take Number.

ANIMATORS MUST NEVER ALTER OR CUT EXPOSURE ROLLS.

- 45 -

Emphasizing
the Accents
in Action

It is advisable to anticipate accent poses
to make them more emphatic.  This means
you may hit the accent position in the
action, as many as 2 frames before the
mouth action (which still must be on the
"nose".)  The scale below gives the antici-
pated lengths allowable.

> Accents occurring from 2 to 7 ex-
> posured apart must be on the "nose".

> Animation for accents occurring
> from 8 to more frames apart,
> may be anticipated by two frames.

> Animation for accents occurring
> from 13 to more exposures apart
> may be anticipated by two frames.

If found necessary to anticipate any
action more than 2 frames ahead, it must be
taken up with the Music Department and an
initialed O.K. (dated) must appear in the
music column on the frame where this pose
is to be.

You cannot secure accented action with
smooth running, evenly spaced action.  You
must devise a change of pace to emphasize
the accent.  In some cases, it might be a
slowing up between accented positions,
as an anticipation into the next accent.
In other actions, it might call for an increase in speed to point out the accent.
But in any case, there <u>must</u> be a change of
pace between accents.

<u>The greater the change in speed between the
accents, the more emphatic the accent.</u>

HOW SOUND ANALYSIS SHOULD BE INTERPRETED INTO ACTION

(Do not confuse these directions for animation action, with
the directions for mouth actions, explained in, "HOW TO
TRANSFER SOUND ANALYSIS INTO MOUTH ACTIONS, "pages 49.)

Animation Action        In animating a bit of dialogue or singing,
& Mouth Actions         the mouth actions are really secondary.
                        To make it convincing, the action itself
                        is the important thing.  This does not
                        mean that mouth actions should be
                        slighted.  They must be on the "nose"
                        (accurate) and convincing, but perfect
                        mouth-actions mean nothing, if the action
                        itself is not convincing.

Reading of              The wide Red Symbols are the most empha-
Analysis for            tic Accent positions in a series of words.
Planning Out
Animation               The wide Brown Symbols are the secondary
Action                  accent positions, and must never  be more
                        accented in the action than the Red
                        positions.

                        Wide Blue Symbols represent the sounds of
                        least importance.  These are only "carry
                        thru" positions in action, and should
                        never be emphasized to the extent of
                        confusion with the Red and Brown accents.

Planning the            DO NOT tear headlong into a dialogue scene
Action to Fit           by starting at the first frame of sound
the Sounds              and animating to the end of the track,
                        expecting to obtain convincing action.
                        DO NOT try to create an action to put
                        each word over.  This tends to make it
                        look confusing.  Simplicity will do it!

                        Listen first, to the acetate record, and
                        study the dialogue you are to animate.
                        You will find there is one important accent
                        pose in every series of words, (the Red
                        accent positions).  Roughly, plan out
                        these poses.  Then continue roughing
                        out the Brown accent positions, which
                        should give you all the positions nec-
                        essary, to put that particular dialogue
                        over.

- 47 -

| | |
|---|---|
| Preparatory Gestures | A Preparatory gesture is a supplementary action preceding an emphatic action. |
| How to Use Preparatory Gestures | The greater the distance between the Preparatory gesture and the accented action, the more emphatic the accent becomes. This distance varies with the personality and attitude you are trying to put over. For example: |

A girl stamps her foot and says, "No"!
If she stamped her foot and said, "No" at the same time, it would weaken her attitude; but if she first stamped her foot and then accented the word "no" about 1½ feet later, it would carry more weight.

| | |
|---|---|
| Action on TWOS | For the sake of animating on TWOS, it is permissable to hit any sound one exposure before the planned frame. In any case, do not plan to have any action hit after the sound it accompanies. |

Sound Effects
and Music to
Sound Analysis

The first reaction drawing after a hit
or contact point, should be considered
the beat or accent position of the
sound.  For Example:

     An object hits a hanging dishpan.
     The contact or hit position is
     one exposure before the sound.
     The first reaction drawing of the
     dishpan occurs on the beat or
     sound position.

It is desirable to anticipate repeti-
tious actions in music or sound effects
to make them more convincing.  The
following scale will guide you in
judging the length of this anticipation:

Reactions occurring from 2 to 7 exposures
apart, should be on the "nose".

Reactions occurring from 8 to 12 exposures
apart, may be placed on exposure before
the beat or sound position.

Reactions occurring from 13 exposures to
more, apart, may be placed two exposures
before the beat or sound position.

If it is thought necessary to anticipate a beat or sound effect by more than
2 exposures, the Music Department must
be consulted and an initialed O.K. (dated)
must appear on the frame planned, in the
Music Column of the Exposure Sheet.

Walks to be
done to Music

If a walk is to be planned to music,
do not plan to have the heel come down
on the beat.  The flat boot position
must be considered the beat.  Avoid
having the foot come down heel first,
if possible.

After completing all of the above, you
are ready for applying mouth positions.
(See sample exposure sheet (How to
Transfer Sound Analysis into Mouth
Actions." Page 49.)

FLEISCHER STUDIOS INC.                           SHEET No.

| MUSIC | ANIMATION | CAMERA |
|---|---|---|

Ⓕ B-92
Ⓟ 954A
Ⓣ 2

ANALYZED 1/3/40
BY L.H.

(The following pertains to MOUTH ACTIONS only. See "How Sound Analysis Should Be Interpreted Into Action" first.)

HOW TO TRANSFER SOUND ANALYSIS INTO MOUTH ACTIONS.

Wide RED symbol represents the most emphatic and loudest vowel sound in a series of words.

Wide BROWN symbol represents the secondary vowel sound and MUST NEVER be more emphatic than the RED.

Wide BLUE symbol represents the vowels of least importance. The BLUE should be the mildest of the three so as not to confuse with the RED and BROWN.

A straight line represents the mouth in position to produce the sound indicated.

A tapering line, as illustrated, indicates an increasing or decreasing sound.

A line across at the beginning represents the start of a series of sounds.
A line across at the end represents the finish of a series of sounds.

In exceptional cases, where a single vowel or other single sound has accents within itself, these will be indicated by use of the colors as shown above for accents in different vowels.

The mouth MUST BE OPEN where the wide striations are shown. The size of opening and shape are left to the discretion of the animator. Either the mouth or the teeth MUST BE CLOSED where the following letters are shown: B, D, F, J, L, M, N, P, S, T, V, Z, CH, SH, and TH.

The sound reading is only an analysis of the modulations on the sound track and mean nothing without the words beside it. The words are to show WHAT IS BEING SAID. The sound analysis shows HOW IT IS BEING SAID. Work with BOTH to get the best results. One means nothing without the other.

The personalities, attitudes and moods of the characters also have a direct bearing on the size and shape of the mouth actions. Listen to the acetate record to determine this.

Sound effects are to be interpreted also by the same basic principle as the dialogue reading.

- 50 -

ANIMATION AS RELATED TO MUSIC

1.    All timing is based on the speed with which film runs
through the projector - a rate of 90 feet per minute, or
the equivalent of a foot and a half per second.  Since
a foot of film has 16 exposures, this makes 24 exposures
per second.

2.    If we wish to determine how many exposures a certain
action takes, say an action from "Now" to Now", guesswork, or judgment would invariably prove to be inaccurate.

3.    Instead, we click a stop-watch from "Now" to  "Now".
This method is more accurate.  We can not be very far
off.  But we can't read this timing very closely either.
The error in starting the watch (personal and mechanical) and the possible error in reading may be six or more
exposures off.

4.    But we can time an interval very accurately and conve-
niently.  16 beats of music at a 12 exposure beat is 12
feet, 16 beats of 14 exposure beats is 14 feet, etc.
If you use a stop watch which reads in feet of film,
time a repetition of the interval  16 times.  In doing
so, if you start counting "one" at the start of the
first interval,  you must finish at "seventeen".  For
when you counted "two", only one interval  elapsed.
Now, this total number of feet for the 16 intervals
determines the number of exposures for one interval.

5.    For example, if you clock 16 times a certain interval
and the watch reads 12 feet, then you have been timing
a 12 exposure interval.

6.    This method is very convenient because music runs in
phrases of 8 and 16 beats.

7.    If your stop watch reads in seconds, you should time
24 intervals, stopping at the count of "25".

8.    Where music is not laid out for a scene, the progress of tempo throughout the picture should be considered.  In general, the beat could start at about
12-ex. or 11-ex. and as the story progresses get
faster down to about 9-ex.  In the case of a very
wild finish we can go down to a minimum, or the fast-
est beat of 7-ex., but  remember that beats below 9-ex.
are for really wild action (such as a machine out of
control).  At this rapid beat, action or hits may be
to 14-ex. instead of 7-ex.

- 51 -

9.    Popeye pictures - unless music is laid out - might start at a 12-ex. beat, work faster as the story progresses to a 10 or 9-ex. The spinach episode should be 9-ex. and after the spinach a 15-ex. which is really alternate 8 and 7-ex.

10.    In general, the pictures should progress down from a 12-ex. to 9-ex. and to a 7-ex. in exceptionally fast cases.

11.    Do not select a beat above 12-ex. without consulting the Music Department.

12.    What may be a fast beat for a particular piece of music, may be a slow beat for another, but in general, the beats mentioned above are most practical.

13.    When you time a particular action, do not clock the timing and then go right ahead and use that beat. Consider what the beat of the picture should be at that particular stage of the story, and try to adjust the timing so that it may go to the desired beat. One may argue that it would spoil the animation to change it, but in most cases, it can easily be made to fit the desired beat without much difficulty.

14.    If an animator times various actions in a picture, all within a short period of time, and all with different beats, the music score cannot follow it, and many good opportunities for synchronous action become too difficult to handle and consequently lost to the picture.

15.    Do not get the impression that the beat is some thing to worry about all through the picture. It is only repeat actions that suggest rhythm, and walking steps that require consideration of a beat. Otherwise, the animation can be entirely ad lib, with no regard to a beat.

16.    If an action occurs several times, and it is desirable to have it happen, either every single beat, every two beats, four beats or eight beats. Multiples of four or eight beats are more desirable.

17.    In attempting to time an action, should you have difficulty in tapping out two, three or four taps to a beat, the following method is suggested:

18.    With a metronome in action, when you want one tap to a beat, say the word "chair" to every beat, tapping once with each word.

19.   When you want two taps to a beat say the word "table" to each beat and tap to each <u>syllable,</u> thus giving two taps to each beat.

20.   For three taps per beat, say the word "regular" and tap once to each syllable.

21.   For four taps say "pitter-patter" being sure to say the entire word for each beat.

22.   Where music is laid out to a scene, and you seek a logical spot for a particular action to occur, the tendency is to find an emphatic note or word of the song and place it there, but most often that is the least desirable spot for a sound effect. Usually, the best place is a beat that has no note or word on it. However, it required a knowledge of music to find the most desirable spot and it will usually be found worthwhile to consult the Music Department. They may find a good place between two certain beats, depending of course, on the music.

23.   In showing sparks for a hit, it is unnecessary in small hits to animate the sparks away. Two alternating drawings not traced up, giving an off-register is usually sufficient.

24.   Musical taps which have sparks animating away invariably give the effect of the picture being late, since the eye doesn't see the tiny sparks but does see the larger ones, when it is too late for good synchronization.

25.   If it is desired that the eye see fast synchronization objects that hit quickly, in a rapid succession, these must not be far apart on the screen.

26.   Sometimes we animate a crowd clapping hands and stamping its feet. If done to music, it is best to consult the Music Department. In general, however, it is better to have the "stamp" on the beat and the "clap" on the half beat, rather than the stamping and clapping simultaneously.

27.   Scene changes are best done on the first beat of a phrase, or sentence or music, but the actual cut should be on the half beat. Never cut to a scene on the beat, except for a special effect in the music.

28.   Do not start dialogue or singing on the first frame of the cut. It should be at least six exposures <u>after</u> the start.

29.   Never cut away from a repeat with the action going toward the next beat located in the ensuing scene. In repeats, cut on the action coming out of the last repeat only. There is a tendency to underestimate the amount of time required for a character to react to something it hears or feels. When in doubt about anything concerning a synchronization, consult the Music Department.

- 52 -

19.    When you want two taps to a beat say the word "table"
to each beat and tap to each <u>syllable,</u> thus giving two
taps to each beat.

20.    For three taps per beat, say the word "regular" and
tap once to each syllable.

21.    For four taps say "pitter-patter" being sure to
say the entire word for each beat.

22.    Where music is laid out to a scene, and you seek a
logical spot for a particular action to occur, the
tendency is to find an emphatic note or word of the
song and place it there, but most often that is the
least desirable spot for a sound effect. Usually,
the best place is a beat that has no note or word on
it. However, <u>it required a knowledge of music to find
the most desirable spot and it will usually be found
worthwhile to consult the Music Department. They
may find a good place between two certain beats, depending of course, on the music.</u>

23.    In showing sparks for a hit, it is unnecessary in
small hits to animate the sparks away. Two alternating drawings not traced up, giving an off-register
is usually sufficient.

24.    Musical taps which have sparks animating away invariably give the effect of the picture being late,
since the eye doesn't see the tiny sparks but does
see the larger ones, when it is too late for good
synchronization.

25.    If it is desired that the eye see fast synchronization objects that hit quickly, in a rapid succession,
these must not be far apart on the screen.

26.    Sometimes we animate a crowd clapping hands and stamping its feet. If done to music, it is best to consult
the Music Department. In general, however, it is
better to have the "stamp" on the beat and the "clap"
on the half beat, rather than the stamping and clapping
simultaneously.

27.    Scene changes are best done on the first beat of
a phrase, or sentence or music, but the actual cut
should be <u>on the half beat.</u> Never cut to a scene
on the beat, except for a special effect in the music.

28.    Do not start dialogue or singing on the first frame
of the cut. It should be at least six exposures <u>after</u>
the start.

29.    Never cut away from a repeat with the action going
toward the next beat located in the ensuing scene. In
repeats, cut on the action coming out of the last repeat only. There is a tendency to underestimate the
amount of time required for a character to react to
something it hears or feels. When in doubt about anything concerning a synchronization, consult the
Music Department.

- 53 -

ACETATE RECORDS

For convenience in handling, filing and reference,
Acetate Recordings are divided into eight classifications according to the purpose for which the
ACETATE is to be used.  These classifications
are given the following names:

Types of Record-     1.   DUMMY              ACETATE
ings on Acetate
                     2.   O.K. TAKES            "

                     3.   AUDITION             "

                     4.   TEST                 "

                     5.   P.B.G. ROTO          "

                     6.   P.B.G. SOUND         "

                     7.   SYNC RECORDING       "

                     8.   MIXING               "

Explanations         (The first two types concern animation
                     only.)

                     1.   DUMMY ACETATE is a recording of
                          music or sound providing a tempo,
                          mood or background for animation,
                          and is not a final sound.

                     2.   O.K. TAKES is a record of selected
                          takes from pre-sync sound on film
                          to aid animators in visualizing
                          action.  When possible, individual
                          speeches, songs or sounds will be
                          recorded in the order of the script,
                          with a short, silent space between
                          each.

                     3.   AUDITION ACETATE is a record of possible
                          talent made to determine microphone
                          qualities, and may, or may not be
                          kept on file according to Director's
                          instruction.

                     4.   TEST ACETATE is a record made for
                          technical purposes and is filed
                          only in the Sound Recording Depart-
                          ment.

- 54 -

5.  P.B.G. ROTO ACETATE (meaning)
    PLAYBACK GUIDE FOR ROTOSCOPE)
    is a record of pre-sync dialogue,
    songs or sound which is played in
    sync with the camera, to guide an
    actor when being photographed for
    rotoscope.

    All such records should be made with
    not less than 4 beats in the tempo
    of the sound just preceding it, as
    an Attack Cue.  Thus the  actor knows
    that sound begins on the 5th beat.

    If silent action precedes a sound,
    or occurs between two sounds, Tempo
    Beats should be provided.  Should
    these beats be more than 8 in number,
    spoken numbers should be called into
    the recording as an aid in spacing
    silent action.

    Sound Film prepared for such record-
    ing, should have a Start Mark on
    leader of 192 frames in advance of
    the sound. The last 5 feet of this
    leader may be used for cue beats.

6.  P.B.G. SOUND ACETATE (which means
    PLAY BACK GUIDE FOR Recording
    Sound.)  is a record of sound or
    accompaniment to be played back to
    a singer or speaker through earphones
    as a pitch or tempo guide in making
    further recordings.

    In all cases, not less than 4 beats
    in the tempo of the sound should be
    recorded preceding its beginning
    as Attack Cue.

    Also, the title and musical key
    of the number should be called into
    the recording when possible.

7.  SYNC RECORDING ACETATE - any record
    on acetate to be played with picture.

    This type of recording must be made
    with a spiral Start Mark.

    Always provide a leader with Start
    Mark exactly 192 frames in advance of
    the sound or of the picture contain-
    ing the sound (if not recorded with
    the picture).  If the latter case
    prevails, use the Standard Start
    Mark of the picture, which is also
    192 frames in advance.)

    This name (SYNC. RECORDING ACETATE)
    also applies to the Playback Record
    made simultaneously with a short
    recording on film.

    The OKAY TAKE of such a recording will
    probably be kept permanently in
    the file. Other takes should be
    disposed of upon release of picture.

8.  MIXING ACETATE is a record of any
    sound to be mixed into a later
    recording and should always have a
    Spiral Start Mark except when the
    sound is for background or is non-
    synchronous.

Note: Each record will bear a chronological serial number
    for filing with the type name and other identify-
    ing matter.  The file for all records except Text
    Records will be maintained by the Music Department.
    Records should be returned to this department
    promptly.  The Sound Department will keep a chronolo-
    gical record of all Acetate Recordings.

Hand-          Remember that Acetate Records are not
ling:          as sturdy as the commercial type of
               disc.  They should be kept free of
               dust and played only with the special
               steel needle provided for the purpose.
               When playing, raise and lower pickup
               head carefully.  Do not permit the
               needle to slide laterally across the
               grooves, as one such scratch destroys
               the record.

               When the record is not being played, keep

- 56 -

It in its protective envelope and
return it to the files as soon as
possible.

Ordering
Acetates

When ordering Acetates, use the
form provided for that purpose and
give the name of the type of recording required. See to it that
Sound Film is prepared to suit
the nature of that recording.
Orders for acetates by the animators must be O.K'd by either
Izzy Sparber or Seymour Kneitel.

TABLE OF CONTENTS

TABLE OF CONTENTS
(Cont'd.)

| | |
|---|---|
| <u>Animation Board</u> | The regular drawing board used in all departments, equipped with a set of three pegs to hold the drawings in place; constructed with a built-in glass that has a light underneath and one above, both controlled by a switch on the left side of the board. |
| <u>Animating</u> | The process of making a series of cartoon drawings that will produce an optical illusion of motion when the drawings are photographed in rotation - These are the original drawings laid out by the animator. |
| <u>Animation Paper</u> | Paper with holes punched on the top to fit all animation boards and used by the animators to make their pencil drawings. |
| <u>Assistant Animator</u> | One who works under the supervision of an animator, animating from rough sketches drawn by the animator. |
| <u>Background</u> | The scenery behind, or underneath, the cartoon action. |
| <u>Beat</u> | Repeated pulsations of time in the rhythm of music or otherwise. Beats are indicated by a circle on the exposure sheet a certain regular number of drawings apart. |
| <u>Bottom Cels</u> | (See Cel definition) |
| <u>Breaking Down</u> | To assist an animator in his work. (See Assistant Animator) |
| <u>Camera or Cartoon Camera</u> | A motion picture camera mounted on a stand and geared up to photograph one picture at a time. |
| <u>Camera Frame</u> | A part of the camera constructed to hold the celluloid drawings and background intact while they are photographed. |
| <u>Cels</u> | Transparent sheets of celluloid properly punched to fit the pegs on all animation boards and camera. The cartoon drawings are transferred to sheets of celluloid to |

- 2 -

| | |
|---|---|
| <u>Cels</u> | permit the scenery, or background, to show through. As many as four cels may be used at one time, each with a different action drawn on it. When these are placed one on top of the other, with the background showing through, they form one complete picture. When used in combination the celluloids are designated as Top, Middle, Bottom Double Bottom or Double Top. |
| <u>Coloring</u> | Term used for painting on the reversed side of the celluloid drawings with opaque paint in any color. |
| <u>Continuity</u> | The smooth relation of one scene to another, or the complete story written and presented in such a way that the audience can follow the intended presentation. |
| <u>Cross Dissolve</u> | The fading out, or disappearing, of one scene at the same time another scene is fading in, or appearing. |
| <u>Cut-Out</u> | An object in the scene, or a part of an object, that does not animate, usually a drawing on a piece of paper cut out around its outline, placed in the scene and held for a certain length of time. |
| <u>Cutting (Or Editing)</u> | Putting together the final film in its proper sequence when it is finished. |
| <u>Dial No.</u> | A recorded number that registers the number of pictures that have passed through the camera. |
| <u>Dissolve</u> | The fading out, or disappearing, of the entire scene or an object in the scene. This is done by the gradual closing of the shutter on the camera. |
| <u>Double Bottom</u> | (See Cel definition) |
| <u>Double Exposure</u> | The photography of one object over another which has already been photographed; two exposure on the same section of film. |

| | |
|---|---|
| Double Top | (See Cel Definition) |
| Exposing | The method of deciding how many times each picture should be photographed. |
| Exposure | The photography of only one picture. |
| Exposure Sheet | A chart informing the camera-man what combination of cels is to be used, and the amount of time to photograph them. |
| Extremes | Drawings of the beginning and end of a particular action in animation. |
| Field Line | An ink line drawn on all animation boards indicating the farthest the camera can photograph on all sides of the picture. |
| Folder | Flaps or coverings used to keep scenes in. |
| Footage | The number of feet of film. |
| Frame | One picture on a strip of film. |
| Gag | An idea for an incident, or action that will bring a laugh from the audience. |
| Hair Line | A thin line drawn with another color to separate a place in the cartoon drawing where two colors that are alike have met. |
| Half Beat | An extra beat of time exactly between two beats. (See beat definition) |
| Hold | An action, or drawing, that is photographed more than one time to make a longer impression on the eye. |
| Hook-up | A drawing at the end of a series of drawings, made almost like the one at the beginning, to connect the entire series so the same action may be photographed over again, or repeated. |

- 4 -

| | |
|---|---|
| Inbetweening | Where the animator does not draw all the necessary drawings to complete an action, an inbetweener makes drawings to be inserted to complete the necessary number of drawings called for by the animator. |
| Inking | The transferring, or tracing, of the pencil drawing on to a transparent celluloid in ink. |
| Lead Sheet | A music chart showing where certain actions take place in the time of the music. |
| Matching | The final check-up on the finished drawings to see that everthing is correct before photography. |
| Metronome | An instrument used to show the length of time between beats. |
| Middle Cels | (See cel definition) |
| Mouth Action | The proper drawings of a mouth to correspond with the sound that is to be heard. |
| Off Register | Two drawings almost alike, with one made slightly different to cause an illusion of shivering. This is done by photographing first one then the other several times. |
| Opaque | The paint used to color the celluloid drawings. |
| Overlay | Part of a scene to be placed on top, or in front, of other drawings when they are photographed. |
| Pan or Panorama | A drawing on a long sheet of paper, or celluloid that moves past the camera field to give the impression to the observer that the camera is moving. |

| | |
|---|---|
| Pegs | Three pieces of metal built on all animation boards and camera alike, for accurate registration of the drawings. |
| Peg Holes | Three holes punched in all animation paper and cels alike, to fit accurately on the pegs of all animation boards for registration. |
| Planning | Examining a scene to decide which cels are to be top, middle, or bottom, and to check the action of the animation looking for any mistakes whatsoever. |
| Planning Sheet | An information chart made by the planner that describes which cels are top, middle, or bottom. |
| Plot | A short synopsis of the story, preferably in a paragraph of about one hundred words. |
| Post Sync. | If the sound is made after the cartoon is produced it's called Post Sync., but if the sound is recorded before the cartoon is produced it is called Pre Sync. |
| Pre Sync. | When sound is recorded before any work is done on the cartoon it is called Pre Sync., but if the sound is made after the cartoon is produced it is called Post Sync. |
| Projection | The showing of the picture on the screen. |
| Projection Machine | A machine used to show the picture on the screen. |
| Punch | A machine that is used to put the holes in the paper and celluloid. |
| Punch Marks | Holes that are punched into a section of motion picture film for any information regarding recording, or otherwise. |

- 6 -

| | |
|---|---|
| Recording | Putting sound on film. |
| Repeat | A cycle of drawings of a particular action used over and over again to save the work of making many drawings. |
| Safety Line | A line drawn on all animation boards to indicate where most of the action will safely be seen on the screen. |
| Scenario | A complete story. |
| Scene | .A location in the story. Whenever an action changes to another location it is called another scene. The drawings in each scene are usually kept in separate folders. |
| Set Back | Scenery constructed to produce depth, or third dimension effects. |
| Sliding Cel | An action drawn on a long strip of celluloid that is moved past the field of the camera. |
| Sound Track | A space on the left side of all motion picture film set aside for the photography of the sound. |
| Still Cel | A celluloid that contains a drawing which does not animate, usually held through a certain length of time in a scene. |
| Synchronizing | The process of making the sound to fit a particular action, or making an action fit a particular sound. |
| Timing | Checking the action in the scenes to see whether they are properly timed or exposed for the camera and to check the action of animation, looking for any mistakes whatsoever. |
| Top Cel | (See Cel definition) |
| Tracing | Transferring the pencil drawings onto transparent sheets of celluloid in ink. |
| Underlay | A part of the scene placed underneath all the transparent sheets of celluloids. |

-.7 -

Washing Cels          the celluloid after it has been
                      photographed, in order that the
                      cel may be used again.

Wipe-Out              When one scene gradually covers
                      another scene starting from one
                      end of the picture and going
                      to another, a method of trick
                      photography.

GENERAL SYNOPSIS                    - 8 -

Inking, often referred to as Tracing, is self-explanatory.  It is the act of transferring the pencil drawing to a sheet of celluloid.  The materials used for transferring are india ink, and pen.

It is a known fact that an inker can seriously effect a scene through carelessness and lack of understanding of facts and details explained in the following paragraphs:

INKERS GUIDE

1.  What to look for in starting a scene:  These are the papers that <u>must</u> be in a scene:

        1.  Exposure Sheets
        2.  Pink Card
        3.  Background Sketch
        4.  Sample Drawings
        5.  All essential drawings

11.  These may also be found in a scene:

        1.  Field guides
        2.  Shift Charts
        3.  Tracing Guides
        4.  Overlays and Underlays
        5.  Overlay or underlay sliding cels

111.  Reasons for above stipulations:

    1.  Exposure Sheets. (Their significance for the Inker.)

        A.  Exposure sheets are the final keys for all information in a scene.

        B.  They are read from left to right for each exposure or complete picture frame.  All references to action may be found by reading exposure sheets in this way.

        C.  They are divided into three main sections:

            1.  Music
            2.  Action
            3.  Camera

The inker is concerned only with sections two and three.

1.  D.  Inkers are not to change anything on
        Exposure Sheets under any circum-
        stances unless O.K'd by Department
        Manager.

2.  Pink Card

    A.  The Pink Card is a source of general
        information to all departments.

    B.  Inker should read entire card and
        use notes or instructions applying
        to inkers only.

3.  Background Sketch

    A.  In every scene, a tracing of original
        background will be found.  It is
        referred to as Background Sketch.

    B.  Inkers are to use this Background
        Sketch for the purpose of matching
        characters to background.

    C.  If it is a moving pan, moves will be
        indicated thereon.  If action has to
        match to background, it should be
        moved as called for on exposure
        sheets, by registering pan positions
        to center of center peg.  (No
        matching is necessary on Set-Back
        Backgrounds.)

    D.  Also read "Background" Section of
        book.

4.  Sample Drawings

    A.  These will be called for on the Pink
        Card under the caption "Coloring
        Department".  They will be called
        for by number, and will bear ink-
        ing instructions which must be
        followed accurately.

5.  Essential Drawings

    A.  If, while inking a scene, necessary
        drawings are missing, call this fact
        to the attention of the Department
        Manager immediately.

- 10 -

II    1.  INKING FIELD GUIDES:

    (a)  Inking field guides will be found
        in approach scenes only, drawn on
        blue paper, large or small, depend-
        ing on the size necessary.

        They will also be noted on pink
        cards and exposure sheets by num-
        bers or letters.

    (b)  The field guide is the area that the
        camera photographs and all action
        must be kept within this area.
        Also, it is a guide to eliminate
        any unnecessary inking that would
        not show on the screen.

    (c)  Be sure that cels used cover com-
        plete area of field guide.

    (d)  Inker is to work within these field
        guides at all times and is to ink
        up to these edges only.

    (e)  On standard fields, inker is to
        carry inking at least one-half
        inch outside of cutting field.

    (f)  If the action in the scene you are
        inking is not completely within
        the ink-field guide, bring it to
        the attention of your department
        manager immediately.

II    2.  SHIFT CHARTS:

    (a)  Shift charts will be found noted
        on pink card only.  They will be
        found on yellow paper in each
        necessary scene, called for by
        number or letter.

    (b)  Shift charts are used to bring an
        action into or out of a field.

        They are also used to raise or
        lower an action or for shifting an
        action over in the field.

    (c)  Place the shift chart on the pegs.
        Inker is to register drawings which
        having crosses on them, to posi-
        tion called for on the shift
        chart.  Then overlay a cel,
        registered on the pegs, and pro-
        ceed to ink.

4.   (c)   If they are made on background
           paper and not mounted on a cel,
           they are not considered a cel in
           planning for a one, two, three,
           or four cel level scene.  If they
           are mounted on a cel, they are
           counted as an additional cel; for
           example, a regular three-cel level
           scene becomes a four-cel level
           scene with an overlay cel.

     (d)   Inker is to work with this overlay
           or underlay at all times.  If not
           available, make an accurate tracing
           of same to use for matching
           purposes.

- 15-

II     5.     SLIDING CELS ON PEGS:

(a)  Notes for sliding cels on pegs
will be found indicated on pink
card under Inking Department.
If not, instructions to use "Sliding Peg Camera" on the pegs will
be noted on the pink card under
"Camera Department" or "Exposure
Sheets". These notes will also
appear on essential drawings.

(b)  Inker will find a diagram on either
a drawing or the Pink Card similar
to this

| Blank | Action | Blank |
|-------|--------|-------|
| o o o | o o o  | o o o |

which means
If action is to be traced on a
three field cel, and is moving in and out of scene, Inker is
to ink action in the middle
field.  If action is to move in
or out, a blank field will be
called for depending on which
of these two is happening at
the time.  (Also see sliding
cels for general information.)

- 15 -

A. If several actions are on the same perspective level, the manner in which they
are exposed will dominate in the deter-
mination of top, middle or bottom. For
example, an action exposed on threes,
or "holds" will be "bottom", that action
exposed on twos, will be "Middle"; that
action exposed on ones, in a repeat, or
a continuous action, will be "top".

B. If several actions are on different perspective levels, that action in the foreground is placed on the top cel; the
action in the background is placed on the
bottom cel; and the action inbetween,
on the middle cel.

C. If the scene is one of four cel levels,
determine whether the fourth level is
"T"-Top" or "B.-Bottom." In either case,
the action used as "T.-Top" or "B.-
Bottom" must be held as such thru-out
the scene.

D. There are many exceptions to the general
rule, and these exceptions can only be
determined by studying the drawings and following the action thru-out
the scene. If in doubt, nothing should
be taken for granted, the Department
Manager should be questioned.

IV. Determine size of cels necessary.

Reasons:

1. Since a field must be covered by cel
or cels at all times, the size
of cel used, becomes a very important factor. Failure to use correct
size results in a great waste
of work, since they cannot be used.

A. In a standard field, small cels are used.

B. In an approach field within the standard
field, small cels are used.

C. In any other field, larger than standard
large field cels are used.

- 16 -

V.   Determine Sliding Cels.

A.  Reasons:

1.  Sliding cels are used for the sole
purpose of saving work in animation.

2.  For example:  If an action will repeat in a scene, but must be first
brought into the scene, it becomes
unnecessary to animate action in,
and again, in a repeat.  In such
cases, sliding cels are used.  The
same thing applies, if an action
in repeat has to be taken out of
a scene.

3.  There are other times when sliding
cels are used, but in each case,
for the purpose of saving work.

4.  Since registration is a very
important factor in cartoons,
special care should be excercised
in registering sliding cels
against  pegs when registration on
pegs is not used.

5.  For further information refer
to index on sliding cels.

B.  Sliding cels will be called for on the
Exposure Sheets, Pink Card, or drawings.

There are several types and lengths of
sliding cels in small and large fields.

(a) Horizontal sliding cels
(b) Vertical sliding cels
(c) Diagonal sliding cels
(d) Top and Bottom punched sliding
cels or, as often called,
sliding cels for moving pegs.

The proper length is determined by the
action as to whether it pans in or out,
or continuously.

1.  A blank field must remain on either
side of sliding cel, depending on
whether an action is panning in or
out.  For example, if we are to bring
in an action, we start with a
blank field.  If we pan out an
action, we end with a blank field.

- 17 -

In all cases, the center peg should be used for registration of cels.

    2.    All type sliding cels must be large enough to cover the given field. Be especially careful when laying out a diagonal sliding cel.

    3.    If no information is given as to whether to use "Top" or "Bottom" Pegs for "Sliding cels on moving Pegs," Department Manager should be questioned.

VI. Determine weight of Ink lines.

    A. 1.    Ink lines play a very important part in characters. Heavy lines tend to make character appear almost black, due to lines appearing to converge. This is especially true on small drawings.

    2.    On approach shots, the ink lines are magnified in proportion to the field. All lines must be kept thin on approaches, to avoid heavy reproductions and blurs.

    3.    On color pictures, thin lines must be used, since a triple negative is required to make a positive print. The super-imposing of one negative over the other will tend to widen ink lines and cause blurs and over-weight lines.

    B. Weight of Ink line is determined by type of picture and size of character or object. Special care and emphasis should be given to facial expressions such as, eyebrows, eyes, wrinkles, and mouth.

    1.    A fine line should be used when characters or objects are in the background, or very small.

    2.    Lines must graduate in weight, same as character graduates in size.

    3.    Colored pictures and approach shots must carry very fine ink lines. This does not mean that facial details and expressions are to be lost due to the thinness of lines.

18 -

4.  Before starting a scene, an inked
    sample on all action must be
    shown to Department Manager for
    final O.K.

INBETWEEN DEPARTMENT

Before starting a scene, an inbetweener should
become thoroughly familiar with all details of that
scene in the following manner:

1. READ THE PINK CARD

    (a) The pink card should be read
        thoroughly, particularly that
        section devoted to the Inbetween
        Department.

    (b) All data such as Background
        Sketch, Tracing Guides,Shift
        Charts, Exposure sheets, etc.,
        mentioned on the pink card,
        should be with scene.

2. FLIP SCENE BEFORE STARTING WORK

    (a) A scene should be flipped before
        beginning work, to acquaint
        the inbetweener with the action.
        Careful study of the scene will
        often remove any doubt from the
        inbetweener's mind as to the
        type of action desired by an
        animator.

3. STUDY EXPOSURE SHEETS

    (a) Exposure Sheets should be looked
        over before starting a scene
        to ascertain whether any approach
        fields or special circles, not
        mentioned on the pink card, are
        with the scene. (Standard circles
        are used only when circling in
        or out to the center of a
        standard or large field.)

    (b) Following the Exposure Sheets,
        lay out your work so that you
        inbetween the bottom, middle and
        top level actions in that order.
        Doing this enables you to have
        any drawings, necessary for
        matching, ready when the draw-
        ings which have to be matched,
        are started.

        The most common example of this
        is where a repeat cycle of a walk,
        is used while mouth actions are

3. STUDY EXPOSURE SHEETS

(b) used on a separate cel. It is necessary to have the walk cycle complete, so that the mouth actions may be matched to the proper drawings as per the Exposure Sheets.

(c) All hook-ups listed on Exposure Sheets, are circled with a red pencil. These hook-ups should be checked with inbetweening notes on animator's extremes.

(d) An inbetween drawing should never be called for as a "hold" on the Exposure Sheets.

(e) If you are missing certain drawings called for on the Exposure Sheets, consult Tracing Guide or Shift Chart to determine whether the missing drawings are listed thereon. All drawings in scene should be accounted for on Exposure Sheets, Tracing Guides, Shift Charts or on all three.

(f) Spacing of "off-the-peg" inbetweening should be checked against the pan moves as exposed on the Exposure Sheets. "Off-the-peg" inbetweening should not be done unless authorized by the animator or department head.

4. INBETWEENING

(a) Before making an inbetween, be sure you are acquainted with all notes, such as spacing, C.D's, Tracings or Trace-backs, O.R. (Off Register), etc., that may be on the two extremes you are working with. Do no make an inbetween if there is any doubt in your mind as to the accuracy of a note or a C.D. without first questioning it.

(b) No tracings are to be made by an inbetweener unless there is a special note to that effect. However, the inbetweener should indicate the proper tracing notes

4. INBETWEENING

(b) on his inbetweens. In a case where
one extreme is only partially drawn
with a tracing note calling for the
balance of the drawing to be traced
from another drawing, and the other
extreme is a complete drawing, it is
necessary for the inbetween to be a
complete drawing.

(c) In drawing an inbetween, the drawings
should be placed on the pegs in the
following order: 1st-LOWEST numbered
extreme, 2nd-HIGHEST numbered extreme,
3rd-the inbetween.

(d) The inbetweener must be sure that all
drawings are carried at least one-half
($\frac{1}{2}$") inch outside the extreme cutting
edge of any field he may be using.
If extremes are not carried out to
this point, this fact should be questioned by the inbetweener.

(e) All lines separating color areas must
be completely closed. Question any
extremes on which this rule is
ignored.

(f) Whenever they are available, model sheets
should be referred to continuously, to
make sure that all detail and construction has been followed out as indicated
on these charts.

(g) It is extremely important that details
be followed throughout a scene.
Should the extremes be inconsistent
in this respect, they are to be questioned before working on the scene.

(h) All hook-up notes must coincide with
the exposing on Exposure Sheets.

(I) Should any series of drawings you are
working with be listed on a Tracing
Guide, instead of the Exposure Sheet,
the Tracing Guide is to be used exactly as an Exposure Sheet for that
particular series of drawings.

(j) In no case is an inbetweener to make an
extreme mouth position on any of his
inbetweens, unless an animator leaves
a note to that effect.

- 4 -

4. INBETWEENING

(k) Backgrounds or other stationary objects, which may have obstructions
in the path of an action, should be on
the pegs to insure the action clearing
these obstructions.

(l) Should it be necessary to divide a scene
among a number of inbetweeners, the
condition of the finished scene becomes the sole responsibility of the
person to whom it was originally
assigned.

(m) Any inbetweener who may be breaking
down a scene for other inbetweeners,
must indicate on his breakdown drawings any special spacing that the
animator may have called for.

(n) The inbetweener is responsible for
all necessary shift crosses being on
the proper drawings. All these crosses
must be traced from one master cross.
The peg holes of this master cross
must be reinforced before being put
to use.

(o) Only the Exposure Sheets are to be used
to determine the drawing count to be
entered on the window card on the
folder. All drawings having a letter
or number must be entered in this
count.

(p) Before resuming work on an uncompleted
scene at the beginning of the day,
it is a good policy to flip thru
both the finished and unfinished work
in the scene, to make sure something
that should have been kept in mind,
has not been forgotten.

(q) Before turning in a completed scene,
it should be flipped in an effort to
detect anything which may have been
omitted. A final check should also
be made to make sure that all necessary
production data originally accompanying the scene, has been put back in
its proper place.

### PLANNING DEPARTMENT

The Planner should:

Read the pink card and note all special
instructions.

Study the Exposure sheets to determine the number of cel levels in the
scene.

Note camera called for on the pink card
and check as to the correctness of this;
i.e., if an approach scene, the approach
camera should be designated; if a
sliding cel scene, the sliding peg
camera should be designated, etc. (See
special instructions for sliding peg
scenes.)

Check all Tracing guides and Shift
charts.

Always work with the fields indicated
on the pink card of each scene. Be
sure the action is carried one-half inch
beyond the cutting field.

Scenes may be 1, 2, 3 or 4 cel level scenes on
the black and white pictures, but, as a rule,
only 1, 2 or 3 cel levels on the color pictures.
A 4 cel level scene in color is permissable, if
it be absolutely necessary to cut down an exceptional amount of trace backs.   THIS SHOULD ONLY
OCCUR IN RARE INSTANCES.

All 4 cel level scenes must be O.K's by Seymour
Kneitel or Izzy Sparber.

One cel level scenes are planned under the "Bottom"
column of the Planner sheet. (See sample Planning Sheet following). These scenes are unmarked
for color since in all one cel level scenes only
pure colors are used.

Two cel level scenes are planned under the "Middle"
and "Bottom" columns of the Planning sheet and should
be correspondingly marked for color.

Three cel level scenes are planned under the "Top",
"Middle" and "Bottom" columns of the Planning Sheet
and should be correspondingly marked for color.

- 2 -

Four cel level scenes are planned as either Top-top
(TT), or Bottom-bottom(BB), in addition to the same
procedure as noted above for three cel level scenes.

When planning a scene, all cels making up each
exposure must be combined on the pegs and the required matching done, using the combination as
called for on the Exposure sheets.

In marking a scene for color, it should be done in
the upper right hand corner of the cel, marking it
"TT" for Top-top; "T" for Top, "M" for Middle,
"B" for Bottom, and "BB" for Bottom-bottom.

All errors or questions must be first referred to
the department head. He will determine course of
action thereafter.

### INFORMATION FOR PLANNING SLIDING PEG SCENES.

A Cel registered on the top pegs, should contain
an outline guide or tracing of the figures on the
Background, plus the figures on the Top, Middle,
and Bottom Cels used in the first exposure, as a
guide for the starting position of the scene. This
same procedure  should be followed for three or
four positions thru-out the scene.

            NOTE:  (Same as the Cel Cutout
                    guides used today)

Whenever a pan background is used in a sliding peg
scene the position of the right hand clamp should
be traced on the pan Background.

The inches or fractions of an inch representing the
stop position of the Top and Bottom sliding pegs
should be written on the exposure sheets (see
sample exposure sheet.)

The numbers used for this registration should be
taken from each  stop position of the sliding pegs
against the  steel rule mounted on the camera
stand for that purpose.

The Pan moves written on the exposure sheets should
be in the form of how much the handle is to be moved
rather than the distance of the pan move.  Also
an arrow indicating the direction.

PLANNING SHEET

| SCENE | | JOB | |
|---|---|---|---|
| TOP | MIDDLE | BOTTOM | |
| (one cel level) | | 1 - 54 | |
| (two cel levels) | 1 - 34 | 35-54 | |
| (three cel levels) 1 - 20 | 21 - 44 | 45 - 54 | |

(four cel levels)

| TOP-TOP | TOP | MIDDLE | BOTTOM | |
|---|---|---|---|---|
| 1 - 6 | 7 - 12 | 13 - 18 | 19 - 54 | |

(four cel levels)

| TOP | MIDDLE | BOTTOM | BOTTOM-BOTTOM |
|---|---|---|---|
| 1 - 6 | 7 - 12 | 13 - 18 | 19 - 54 |
| | | | |
| | | | |
| | | | |
| | | | |
| | | | |
| | | | |

## SPECIAL EFFECTS

The functions of this department include color
marking, application of speed effects such as
multiple images, blurs, and dry-brush work, and
the application of transparent and semi-transparent
shadows. This department also prepares preliminary
and final color samples to be used by the Coloring and Background departments.


1. READ THE PINK CARD

    No work should be attempted before the Pink
    Card is read and understood with specific
    emphasis on those instructions govern-
    ing your department.


2. STUDY SPECIAL EFFECTS CARD (See page 16)

    Equally important is the yellow Special
    Effects card filled out by the department
    head on which is designated the number and
    numbers of cels to be done, and also the
    kind or kinds of effects desired. Every
    heading of this card should be filled out
    by the proper person to whom the various
    responsibilities are designated. Before
    a scene is completed, make sure you have
    signed this card.


3. WORK WITH EXPOSURE SHEETS

    It must be understood that the Exposure
    sheets are the final authority of the scene
    and should be used carefully in connection
    with the progress of your work. Parti-
    cular care should be exercised in the case
    of hook-up actions to make sure that the
    special effect called for carries through
    smoothly and as intended.


4. COLOR MARKING

    When a scene is to be marked for color, it
    arrives from the Timing Department before
    it is inked, and usually, before it is
    inbetweened. Certain drawings, best illus-
    trating the detail of character and draw-
    ing, are selected by the department

## 4. COLOR MARKING

manager to be traced for "samples".

The drawings so selected are traced in ink on cels, and also in pencil on paper before being returned to the Timing Department. After the preliminary sample cel is colored, it is submitted to the Director of Production, Director of Animation and the Background Layout man, for approval or correction. When these are satisfactory, the Director of Production or a duly authorized assistant, will sign the Special Effects card. Care should be given to make sure that the card on every scene in process of production bears this signature or okay.

Corrections being made, the final color samples on cels are sent to the Background Department. The penciled tracings of the original drawings are marked correspondingly and sent to the Coloring Department.

## 4. SPEED EFFECTS & SEMI-TRANSPARENCIES

A scene requiring speed effects involving either dry-brush work or multiple images or both, or a scene requiring semi-transparent shadows, will enter this department from the Coloring Department. Semi-transparencies may be used for effects such as smoke, dust, glass, water, etc. Once completed, the scene is returned to the Coloring Department. Make sure the yellow Special Effects card is signed before turning in the completed scene.

## 5. TRANSPARENT SHADOWS

When a scene requires transparent ground shadows, it comes directly from the Planning Department, before the scene is colored. Care should be taken not to confuse the transparent shadow with the semi-transparent effect.

## MATCHING

1. READ PINK CARD

   Be sure that you understand what is happening in the scene. Check to make sure
   that the correct number of exposure sheets,
   as designated on the pink card, are with
   the scene.

2. CHECK SAMPLE DRAWINGS CAREFULLY

   The scene should be checked against the
   sample drawings to make sure that colors
   and details are being followed accurately.

3. EXPOSURE SHEETS

   Read the Exposure Sheets carefully as you
   match the cels. In checking hook-up actions,
   look for color flashes, consistency of cel
   levels, and other details. Also, make
   sure the scene contains every cel called
   for on the Exposure Sheets.

4. THE COMPLETED SCENE

   (a) Check one area of color at a time
   (b) Watch out for color flashes
   (c) Look for missing or incompleted ink
       lines, or objects that are not com-
       pletely drawn
   (d) Check for consistency and smoothness
       of action

5. CHARACTER AND OBJECT CONSISTENCY

   Be sure that every character or object is
   carried throughout the scene. Nothing
   must be allowed to either appear or
   disappear abruptly, in the scene.

6. SHADOWS

   Check for opaque shadows only, making sure
   they are carried through consistently. All
   transparent shadows and speed lines are the
   responsibility of the Special Effects Dept.
   However, it is the responsibility of the
   matcher to see that all special effect

6. SHADOWS

> treatments are correctly carried out.

7. CUTOUTS

> When cutouts are used, be sure they con-
> form to Cutout Guides and that color
> hookups match.

8. POLISHING

> Having completed the matching of a scene,
> the matcher should first count all cels
> and compare this count to the Worksheet
> listing, before signing the pink card and
> turning the scene over to the polishers.

9. RETOUCHING

> If part of the scene is to be retouched
> by the Background Department, turn the
> scene in to the Department Manager with
> necessary instructions.  If no retouch-
> ing is called for, and the scene is com-
> pletely matched, the scene should be
> placed on the Department Manager's desk.

Milton Keynes UK
Ingram Content Group UK Ltd.
UKHW030856180424
441376UK00011B/286